A Powerful Peace
The Integrative Thinking Classroom

Warren Heydenberk

Lehigh University

Roberta Heydenberk

The Peace Centers, Bucks County, Pennsylvania

Foreword by **Margery Baker**

Past President, National Institute of Dispute Resolution

Founder, Youth Vision

Allyn and Bacon

Boston ■ London ■ Toronto ■ Sydney ■ Tokyo ■ Singapore

Executive editor: Stephen D. Dragin
Series editorial assistant: Bridget Keane
Manufacturing buyer: Suzanne Lareau
Marketing manager: Stephen Smith

Library of Congress Cataloging-in-Publication Data

Heydenberk, Warren.
    A powerful peace : the integrative thinking classroom / Warren Heydenberk and
Roberta Heydenberk
        p.   cm
    Includes bibliographical references (p.) and index.
    ISBN 0-205-29360-3
    1. Critical thinking—Study and teaching.   2. Creative thinking—Study and teaching.
3. Conflict management—Study and teaching.   4. Communication in education.
5. Activity programs in education.   I. Heydenberk, Roberta.   II. Title
LB1590.3 .H49 2000
370.15'2—dc21   99-053863

Printed in the United States of America
10 9 8 7 6 5 4 3 2   08 07 06 05

Dedicated to

Robert K. Stern
and
Robert C. Heydenberk

Contents

Foreword   xi

Preface and Acknowledgments   xiii

PART ONE   **Critical Thinking, Communication, and Cooperation**   1

Introduction   1
Safety and Skills: The Synergy of the Integrative Thinking
   Classroom   6
Social Skills: Where There Is Hope, There Is Life   10
Attitudes and Achievement: The Alchemy of the Integrative
   Thinking Classroom   13
The Tools of Academic Achievement: The Tools of Peace   22

Chapter 1   Communication and Comprehension   27
   Active Listening   27
   Introduction to the CR-CT Portfolios   27
   Sound Scavengers   28
   Stop, Look, and Listen   29
   Context Clues   32
   Sound Off   33
   Inference Cartoons   33
   Tales from the Tones   34
   Looking In–Looking Out Journals   36
   Timing Is Everything   37
   Introduction to ACE Paraphrasing   39
   Metalistening   40
   Listening Tip of the Week   42
   The Listener Interview   42
   The Listening Gauge   44
   Questioning for Clarity   45
   Clarification Questions   45
   Question Card   46
   Cooperative Re-Quest   47
   Question Mark   48
   Cooperative Questioning   49
   Prediction Detectives   50
   Inner Dialogue and Quiet Questioning   51

Mapping Understanding   52
Start with Art   53
MIS-MAP: Main Idea Summary Maps   53
Summary/Paraphrase Partners   55
Story Maps   56
Mirror, Mirror   57
RSVP: Read, Summarize, Verbalize, Paraphrase   58
Socrates Says   59
Summary Table   60
Character Maps   61
Me and My Shadow   62
Moccasin Miles   63
Different Lenses   65
Conflict Maps   66
The "I" of the Storm   67
The Three C's: The Simple "I" Statement   67
Meeting Maslow   69
Me Map–We Map   70
Do You See What I See?   71
The United States Constitution   72
Life, Liberty, and the Pursuit of Happiness   74
The Twister: A Backdoor Introduction to the Classroom
    Constitution   75
Rights and Responsibilities: A Skill Storm   76
The Classroom Constitution   77
Introduction to Restitution   78
Weaving Straw into Gold   80
From Sorry to Solution   81
Toolbox Tour   82

Chapter 2   Creative and Critical Thinking   84
Quantum Questions   84
Fantastic Flops   84
Interviewing Einstein   87
The Grass Is Always Greener on the Other Side   89
The Brainstorming Banquet   91
Time Machine   92
The Right Question   94
The Invention Question   95
Creatography   97
Question Bridge   99
Concrete and Concept Questions   100
Brain Boosters   101
Goal and Question Power: QP   102
Quantum Question   104
Carpe Diem: Using Quantum Questions Every Day   106
Bioscape   107
Analogies   108
Introduction to Analogies   108
Analogies: Common Characteristics   110
Analogy Attributes   111
Connection Sentences   112
The ABC Activity: Analogy Brainstorm Concepts   113

The Cause–Effect Analogy Map   113
Critical Concept Maps   114
Critical Concept Feature Matrix   115
Brainstorming   116
Introduction to Creative Brainstorming   117
Hitchhiker's Guide to the Universe   117
Brain Frame   118
The Creativity Twister   119
Brainwriting and Brainboarding   120
Metamorphing and Simile Solutions   121
Magnificent Metaphors and Stunning Similes   122
Tantalizing Twisters   123
Synthestorming   124
Metaquest   124
Toolbox Tour   125

Chapter 3   Integrative Solutions   127
Potholes, Brain Blunders, and Solution Snags   127
Wrong Exit   127
Asleep at the Wheel: Examining Unstated Assumptions   128
Stretched to the Breaking Point   130
Mental Floss—Reasoning and Relevance   131
Polar Bear   133
Oversimplification   134
Mirage: Mistaking Evidence as Proof   135
Foolish Fishing or When to Throw It Back   137
Hitchhiking on the Bandwagon   138
Sphinx Thinks Matrix   139
Group Think or Group Sink   141
The Non Sequitur: Slippery Slopes on the Road to Reason   142
Potholes on the Road to Reason   144
Criteria by Design   145
The Sun and the Moon   145
Creating Criteria: Safe, Smart, and Successful   147
Picking Priorities   148
Criteria Design   150
Cause–Effect Maps   152
Bounce or Break Blues   152
The Pros/Cons Questions (PCQ)   154
Wishbone Thinking   155
Super Solutions: The Synthesis Shift   156
Protection: A Prevention Plan   158
Introducing Controversy   159
Academic Controversy   159
Toolbox Tour   160

**PART TWO   Conflict-Positive Communication
and Cooperation**   163

Conflict Resolution: The Promise of Prevention   163
From Alienation to Activism: Attachment in the Integrative
Thinking Classroom   167
The Biology of Success in the Integrative Thinking Classroom   168
The Cooperation-Conflict Resolution Cycle   170

Chapter 4   United without an Enemy: The Conflict Resolution Program   175
Exploring Attitudes about Conflict   175
Conflict Resolution Twister   178
Conflict Resolution Styles   179
The Three R's of Conflict Resolution   181
Conflict Style Theater   183
Communication Keys   184
Boomerang   185
Meeting on the Mobius Strip   187
Ground Rules, Guidelines, and Goals   188
Active Listening   189
Feelings Word Wheel   191
ACE Paraphrasing   192
The Alternative "I" Messages   193
The Blame Frame   195
Appreciation and Affirmation "I" Messages   197
Brainstorming Breakthrough   198
"Peacing" It Together   198
Conflict Journalism   199
Conflict Resolution Table   200
Conflict Resolution Toolbox Tour   201

Chapter 5   Lions and Tigers and Bears: No Problem   203
Conflict-Positive Cooperation (CPC)   203
Conflict-Positive Cooperation Plan: Skill Storm   205
Cooperation Crunch Twister   207
Framing Feedback   208
Each One Teach One   209
Help Wanted   210
Cooperative Metaquest: Questioning Our Questions   211
Team Check-Out List   211
Cooperative Critical Incident Reports   212
Introduction Interviews   214
Circle the Elephant   215
Cooperative Consensus   216
The CPC Class Meeting   218
Town Teams   219
Introduction to Check-Ins   220
Kids Can, We Can   222
CPC Project Plans   224
The Vocabulary of Understanding   225
Common Ground   226
Beating Bias   227
Lead Letter Days   229
Going Global   230
Culture Clash   232
Dynamic Differences   235
Stranded with Same Sam   235
The Parent Pack   236
Toolbox Tour   237

Bibliography   239
Name Index   249
Subject Index   253

Foreword

In recent times the public focus on education policy has appeared to be a pendulum swinging back and forth between concerns about violence and concerns about academic rigor. Triggered by horrific and unthinkable acts of violence by and against youth in our nation's schools, we look for ways to prevent further eruptions. As our memories of the latest incident fade, headlines re-emerge about a need to focus on academic achievement, accountability, and standards of performance.

Neither of these concerns should be minimized in any way. What conflict resolution educators know—and what the authors of *A Powerful Peace: The Integrative Thinking Classroom* so cogently capture—is that teaching the skills and values of conflict resolution and critical thinking provide sound foundations for wrestling with both concerns.

No one—neither youth nor adult—can learn in an environment that does not feel physically or emotionally safe. Effective conflict resolution education programs teach us to understand the needs and interests that drive potentially harmful conflicts and to hone the skills to wrestle with those conflicts constructively, peacefully, and with justice. At its core, conflict resolution education focuses on making classrooms, schools—even homes and communities—physically and emotionally safe places to learn and grow. It helps us to create the havens of safety that we all need to become lifelong learners.

Conflict resolution education emphasizes the **value** of thinking creatively and analytically, and it teaches what Crawford and Bodine call the "foundational abilities" **to act on** these values (orientation, perception, emotion, communication, creative thinking, and critical thinking). These abilities, together with the feelings of **self-actualization** that flow from the knowledge that one can, indeed, solve problems for oneself, are at the root of successful academic performance. It is no accident, then, as the authors share with us in their introduction, that participation in conflict resolution education programs correlates with heightened academic success.

One of the most salient contributions that *A Powerful Peace* makes is in helping us to bridge these two domains. It takes us step by step through exciting, interactive lessons on communication and comprehension, creative and critical thinking, developing integrative solutions, and conflict resolution processes. And it does so throughout by showing us how to embed the teaching of these lessons within core academic subject matter. It models the most important lesson—that empowering youth and adults to create safe havens is inextricably intertwined with empowering them for academic success. It is no wonder that *A Powerful Peace: The Integrative Thinking Classroom* has been receiving rave reviews from educators who have been field-testing the curriculum.

Solid education policy will produce young people who understand their own potential to meet the life challenges they confront—whether it is the bully in the schoolyard or college entrance exams. The greatest gift that adults—teachers, parents, and mentors—can give to young people is the confidence that they can realize that potential. That is the message embedded in this effective conflict resolution curriculum—*A Powerful Peace* sings with hope and expectation to help all of us rise to that challenge.

Margery Baker
Past President, National Institute of Dispute Resolution
Founder, Youth Vision

Preface and Acknowledgments

HOW TO USE THIS BOOK

A Powerful Peace: The Integrative Thinking Classroom is designed to be used in upper elementary through high school levels. The text is organized into two major sections. The first part, comprising Chapters 1, 2, and 3, is a comprehensive critical thinking, communication, and cooperation curriculum. The second part of the book, consisting of Chapters 4 and 5, is designed to teach students the essential skills of conflict resolution and conflict-positive communication, characterized by the use of constructive conflict resolution skills and appreciation for the opinions and insights of everyone in the integrative thinking classroom. The last chapter, "Lions and Tigers and Bears—No Problem," provides activities that increase cooperation and build classroom community.

The activities were created with busy teachers in mind: none of the activities requires much preparation time or any extra materials beyond standard school supplies. Each new concept is introduced with a specialized activity or two. However, the majority of the activities in the book are designed to be used with whatever curriculum or content materials the teacher would generally use. Many of the strategies, as well as terms introduced in the activities, will be useful in many contexts in the classroom beyond the activity itself. All of the activities are designed to increase comprehension, critical thinking, and cooperative interaction as students process content in the classroom.

Although many of the chapter activities are presented in a developmental sequence, teachers may pick and choose the activities that best serve classroom content needs and the social development needs of students at any given time. However, because of the short time it takes to introduce most of the communication activities, it is a wise investment to use all of the activities: Increased student listening and effective communication save time and increase content area achievement in the long run. Many of the activities close with a section called Extending Activities. Contained therein are extra questions and activities such as journal writing to be used as homework or as in-class activities, as time permits.

The CR-CT (Conflict Resolution–Critical Thinking) Portfolio system is integrated throughout the book after its introduction in Chapter 1. Although many of the activities are marked with the recommendation **Portfolio Pick**, you are encouraged to develop the CR-CT Portfolio according to your curriculum needs or simply to integrate these portfolio activities into your existing portfolio system.

In addition, each part of the book provides a theoretical and research background for the chapter activities. We hope this will be enlightening and will serve as useful information for educating parents and the school community about your curriculum.

ACKNOWLEDGMENTS

We thank the staff of the Peace Centers and the staff and students of the Carl Sandburg Middle School, Haycock Elementary School, Little Caboose School, Morrisville Schools, Neshaminy Schools, S.T.A.R. Academy, Stearne Elementary, and Strayer Middle School. As well, we are fortunate to have the support and inspiration of Dr. Don Campbell, Dr. J. Kender, Dr. J. Manni, Dr. A. Moe, Dr. H. Rubenstein, Dr. G. Smith, K. Winters, and S. Bailey. We are especially grateful to our family members: Carol, Bob, Dan, Nanna, Nina, Greg, Judy, Lucille, Celeste, Marion, Robert, Eric, Laurel, Trapp, and Susan.

We extend our appreciation to John Parr, Iris Anderson, Diana Taylor, and Kelly Huff-Benkowski for their critical reviews of the text. And finally, the text would be much diminished without the astute editing and patience of Bridget Keane of Allyn and Bacon and Nancy Crompton of Stratford Publishing Services, Inc.

A Powerful Peace

PART ONE

Critical Thinking, Communication, and Cooperation

INTRODUCTION

One morning many years ago in a small rural farm community, Jane Elliott greeted her elementary school students. They were very upset. Her class wanted to know why someone had killed Dr. Martin Luther King the day before. Ms. Elliott struggled to answer their questions. Finally, she devised a very simple, quick plan.

Ms. Elliott made collars by cutting strips of brown felt. She put the collars on all of her blue-eyed students. The blue-eyed students were discriminated against that day. The students with collars had quietly lost their rights. They sat in the back of the room as the brown-eyed students went to the water fountain and engaged Ms. Elliott in conversation, laughter, and comments about their studies. Every time a student wearing a collar made a comment, it was ignored or criticized. Every time a student wearing a collar made a mistake, it was exaggerated and generalized to all students wearing collars. The students wearing collars began to suffer academically, taking up to twice as long to complete simple tasks. They fought with their brown-eyed friends. As the day wore on, collared students became hopeless and helpless. The next day, the brown-eyed students wore the collars that the blue-eyed students had worn the day before. The same hopelessness and helplessness overcame them.

When it was over, Ms. Elliott noticed all of the expected changes: improved understanding, improved empathy, and compassion. The experiment had worked: she had opened these young students' hearts. However, there was one change that no one had expected. Ms. Elliott's students had changed academically, as well. Somehow they had magically increased performance on academic tasks. Ms. Elliott had opened their minds as she opened their hearts.

For many years, we have searched for the key to this "Elliott Effect." We have worked with teachers who share Ms. Elliott's concerns and commitment. We have worked with their students in diverse school communities—rich, poor, rural, and urban. These teachers and their students have a strong sense of justice. They are committed to being skilled communicators and thinkers; they resolve conflicts creatively. Their classrooms are characterized by a sense of safety and a sense of belonging. They appreciate and learn from one another's unique perspectives while nurturing their common humanity. This is the essence of the integrative thinking classroom.

What we have found from Ms. Elliott's work, and similar work of others, is that if anyone in the classroom or school is bullied or victimized, we are all diminished. Being in an environment that supports or even tolerates fear and injustice will affect everyone's performance, not just that of the immediate victims. As we have learned from Ms. Elliott's work, we all have our collars on until all the collars are gone.

The integrative thinking classroom benefits all students in profound ways. What does *integrative thinking* mean? The term was inspired by the term for win–win negotiation style; integrative negotiation is characterized by a commitment to constructive problem solving and conflict resolution. The first step in this process is to expand our understanding and to make sure that everyone's perspective is clear. The second step in integrative negotiation is to carefully define problems as mutual concerns, to separate problems from people, and to avoid personal attack. When students begin to communicate and solve problems in an integrative way, the classroom climate begins to change and eventually the school culture is affected. In some cases, the community culture is affected, as well.

When students realize that they have the ability to solve problems constructively and creatively, they begin to see problems as opportunities to increase understanding and to hone communication skills. They begin to tackle problems that they would have avoided before—in both the academic and social domains. These students are not only less likely to be perpetrators of violence, they are also less likely to be victims of violence. They think in more creative and comprehensive ways. Hope and achievement increase, and we are all safer.

The Conflict Resolution–Critical Thinking Curriculum (CR-CT) represents a synthesis of research on how students learn and the authors' own research in this area. An integrative thinking environment enhances student learning and cooperation in three ways. First, the sense of safety in the integrative classroom prevents downshifting, a neurological fight-or-flight reaction that makes critical thinking impossible. Second, with fewer discipline problems, students enjoy school; with less alienation, they spend more time on task and develop a stronger sense of school attachment or belonging. Third, students begin to engage automatically in integrative thinking. Integrative thinking develops in an environment characterized by a sense of safety and a sense of belonging. However, these two essentials alone do not create integrative thinking—it depends on a strong grounding in critical thinking, as well. This constellation of related changes represents a shift that has transformed education in conflict-positive schools.

Two cornerstones of successfully building resilience in a child are social skills and academic skills, which are interdependent. The third cornerstone is a sense of community. As Maslow and other psychologists posited years ago (and as is now corroborated by research in neurology), children's environments

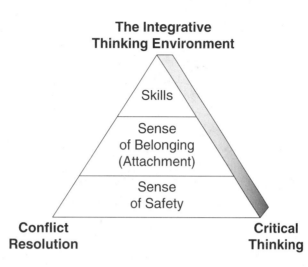

**The Integrative
Thinking Environment**

Skills

Sense
of Belonging
(Attachment)

Sense
of Safety

**Conflict
Resolution**

**Critical
Thinking**

must be free of physical and psychological threat for cognitive growth to occur. The CR-CT curriculum embeds the most effective academic strategies to help us achieve critical thinking and conflict resolution goals simultaneously in the classroom.

The CR-CT curriculum addresses the concerns of those who may feel that conflict resolution represents just another "feel good" program and, accordingly, that it would be a bad direction to take at a time when critics of education champion academic achievement. Critics' doubts should be allayed by knowing that conflict resolution, social skills, and a feeling of safety are requisites of academic achievement. Learning is severely hampered, if not impossible, in an environment of fear and hostility. Creativity and critical thinking are severely limited in an environment where social and psychological safety are threatened.

The CR-CT curriculum teaches the skills that increase physical and psychological safety in our classrooms. These essential life skills are also necessary for academic performance: listening, analyzing, brainstorming, considering multiple perspectives, and communication are all essential for developing the critical-thinking skills that will enable our children to succeed in the information age, as well as being skills that are necessary for resolving conflict and building our communities. The CR-CT curriculum is designed to strengthen both conflict resolution and critical-thinking skills, resulting in our teachers spending less time on disciplinary issues.

Just as academic growth cannot be fostered in a psychologically or physically unsafe environment, neither can social or emotional growth occur in an environment where a child experiences chronic academic failure. Decades of research have shown us that low-academic-performance children "seemed ashamed" (Marrett & Leggon, 1979, p. 136; Hawkins, 1995). Often their later aggression was used as "a means of enhancing or safeguarding self-esteem" (Marrett & Leggon, 1979, p. 137) that was lost in their academic failures. Such school behavior will affect peers and teacher expectation, which will further predict lower self-esteem, future academic failure, and aggression (Marrett & Leggon, 1979; Rosenthal, 1973). It is not IQ, but "specifically the experience of failure that appears to escalate the risk [of destructive behaviors] rather than ability per se" (Hawkins, 1995, p. 13).

Alienation has a dramatic impact on academic performance. Classroom interventions that improve the classroom climate have shown "clear superiority over relationship therapy" (Mash & Barkley, 1989, p. 87) for many student problems. As many educators will affirm, "children whose belief in their own intelligence is confirmed by others subsequently behave more intelligently" (Lipman, 1993, p. 377). We know from Piaget, and more recently from brain research, that cognitive growth is facilitated in a socially rich environment (Gibb, 1978).

Furthermore, research has shown us that simply posting the rules of decision making and behavior, the mainstay of stand-alone programs, is "not enough to provide long-term measurable change in students' critical-thinking or conflict resolution behavior" (Prothrow-Stith, 1994). Integrated conflict resolution–critical thinking programs show consistent results in improving school climate (National Institute of Dispute Resolution [NIDR] 1998). School cultures have been positively transformed by such programs (Heydenberk & Heydenberk, 1998a) sometimes extending from the school to the community.

Classroom conflict resolution and critical-thinking programs that help children learn the cognitive skills that they will also use socially are the most promising. Students become more skilled at explaining their viewpoints without the use of force, having successfully replaced frustration and aggression with effective communication avenues. Children who learn these skills are more hopeful and form healthier bonds in the school community. An increased sense of hope correlates significantly with continued or increased academic success, positive peer attachments, and higher ratings of global self-worth (Snyder, 1994).

However, in order to increase critical thinking and academic performance, children first need a safe school environment characterized by high and clear expectations, teacher and peer support, and psychological and physical safety. We know that depression, aggression, and school failure are all linked to poor social skills (Mash & Barkley, 1989). The classroom presents the perfect arena in which to improve these skills, increasing resilience and academic performance, as decades of research have shown. In a variety of classroom settings, cultures, and countries, Johnson and Johnson's (1995) conflict resolution evaluations showed safer classrooms and schools, where children consistently retained knowledge of the conflict resolution skills, transferred use of the skills to the home, chose win–win negotiations over win–lose, and increased their academic achievement. Continued exposure to a conflict-positive environment produces children who are integrative thinkers, who engage in a broader synthesis or win–win thinking rather than the common distributive (win–lose) thinking style.

Contrary to widespread perceptions about the nature of conflict and conflict resolution programs, good programs recognize the need for conflict and enable students to learn from it and to use conflict constructively rather than becoming its victim. We will never have a conflict-free environment: a conflict-positive environment is our goal. As Simonton researched the conditions for a creative renaissance, he noted the significance of conflict and diversity of ideas in the environments of the city-states of ancient Greece: Corinth, Athens, Sparta, and Italy were "bubbling" with diversity and conflicts (Goleman, Kaufman, & Ray, 1992, p. 171). Differences may be essential to creativity and growth as long as the "attitudes toward innovation" and the "organizational climate" allow people to "feel secure enough to express new ideas without fear of censure," ridicule, or worse (Goleman, Kaufman, & Ray, 1992, p. 128). We wish to teach our children to appreciate diversity and embrace conflict before conflict embraces them.

We are naturally social beings with a basic need for bonds and attachment to others, a need as important as our need for food and shelter. If we build our communities in a way that facilitates strong bonds we will also facilitate academic growth. Cooperation is our natural state. We invite problems when we ignore this in our schools. Children are born capable of love, empathy, and natural curiosity. Studies show that people of different races, cultures, incomes, and intellectual abilities feel better about themselves and are physically healthier when they have the opportunity to become involved in their community and help each other. Children who are encouraged to interact socially form friendships, increase their language skills, and feel safe and productive. Furthermore, such children are less likely to join destructive groups and gangs in search of attachment.

A sense of safety and belonging are not guaranteed, but rather they must be created to effect a good learning environment. Unfortunately, for too many of our children safety and attachment are lacking. Our teachers feel that aggression and misconduct significantly interfere with learning in their classrooms; we have had a significant increase in homicides of children under eighteen in recent years; many school crimes involve a weapon; for every child murdered in our communities, another eight are injured (Catalano et al., 1993). The psychological consequences of violence to bystanders and victims are lifelong (Regier & Cowdry, 1995).

Building our community bonds is an urgent issue because it is the most significant protective factor against youth involvement in violence. Schools can provide a place "to create positive connections across group lines" (Eron, Gentry, & Schlegel, 1994, p. 305). The community component of our curriculum includes a conflict resolution program for teachers and students who will be able to model what they learn and help build bridges between the school and the community. Some evaluations have shown a "ripple effect," in which students, parents, and siblings resolved conflicts at home by using strategies taught in the schools (Heydenbderk & Heydenberk, 1998a; Stomfay-Stitz, 1994, p. 280). We first need to convince our students that a better model for human behavior and interaction is possible, that people all over the world have "core values" like "the Golden Rule" (Guinness, 1990, p. 317) and peace, justice, compassion, and respect.

Understandably, students who don't believe a better outcome is possible aren't amenable to change. We must show youth that hatred and violence are not the norm but represent "forms of human pathology" (Sylwester, 1995, p. 117) and that "restoration of our natural tendencies of cooperation" will begin to heal our pathological communities (Davidson & Worsham, 1992, p. 38). Cooperation is not new, but an "ancient legacy," a part of our biological nature that is revealed in our cultural values throughout time—values of cooperation with those we do not fear, with those we understand (Davidson & Worsham, 1992, p. 38). Human beings perish without human contact and flourish without violence, aggression, and war. We must convince our students that one bystander speaking out against violence or injustice will often motivate a paralyzed crowd (Baron, Kerr, & Miller, 1992). In a multiple-risk environment, "a single good relationship may serve to insulate a child against potentially damaging . . . environments" and circumstances (Farrington et al., 1990, p. 312). We can show our children that making one person feel better is likely to increase that person's respect, tolerance, compassion, and acceptance of others (Marrett & Leggon, 1979). And, if one person can do all of this alone, imagine what can happen when we work together.

SAFETY AND SKILLS: THE SYNERGY OF THE INTEGRATIVE THINKING CLASSROOM

Great thinkers enjoy thinking. Studies of high academic achievers and creative geniuses find several common attributes: the ability and curious disposition necessary to seek out information; the ability to connect that information to prior knowledge, form creative associations or find novel associations; and the "willingness to express" those insights (Cropley & Dehn, 1996, p. 7).

The information that the curious and creative minds retrieve is divergently processed and ultimately convergently processed (in problem solving). Flexibility is another key to academic achievement and creative ability (Cropley & Dehn, 1996). Studies of achievers and creative geniuses show us that the noncognitive aspects of academic achievement and productivity are more important markers than the brain's speed of processing, which appears to be completely insignificant as a correlate of IQ (Necka, 1996, p. 99). The "noncognitive" or social-emotional and personality characteristics that characterize great thinkers include "flexibility, sensitivity, tolerance, sense of responsibility, empathy," independence, and even a sense of humor or "wit" (Cropley & Dehn, 1996, p. 9).

Often studies point to what seems like paradoxical markers in that students who are creative critical thinkers may also show high levels of compassion and empathy and independence. These are often students who understand and empathize with classmates, but who are not controlled by a need for approval from their classmates (Goleman, 1995). As creativity researcher Csikszentmihalyi (1990) tells us, the optimal relationships for creativity are both differentiated and integrated.

What does this information about thinking have to do with conflict resolution? There are clear "environmental enablers" (Cropley & Dehn, 1996, p. 13) that foster creativity, compassion, and critical thinking. The first "enabler" is a classroom that is physically and psychologically safe—a classroom that can be characterized as a "socially rich environment" (Gibbs, 1978, p. 39). The opportunity to express one's ideas and reflect on their ideas in an integrated cooperative environment increases critical thinking and decreases destructive conflict (Johnson & Johnson, 1995). Students in a cooperative environment do not just have more opportunities to engage in critical thinking, they actually have the opportunity to develop higher level critical thinking. A classroom characterized by alienation and competitiveness causes shallow, "dichotomous" (Kohn, 1986, p. 127), and flawed thinking.

In the integrative thinking environment, "students create a synthesis that integrates both perspectives" (Johnson & Johnson, 1995a, p. 109) when confronted with conflicting ideas. The positive interdependence nurtured in the integrative thinking environment helps students find the valid points in two perspectives and the joint benefit in any solution. Students' thinking evolves from dichotomous or simple analytical (who is right, who is wrong) to integrative thinking that incorporates a larger perspective and a more creative conceptualization.

Furthermore, in this integrative thinking environment, students are motivated to increase positive, constructive communication skills with teachers and classmates as levels of school attachment increase. This is vital, as attachment may be the most significant predictor of resilience in our children and students. Students are also more committed to their academic goals. Academic failure, poor communication and poor social skills predict alienation or lower levels of attachment and achievement, and vice versa. The integrative classroom fosters both domains simultaneously—each with exponential positive effects on the other. Studies have shown that social skills alone predict life and career success with 4 to 20 times greater accuracy than IQ alone as a predictor. Uncontrolled anger, impulsive, destructive behavior, apathy, and undisciplined behavior ruin more careers than a few points of difference on an IQ test. More failures are associated with lack of emotional control rather than with lack of IQ (Goleman, 1995, p. 27).

Although establishing an integrative thinking environment is not always simple, teachers usually report that any time spent is saved many times over by decreased conflict and increased critical thinking. While theorists prescribe conflict-positive environments, we know that we can't simply place students together and expect them to become integrative, cooperative thinkers (Johnson & Johnson, 1992). Students often come to us with a distributive (win–lose) thinking style and are often unaccustomed to practicing cooperative communication. When a school initiates a conflict resolution program, months may pass before noteworthy changes are documented (Heydenberk & Heydenberk, 1998b). Years of distributive (win–lose) thinking are not forgotten over night.

Complicating the initiative to create conflict-positive, communicative classrooms is the fact that students may come to us from unsafe environments. We know from brain research that the limbic system's amygdala—the "emotional brain" (Goleman, 1994, p. 4)—hijacks the cortex in stress conditions, making integrative, critical thinking impossible in a high-threat environment: A fight-or-flight brain response occurs which we call *downshifting* (Caine & Caine, 1997, p. 41).

To create an academic and physically safe integrative environment, several pieces must be in place. Comprehensive conflict resolution programs create the shift to integrative negotiation, but they must be practiced in a cooperative environment in order to be effective (Johnson & Johnson, 1995). In turn, a cooperative environment is much easier to establish when students are integrative thinkers with conflict resolution training. Clearly, this is not a simple linear relationship in our complex school communities, but often the shift begins with integrative critical thinking, which is the focus of the first part of this book.

Although the risks our children face are numerous, the risk resiliency research, in a "clear and consistent" pattern, identifies school-based interventions that promote significant resilience in our students' school and community bonding and academic success, or, more specifically, "problem solving skills [and] social competence" skills (Wright, 1994, p. 2) that provide protection.

Bernard's review of the resilience literature and research identifies critical thinking, abstract thinking, reflection, communication skills, the ability to generate alternative solutions or problem-solving, and responsiveness to others among the essential skills of the resilient child (Wright, 1994, p. 3).

Many of the social ills our children suffer actually "incorporate a number of characteristics associated with the processes of cognition" (Wright, 1994, p. 2). Effective problem-solving skills have "dramatic significance in social adjustment" (Baruch & Stutman, 1993, p. 11). Among the first recommendations from the APA commission is "school based intervention in classroom management [and] problem solving" (American Psychological Association [APA], 1993, p. 31). The APA's *Report on Youth and Violence* identified a "cognitive handicap . . . that may inhibit not only academic functioning but also their learning of pro-social skills and moral concepts (APA, 1993, p. 20). In fact our students' cognitive skills are not just essential for academic (and eventually economic) success. They are also essential to prevent the feeling of failure that damages school bonding and thereby may affect many other areas of a child's life (Hawkins, 1995).

Our most challenging students in our most disruptive classrooms benefit from conflict-positive classrooms. Bullies are often "motivated by perceived provocation" showing consistent deficits in social cognition (Marano, 1995, p. 65). The National School Safety Commission identified the deficit as a "destructive form of circular reasoning" (Stephens et al., 1995, p. 3). School failure and deficits in problem-solving skills are related to lack of school commitment, lack of attachment, and to delinquency (Empey & Stafford, 1991, p. 240). Academic failure is a "school-related risk factor that is likely to result in violence and other problem behaviors" (Hawkins, 1995, p. 13). This is not a thinly veiled indictment of the less intelligent child. In fact, "poor problem-solving skills and poor school achievement are more important than IQ in predicting violence and aggressive behavior" (Eron, Gentry, & Schlegel, 1994, p. 38). "Lack of reasoning skills," not lack of intelligence, is sufficient to produce failure (Lipman, 1991). Simply put, memorization of facts without the ability to reason about those facts does not work for many of our students (Lipman, 1991, p. 17).

From the resiliency research alone, a very compelling case can be made for stressing critical thinking and problem-solving skills in our curriculum. The Carnegie Council on Adolescent Development (CCAD) suggests that critical thinking skills need to be taught; they are "not automatic" (CCAD, 1995, p. 5). One of the reasons for the council's concerns was that "by the time students master one set of facts, it may be outdated by new developments. Such rapid changes require people to think for themselves, and educators to provide these skills" (CCAD, 1995, p. 5). From the education community's Association of Supervision and Curriculum Development (ASCD) comes agreement that we do indeed "need . . . an expanded version of the basics . . . development and emphasis are needed in teaching skills of problem-solving, reasoning, conceptualization, and analysis, which are among the neglected basics in tomorrow's society" (Costa, 1991, p. 3).

The Institute for Curriculum and Instruction's intended outcome statement recommends that by graduation from high school our students should be able to "consistently and effectively take intelligent and ethical action to accomplish the tasks society legitimately expects of all of its members and to establish and pursue worthwhile goals of their own choosing" (Costa, 1991, p. 6). Among the skills mentioned as relevant were critical-thinking skills such as clarifying, analyzing, evaluating consequences, and using ethical procedures to evaluate a course of action (Costa, 1991, pp. 6–7). Because of the interest in cooperative learning and the emphasis on critical thinking, a teacher's role has changed from information-giver to "facilitator" in many classrooms (Lipman, 1991, p. 15).

This is not a new role for many teachers. Educators, philosophers, and theorists from Dewey to Vygotsky have talked through the years about teachers as facilitators of experience. This wave of concern is inspired to some extent by the many changes in technology and information processing; "during this century, the tremendous increases in knowledge have outstripped our ability to learn or even gather it in a lifetime" (Davidson & Worsham, 1992, p. 14). Hence, the need for information-processing skills and critical thinking gains new attention. Thurow reminds us that the "critical factor for the American community in the coming economic competition will be the facility with which workers learn new technologies . . . The leading industries of the future will all be brainpower industries" (Erickson, 1995, p. 26). The old basics have not become less important or gone away, but we have to consider presenting them differently and letting our students spend more time on processing than on simple recall.

How then are we to reach these goals of competence and compassion for our children? The good news is that the best approach isn't just to add an isolated, rigorous critical thinking program to our teaching day, but instead to embed these skills and processes into the existing curriculum. Teachers may help their students use multilogical strategies; identify connections, similarities, and differences; actively involve students in their own learning; entertain a wide variety of perspectives and views; use diverse teaching strategies; and encourage rational discussions and disagreements in their classrooms. The purpose, then, is not just to teach and reinforce critical thinking but to improve comprehension in content areas and practice conflict resolution skills simultaneously.

Melding conflict resolution and critical thinking into the content areas is not a compromise but a resourceful enhancement of classroom content. Using "real life situations" increases interest in science and other content areas (Cawelti, 1995, p. 132) as well as providing students with an opportunity to solve problems with the increased interest inspired by relevance.

From a review of the research it can be concluded that "students will better learn and use critical thinking skills and strategies if these skills and strategies are taught explicitly in the context of content knowledge with attention to their [various] appropriate applications" (Cawelti, 1995, p. 150). Although both critical thinking and conflict resolution skills may be successfully introduced on their own, incorporating these skills (or subsets thereof) will strengthen their use and transfer, as well as strengthening content area comprehension (O'Tuel & Bullard, 1993).

The good news here is that we have no shortage of real-life problems and conflicts for our students to consider, and no shortage of content area material that we are expected to cover. By discussing our critical-thinking and conflict resolution objectives together we are not suggesting that the critical-thinking and conflict resolution parts of our model are to be thought of or treated as the same entity. We are, however, suggesting that they no longer be considered as unrelated entities; they are a constellation of facets. Reflecting on our review of the research, the relationship between violence and aggression, and social skills and academic achievement is strong and clear. Our critical thinking and conflict resolution community model proposes that we begin to consider problem-solving, critical-thinking skills and conflict resolution skills as occupying different places on a continuum.

It is difficult to successfully accomplish our conflict resolution goals without considering students' cognitive characteristics: their abilities to analyze and reflect; their perspective-taking ability; their listening and comprehension strategies; and their divergent thinking abilities. It is also difficult, if not impossible, to reach our academic critical-thinking goals without considering students' abilities to concentrate, communicate, and work with others. Conflict resolution and critical-thinking skills are not separate or opposite, but instead are related and complimentary skills with many subskills in common—some being closer to the conflict resolution end of the continuum and some being closer to the critical-thinking end of the continuum.

SOCIAL SKILLS: WHERE THERE IS HOPE, THERE IS LIFE

Social and emotional intelligence and abilities may be more important to the child's welfare than IQ, according to Goleman (1995). In one study cited by Goleman (1995), boys with above-average intelligence were failing in school because they were impulsive and anxious. As Goleman (1995) tells us, "Despite their intellectual potential, these are the children at highest risk for problems like academic failure, alcoholism, and criminality—not because their intellect is deficient, but because their control over their emotional life is impaired" (p. 27). The calm, reflective steps of conflict resolution and perspective taking lend well to impulse control. There may be "no psychological skill more fundamental than resisting impulse. It is the root of all emotional self-control" (Goleman, 1993, p. 81).

In the now famous marshmallow test, Stanford researchers gave four-year-olds a marshmallow and told them they could get two marshmallows if they could wait five minutes before eating the first. If not, they would simply have the one they had consumed. Years later, when the marshmallow subjects had graduated from high school, researchers found that "those who had resisted temptation at four were now, as adolescents, more socially competent, personally effective, self-assertive . . . better able to cope. They were less likely to go to pieces, freeze, or regress under stress. . . , they embraced challenges, were self-reliant, confident, trustworthy . . ." (Goleman, 1993, p. 82). Later tests showed that those who were less impulsive at four years were "far superior as students" (Goleman, 1993, p. 82) with a 210-point average difference from the more impulsive students or the SATs. A review of these and other related studies indicates that IQ predicts 4 to 20 percent of career performance. It's significant to note that in the authors' research the most frequent response students give to the question of how they have changed following conflict resolution training has been "Now I stop and think" (Heydenberk & Heydenberk, 1997a). The integrative environment helps students understand themselves and each other and curb their impulsivity.

Emotional intelligence predicts approximately 80 percent of the person's success in life (Pool, 1997, p. 12). The more serious negative effects of poor emotional control and poor social skills include increased risk for delinquency and violence. A child's early antisocial behavior, misreading of social cues, conflict, and impulsivity are "almost three times as powerful a predictor of later delinquency as is their IQ" (Goleman, 1995, p. 237).

Related studies found "when depressed children have been compared to those without depression, they have been found to be more socially inept, to have fewer friends, to be less preferred than others as playmates, to be less liked, and to have more troubled relationships with other children" (Goleman, 1995, p. 243). These children were also doing poorly in school. This depression was tied to "children's own abilities to control what happens in their lives" (Goleman, 1995, p. 244). "In fact, among the younger children, the strongest predictor that they would become depressed was a pessimistic outlook" (Goleman, 1995, p. 245). Some "promising findings" (Goleman, 1995, p. 245) came from an after-school program that included "thinking before acting" (Goleman, 1995, p. 245) and challenging the children's pessimistic beliefs. These social and emotional skills had a significant positive impact on the depressed children (Goleman, 1995; Seligman, 1990).

Snyder's (1994) work with hope, optimism, and emotional control found the same relationship between emotional control and emotional outlook, and performance in academics, athletics, and life. In findings related to Seligman's (1990) work Snyder (1994) discovered that optimism, emotional control, and performance levels were amenable to positive change through problem-solving training. In fact, Snyder's Hope Scale is a measure of students' dispositions about their problem-solving abilities, including:

> I can think of many ways to get out of a jam.
>
> There are lots of ways around any problem.
>
> I can meet the goals I set for myself.
>
> Even when others get discouraged, I know I can find a way to solve a problem. (Snyder, 1994, p. 26)

Snyder's (1994) studies have found that high-hope children perform better in school socially, academically, and athletically. Even when the "previous levels of achievement is taken into account, hope still predicts performance on a variety of outcomes" (p. 24). Hope often predicts "positive outcomes even when one controls statistically for the effects of intelligence" (Snyder, 1995, p. 24). Snyder's Hope Scale Scores are not correlated with IQ. Overall, therefore, the academic performance benefits of high hope "are not simply differences in previous records of scholastic achievement or intellectual ability" (Snyder, 1994, p. 54).

It is known that "children who experience trauma may have difficulty seeing themselves in future roles that are meaningful" (Wallach, 1993, p. 152) as in the case of the Chowchilla School bus kidnapping victims. These lower-hope children "feel they have no control over their lives" and "cannot give their all to the present task of learning and becoming socialized" (Wallach, 1993, p. 162). Social skills and conflict resolution curricula have been shown to positively affect the low level of hope in some children as well as positively affect a related sense of self-efficacy (Heydenberk & Heydenberk, 1997c).

The high-hope scores are closely related to social and emotional problem-solving abilities. Characteristics of high-hope people are that they believe they can solve problems well and enjoy problem solving, they "enjoy interacting with people and they listen to the perspectives of others" (Synder, 1994, p. 197). In fact, Synder's (1994) first prescription for parents to foster hope and related resilience in their children "is to convey the importance of listening" (p. 197) and give children strong social problem-solving skills.

Instead of fixation on worry or blame, high-hope children, like optimistic children, "look outward and problem solve . . . giving attention to the task rather than oneself" (Synder, 1994, p. 59). This is one of the first skills students learn in the integrative thinking environment. The focus on attacking problems rather than people increases hope in the integrative environment. Low-hope children, on the other hand, "aren't very good at making and maintaining friends . . . generally report feeling lonely, [and] have difficulty understanding the perspectives of other people and establishing intimate relationships and friendships" (Snyder, 1994, p. 251). Snyder (1994) indicates that although research shows a positive relationship between social support, and "positive coping and reports of well-being" (p. 251) it is not "the sheer number of contacts" (p. 251) that predict those relationships, but in fact whether or not a subject believes they can communicate effectively with those with whom they have contact.

Social interaction and self-efficacy appear to be so central to a child's well being that some have argued that these motivation systems are "inherent in our species" (Masten & Coatsworth, 1998, p. 208). Children's innate mastery motivation in the area of self-efficacy is "readily observable in the inclination of young children to actively engage with the environment and to experience pleasure [a feeling of efficacy] from effective interactions" (Masten & Coatsworth, 1998, p. 208). Babies exhibit motivation to achieve mastery of social self-efficacy with caregivers (Masten & Coatsworth, 1998) and show distress when they cannot interact successfully.

Self-efficacy affects students' choices of activities, goals, behaviors and "predicts such diverse outcomes as academic achievement, social skills, pain tolerance, athletic performance . . . coping with feared events" (Schunk, 1991, p. 209). In social and achievement settings, much of a student's disposition will be determined by skills: A "high (sense of) self efficacy will not produce competent performances when requisite skills are lacking" (Schunk, 1991, p. 209). Although self-efficacy depends on skill development, "heightened self-efficacy sustains motivation and improves skill development" (Schunk, 1991, p. 213) in turn. In short, when students have an opportunity to resolve their problems successfully and handle problems effectively, they develop the self-efficacy and motivation to continue to function well. In some instances, students who consider themselves good problem solvers not only accept, but may actually welcome an opportunity to mediate a conflict (Heydenberk & Heydenberk, 1997a). Given a chance to first learn the steps of problem-solving, then practice, review and label strategies, students become skilled and develop positive dispositions toward problem-solving on their own. As their social and problem-solving skills improve, students' academic performance and pro-social attachments are strengthened, too.

A report from the Centers for Disease Control states that "training in social skills that includes nonviolent conflict resolution training . . . provides students with appropriate standards of behavior, a sense of control over their behavior and improved self-esteem" (Fenley et al., 1993, p. 14). These students are not only less likely to be perpetrators of violence, but are also less likely to "become victims of violence" (Fenley et al., 1993, p. 14).

Both problem-solving curricula and conflict resolution programs have been related to "long-term academic and social competence gains" (Zins & Forman, 1991, p. 27; van Steenbergen, 1994; Kazdin, Esveldt, Dawson, French, & Unis, 1987). Both types of programs help us prepare healthier, happier, productive, and safe students and community members. By including teaching strategies that may use children's social skills as well as their academic skills, such as structured controversy, integrative thinking, cooperative learning strategies, and other forms of interactive teaching, we give our students more ways to learn, succeed, and get along. Research shows us that students who have some success and develop their critical thinking abilities will "find thinking enjoyable" as opposed to the "poor thinker" who will, in contrast, "need certainty, avoid thinking . . . (and) . . . reach closure quickly" (Costa, 1991, p. 65). As skilled thinkers we can show our children how to enjoy thinking, enjoy problem solving, and embrace conflict as an opportunity for creativity and increased understanding rather than as a crisis.

ATTITUDES AND ACHIEVEMENT: THE ALCHEMY OF THE INTEGRATIVE THINKING CLASSROOM

Academic achievement affects students' sense of school attachment and their attitudes. However, students' attachment and attitudes also powerfully predict academic achievement. Although this is not a simple relationship, it is a critical relationship. Too often, critical thinking has been narrowly defined and taught. Critical thinking has two distinct and important aspects—skills and dispositions (Kennedy, Fisher, & Ennis, 1991). Skills (or abilities) are the more cognitive aspect to critical thinking, whereas dispositions (or attitudes) are the more affective aspect. The importance of dispositions becomes clear when a student possesses a high level of intelligence and thinking skills and is "not . . . disposed or inclined to exhibit or use them" (Kennedy, Fisher, & Ennis, 1991, p. 14). Among the dispositions that Kennedy and his colleagues (1991) consider key are being open minded and considerate of other people. Research on critical thinking shows that "students who undergo thinking instruction gradually do score better on outcome measures than their controls" (Kennedy, Fisher, & Ennis, 1991, p. 14). Researchers suggest that an "overlooked" (Kennedy et al., 1991, p. 15) strategy is to work on students' attitudes and dispositions as well as their abilities.

The dispositional or affective aspects of intellect and the cognitive aspects are difficult to consider separately. Piaget's suggestion that "we must agree that at no level, even in the adult, can we find a behavior or a state which is purely cognitive without affect nor a purely affective state without a cognitive element" (Marzano, 1992, p. 415) is echoed here. Marzano's (1992) summary of the research on attitudes and dispositions holds that "the extent to which learning occurs is a function of the learners' affective tone, attitudes . . . [and] awareness of explicit goals" (p. 417). For Marzano (1992) "dispositions are habitual ways that we approach a learning situation" (p. 424). Many "dispositions, when activated, drastically change the nature of learning" (Marzano, 1992, p. 425). Seeking clarity, being open minded, well informed, sensitive to the feelings of others, and self regulating are important dispositions for effective critical thinking. As Csikszentmihalyi (1990) reminds us, great thinkers tell us they are "motivated by the enjoyment of thinking" (p. 126).

High-ability students who give up easily or simply don't care are far less likely to succeed in life than their average counterparts imbued with enthusiasm, compassion, and a determination to triumph over inevitable challenges and conflicts. This connection or attachment has been the focus of concerted research, the most notable being done by David Hawkins and his colleagues.

Opportunities for success in the classroom and opportunities to participate actively in the learning process promote school bonding (Brewer, Hawkins, Catalano, & Neckerman, 1995). School bonding promotes academic achievement (Wright, 1994; Hawkins, 1995). Academic achievement, in turn, promotes stronger school bonds and provides the attachment that helps children avoid destructive behaviors and choices (Hawkins, 1995; Brewer et al., 1995; Wright, 1994; Baruch & Stutman, 1993).

Developing the skills necessary to become successful in the classroom is always a priority goal. When students experience success their school bond increases as does their motivation to strive for further success (Empey & Stafford, 1991; Hawkins, Doveck, & Lihner, 1988). To assure involvement and success Hawkins suggests interactive teaching. Engaging the student increases mastery with ongoing assessment and checks and provides an opportunity for social growth by incorporating constructive classroom interaction and cooperative learning with great success for students of all ability levels (Hawkins et al., 1988). One of our challenges is to find out how to best help each child succeed; every child "possesses at least one small island of competency, one area that is or has the potential to be a source of pride and accomplishment" (Baruch & Stutman, 1993, p. 12). Finding the islands and building on them in the "ocean of self doubt" (Baruch & Stutman, 1993, p. 12) is the first step most teachers take to facilitate students' success. Looking at all of our student's talents, strengths, and weaknesses and assessing their various multiple intelligences "is an idea whose time has come" (Gardner, 1983, p. 11). Now teachers ask students *how* they are smart, not how smart they are, a much more important and constructive question. In the integrative thinking classroom all students use their interpersonal, intrapersonal, and academic intelligences to strengthen the learning process, making it more meaningful and memorable.

Teachers do not simply encourage growth and achievement in a student's special area of interest or talent but instead use that information about an individual student's strengths to provide that student with opportunities for success and opportunities to enjoy learning. These opportunities in turn build a student's confidence which becomes the engine for new growth in other areas. These experiences of success work to sustain students through the more strenuous and challenging times. "Study after study" (Empey & Stafford, 1991, p. 240) show us that the continual experience of failure at school is one of the best predictors of future destructive behavior. By locating a child's opportunities for success, a teacher has built a "scaffolding" (Zemelman, Daniels, & Hyde, 1993, p. 8) enabling his or her students to continue to build their successes and strengthen their school bonds. This school bond, in turn, strengthens the students' commitment to academic success.

Because researchers now agree that most "learning is . . . socially constructed and often interactional" and "teachers need to create classroom interactions which scaffold learning" (Zemelman, Daniels, & Hyde, 1993, p. 8), teachers are developing a range of new techniques. In HOTS (Higher Order Thinking Skills Program), Pergoff simply masters turning students' questions around with great success for students of all abilities (Hartjen, 1994). The teacher "must help the student learn to focus on a problem and define its attributes" through guided inquiry techniques (Hartjen, 1994, p. 80). Students set out to answer their own questions themselves or in small teams. Evaluations of these teams suggest that most students are so "enthusiastic about their inquires, that the teacher does not have to deal with disciplinary problems" (Hartjen, 1994, p. 82).

Although many textbooks "fragment thinking skills" (Yashin & Shaw, 1997, p. 412), the interaction of the integrative thinking classroom may breathe new life into our content studies. Any social interaction that creates emotional meaning or new associations with content "enhances students' enjoyment" (Sylwester, 1995, p. 76) of thinking as well as their memory of the content. Students are transformed from owners of knowledge to users of knowledge. Students may achieve Csikszentmihalyi's (1990) cognitive flow as cooperation and feedback increases in the integrative thinking classroom.

Through critical thinking "children learn to object to weak reasoning," ask questions, and "practice the art of making good judgments" (Lipman, 1993, p. 337). Through academic debate and interaction students become better at "giving reasons to support another's view even if one doesn't agree" and therefore become "free of the need to always be right" (Lipman, 1993, p. 338) in the classroom. Students become better at understanding the perspectives of others and better at listening to one another. In the integrative thinking classroom students begin to look for the strengths and weaknesses and what's right in each position or idea.

Students working in cooperative groups develop better metacognitive skills (Davidson & Worsham, 1992). Decades of extensive research into various forms of cooperative learning show increased "academic achievement, development of higher order thinking skills, self-esteem and self-confidence as a learner, intergroup relations including cross-race friendships, social acceptance of mainstreamed students, development of social skills and [the] ability to take the perspective of another person" (Davidson & Worsham, 1992, p. 12). Characteristics common to many cooperative learning classrooms include "small group student-to-student interaction, interdependence structured to foster cooperation, teaching of social skills, processing social skills, reflecting, team building, initiating group work, trying ideas together, and perspective taking" (Davidson & Worsham, 1992, p. 12).

Students who have been "stuck in the cycle of low expectations, children who appear to lack the internal resources to control themselves," children whose "anger and self-dislike [is] then acted out," and children who appear to "only respond to rigid controls" (Zemelman, Daniels, & Hyde, 1993, p. 213) may ultimately be our best new team members when the long, hard work of group building and conflict resolution skill building is done. Many of the most challenging students are the first ones to benefit from the increased critical thinking and social skills of cooperative learning environments. Some of our students have "never seen these values (cooperation, deferral of gratification, sharing, responsibility, and self-control) enacted and never internalize them" (Zemelman, Daniels, & Hyde, 1993, p. 214). Many of our teachers "are delighted to discover that meaningful classroom activities yield the side effect of improving children's behavior" (Zemelman, Daniels, & Hyde, 1993, p. 214).

Whatever the methods, in whatever measure the teacher is comfortable choosing, it is clear that discussion and analysis produce more critical thinking in classrooms, improving recall and inspiring more in-depth questioning. In language arts, children's discussion and analysis and writing enable the student to "construct and communicate their own ideas" (Cawelti, 1995, p. 78). In any academic endeavor, "when students are involved in actively constructing their knowledge, with the teacher's guidance based on understanding of the subject matter and the conceptions and misconceptions that the students bring to the learning situation, learning will be both more meaningful and more correct." (John Dewey, quoted in Cawelti, 1995, p. 158).

In consideration of the students' classroom environment, Greenspan's (1997) intensive research has confirmed that emotions "provides purpose and direction" (p. 66) to critical thinking and any cognitive activity. If we ignore a classroom's state of alienation, students "emerging behavior and thinking becomes idiosyncratic and disorganized like members of an orchestra playing without a conductor" (Greenspan, 1997, p. 66). Effective higher level thinking may then be impossible.

On the other hand, positive social interaction enhances performance. In one of Izard's early studies, subjects interacted with a planted actor who was either encouraging, supportive, concerned, and positive or very critical, negative, and hostile. Following the emotional interaction, the subjects who interacted with the more positive actor performed considerably better on tests of creative thinking and intellectual functioning. In another study reviewed by Izard (1991) positive emotion induced by a humorous filmclip or a gift of candy "caused subjects to perform more effectively on intellectual or problem-solving tasks" (p. 167).

Wentzel and her colleagues (Wentzel, Weinberger, Ford, & Feldman, 1990) studied the relationship between social and emotional factors and academic success, because there exists "an important developmental link between social and academic competence" (Wentzel et al., 1990, p. 179) and "there is evidence that affective and self-regulatory problems such as . . . low empathy, aggression, and conduct disorders predict low levels of achievement" (Wentzel et al., 1990, p. 179). The authors suggest that we consider that "social and emotional development may also be important contributors to intellectual development and school success" (Wentzel et al., 1990, p. 189). The authors find "little doubt" (Wentzel et al., 1990, p. 190) that social and emotional abilities "contribute directly to achievement" (Wentzel et al., 1990, p. 190).

Some of the most compelling research on affect and school climate comes from studies of neighborhoods and schools exposed to the same violence, poverty, racism, and other environmental risks, but with very different outcomes (Katz, 1997). What makes the difference in these schools is "the attitudes and beliefs among administrative and teaching staff and the school fostering the acquisition of important social and cognitive skills among the students" (Katz, 1997, p. 97). The schools are not different from each other, nor are the students attending them different; what is different is their response to conflict and school attachment.

Apparently "the human experience can't be made coherent by merely labeling its parts, locating them on a conceptual framework and studying them in isolation" (Beane, 1995, p. 30). In the conflict-positive integrative thinking classroom, students process information and construct knowledge through multiple lenses. Apparently, we learn our conflict resolution and critical thinking skills by listening, comparing, reflecting, processing information ourselves, and discussing it with our teachers and friends. As Aristotle told us "what is called judgment . . . is the right discrimination of the equitable" found through both dialogue and deliberation. Thousands of years later, it is even more critical that we learn to think deeply and to listen carefully to one another.

Superior IQ alone doesn't protect students from decreased academic performance under stress. Goleman's review of 126 different studies "found that the more prone to worries a person is, the poorer their academic performance, no matter how measured—grades on tests, grade point average, and achievement tests" (Goleman, 1995, p. 84). As a child's anger increases, his "energy gets channeled into erecting barriers, rather than into communication and problem-solving," eventually creating "a maze of psychological mines and trenches" (McKay, Rodgers, & McKay, 1989, p. 34) that make it impossible to establish healthy bonds and attachments or to achieve academic success.

For this child (and his or her peers and/or victims), simply posting rules or demanding a behaviorial change isn't effective. Nothing short of a new paradigm in the classroom will have an effect. Chronic anger or chronic fear can make a child "rigid and trigger-happy" (McKay, Rodgers, & McKay, 1989, p. 35), emotionally if not literally. The switch from "defense to appreciation, from vigilance, to any kind of trust" (McKay, Rodgers, & McKay, 1989, p. 35) is not a simple one. We know that simply venting anger actually increases anger (Goleman, 1995).

First our children need to believe that peace, respect, safety, and trust are all possible. In Ritta Wahlstrom's study of hundreds of children, she found that those "who considered aggression and war to be a part of human nature were understandably not inclined to work towards the goal of peace" (McKay, Rodgers, & McKay, 1989). Numerous studies from all over the world confirm her findings (Blumberg and French, 1992).

Hopelessness and a negative affective tone "will inhibit learning" (Davidson & Worsham, 1992, p. 10). The first requisite in our classrooms is "a sense of safety and acceptance. Safety refers to both physical and psychological safety . . . Students must believe that their ideas will be honored and valued and their failures will not be met with ridicule" (Davidson & Worsham, 1992, p. 106). Students are not overburdened by challenge or conflict if they know they have the tools to handle it.

Creating an environment that is physically, psychologically, and socially safe is the first step in restoring hope. In an integrative environment, hope is increased despite all other risk factors (Heydenberk & Heydenberk, 1997a). The ability to constructively handle conflict in high-risk situations changes the student's entire outlook. The conflicts that in the past caused fear, anger, and alienation, are handled skillfully and peacefully—increasing hope.

Closely related to a sense of psychological safety is a sense on the part of students that they are accepted and appreciated by their teacher and peers (Davidson & Worsham, 1992, p. 10). Our school community sanctuary begins in the classroom. Students in a hopeful and safe environment become better critical thinkers and problem solvers as they "believe in their own competence in scholastics, social matters . . . and behavior conduct as well as global self-worth" (Snyder, 1994, p. 119). Controlling for IQ, children who "possess higher hope perform better in the scholastic and athletic arenas" (Snyder, 1994, p. 195) by objective measures. High-hope children are "more facile at understanding the perspective of other people" (Snyder, 1994, p. 94) and are less likely to misplace blame. High-hope children "report less depression and [have] an elevated sense of self-worth, as well as an internal source of control" (Snyder, 1994, p. 113). Because hope is related to social and cognitive resilience skills, these children may overcome obstacles and become stronger as they experience triumphs, developing an "enduring pattern of thinking" (Snyder, 1994, p. 68). Students with hope can build lasting friendships, focus academically, and better meet the challenges of a hostile environment.

In contrast, children without coping skills who live with constant fear and stress may develop learned helplessness. These children suffer from chronic pessimism that pervades every aspect of their lives, "but the pessimism is not fixed and unchangeable" (Seligman, 1990, p. 16). They can learn a set of thinking skills that can set them "free from the tyranny of pessimism" (Seligman, 1990, p. 16). Social competence, including self-regulation and problem-solving style, is one of the most powerful predictors of academic achievement (Wentzel, 1991). In fact, these "interpersonal forms of competence are often more powerful predictors of achievement than intellectual ability" (Wentzel, 1991, p. 1066).

Wentzel's (1991) study of the relationship between social competence and academic achievement found that socially responsible behavior is a significant factor in predicting students' grades and school success. Self-regulated behavior appears to be determined by several components including levels of interpersonal trust, interpersonal problem solving, and a sense of social responsibility (Wentzel, 1991, p. 1067). All three of these subcomponents of self-regulation have been linked "empirically to objective indices of social competence as well as to intellectual accomplishments" (Wentzel, 1991, p. 1067). Wentzel (1991) found that each characteristic of social responsibility, interpersonal problem solving, interpersonal trust, and emotional self-regulation was significantly correlated with grade point average. A socially responsible disposition explained a significant amount of unique grade point average. School success is related to students' abilities to resolve academic and social problems in an adaptive way. As Wentzel (1991) summarizes, "Very simply, students who control negative affective reactions to failure and who persist in trying to solve problems achieve more than those who tend to become emotionally upset" (p. 1068) in social and academic domains. "Although the link between social and academic problem-solving is not well understood," Wentzel tells us that it appears that "the ability to control negative emotional reactions to failure may contribute to both socially and academically competent outcomes" (Wentzel, 1991, p. 1068).

It is important to note that being socially competent is not a popularity contest. Children who are socially competent, capable of higher levels of interpersonal problem solving and relating to peers with respect and trust, but who are not particularly popular, still enjoy the higher levels of social responsibility and higher grade point average scores. Students who are either popular or neglected by peers but socially responsible still enjoy academic success.

There exists a "well-established relationship between academic underachievement and anti-social behavior" (Larson, 1994, p. 151). Although the direction of the relationship is not always clear or uniform, in most cases academic achievement is fostered in an integrative environment (Johnson & Johnson, 1996). We have strong evidence that conflict resolution programs that provide students with some opportunities for skills development in a cooperative context are related to "significant increases on cognitive skills as indexed by the WISC-R (Wechsler Intelligence Scale for Children—Revised)" (Greenberg, 1996, p. 3) and other measures of achievement (Johnson & Johnson, 1996).

Contrary to common perceptions, increased time on task alone does not appear to be the significant factor. Increased motivation and self-efficacy in an integrative environment, as well as increased opportunities to practice authentic problem solving are important factors related to gains in reasoning and academic achievement (Johnson, Johnson, Dudley, Mitchell, & Fredrickson, 1997; Wentzel, Weinberger, Ford, & Feldman, 1990; Schunk, 1991).

Perhaps the most telling evidence comes from those who work directly with students: their teachers. Teachers tell us that students "work harder, achieve more and attribute importance to schoolwork in classes in which they feel liked, accepted, and respected by the teacher and fellow students" (Lewis, Schaps, & Watson, 1996, p. 141).

Children who learn the constructive problem-solving and communication skills related to increased hope and optimism have the "keys to academic success" according to education researcher Joan Girgus (Seligman, 1990, p. 142). Children who learn conflict resolution skills and other "interpersonal problem-solving skills" are more resilient, hopeful, resourceful, and responsible (Baruch

& Stutman, 1993, p. 11). Children who have an opportunity to contribute and solve their own problems "feel they have some control over their lives" (Baruch & Stutman, 1993, p. 13). These students make better decisions and become more hopeful in school and in life (Goleman, 1995; Baruch & Stutman, 1993). Furthermore, they make more friends and have a more substantial support network when they are sick or faced with a tragedy, trauma, or adversity (Snyder, 1994).

There is extensive research support for Hirschi's (1969) assertions about the importance of bonding and creating a sense of community (Hawkins, 1995; Empey & Stafford, 1991). There is also substantial evidence that a safe school community with a conflict resolution program and a committed teaching team is at least as effective as individual therapy alone for many aggressive children (Olweus, 1979; Olweus, 1991; Mash & Barkley, 1989). Positive student interaction and community support for prosocial behaviors may "reduce alienation in the classroom" and promote positive attachments among students which may "in turn reduce the likelihood that students will form alternate attachments with delinquent peers" (Hawkins & Lishner, 1987, p. 273; Howell, Krisberg, Hawkins, & Wilson, 1995) resulting in destructive behaviors. Gangs fill a need and therefore may not proliferate when children have positive school bonds.

In addition to having healthier, safer students, the relationship between conflict resolution and emotional literacy skills, and a child's academic performance is also strong and positive (Center for the Study of the Prevention of Violence ([CSPV], 1996). Among the expected results of reduced conflict and behavior problems, the research has shown significant increases in students' cognitive skills using standard measures.

Conflict resolution strategies have been integrated into classroom work "in ways that promote academic achievement" (Johnson & Johnson, 1995, p. 434). These skills have also been shown to become part of a "lifelong practice of peace" (Meek, 1992, p. 51). When a child feels that he or she is part of a larger community this "larger perspective" (Goleman, 1995, p. 241) provides the psychological safety net that becomes the foundation for resilience. The child's community relationship provides a chance to become socially and emotionally competent, reinforcing skills that are essential for success and happiness in school and life. Anger and impulsivity "in a ten-year-old boy is almost three times as powerful a predictor of their later delinquency as their IQ" (Goleman, 1995, p. 237). In fact, emotional literacy and conflict resolution skills and programs that support "emotional competence" are more significant predictors of a child's future success in life "over and above family economic forces" (Goleman, 1995, p. 256). Social and emotional competence may determine "the extent any given child or teenager is undone by . . . hardships or finds a core of resilience to survive them" (Goleman, 1995, p. 256). Studies of hundreds of children who have faced hardships and risks have shown us that resilient children "share key emotional skills" (Goleman, 1995, p. 256), among them emotional competence, social skills, and "an optimistic perspective in the face of failure and frustration" (Goleman, 1995, p. 256).

The basic social skills are also the skills that children need in order to be successful in the classroom: listening, reflecting, cooperation, perspective reversal, communication, and understanding. Teachers are "looking for new tools" to facilitate and develop students' capacities to understand, express and control their feelings, as well as "relate sensitively and effectively" (Kessler, 1994, p. 34). Violence prevention and conflict resolution "has been another impetus for emotional literacy courses, since cooperation and interpersonal problem solving are fundamental lessons" (Goleman, 1994, p. 34). As creative and committed teachers implement new programs the good news continues to come in (Goleman, 1995; CSPV, 1996). The promising results from the education community are that even in the most challenging high risk environments, creating safe schools characterized by hope and success is possible.

The social and emotional climate of the classroom influence the students' ability to learn (Sylwester, 1995; Restack, 1984). There is "abundant evidence to indicate that positive peer relationships are requisites for mental health and educational success" (Mash & Barkley, 1989, p. 222). Our classroom teachers are in a unique and powerful position to effect change in students' communication and critical thinking abilities. Peer mediation, conflict resolution, and social and emotional literacy programs have grown "geometric in proportion" with some positive results that are "remarkable" (Mash & Barkley, 1989, p. 231). The most "lasting success" in emotional literacy or social skills programs is reported for "interventions . . . when the peer group has also been involved" (Mash & Barkley, 1989, p. 240).

The aggressive child often misreads social cues and attributes hostility to others where there is none. This anger endangers the child and all with whom he has contact; it upsets the school community. The inability to read social cues, empathize, and resolve conflict successfully affects the student's academic performance and may well affect the academic performance of the child's classmates. "Fear, anger, and stress cause a student's performance to deteriorate" (Restak, 1994, p. 175). Even reading becomes "more difficult" (Restak, 1994, p. 175) as stress causes dilation of the pupils. A student under stress or fear may find it "impossible to take in new information . . . recall previously acquired information . . . [or] concentrate" (Restak, 1994, p. 175), much less problem-solve or think critically, or think creatively, or establish empathy.

In an interesting biochemical twist, "the chronically angry bully usually has lower testosterone levels than their peers, indicating that they perceive themselves as lower status," and . . . "they do not consider their chronic aggression to be a successful adaptation, perhaps because they often have few friends" (Marano, 1995). Among different social classes and different communities testosterone "surges" or peaks at different ages. These hormone levels are to some extent affected by environmental interaction and status and stress; "winners gain not only status, but surges of T [testosterone]" (Kemper, 1990, p. 78). Bullies do not see themselves as winners.

We cannot achieve our academic goals if we must live with the fear, aggression, stress, and anxiety caused by bullies. In *Creating Sanctuary*, Dr. Bloom (1997) states that, "affect draws our attention to something, determines what information reaches our consciousness and motivates our behavior." (p. 41). If students or teachers can't eliminate the stress, alienation, or fear they feel, they can't function optimally.

Testing thousands of students in New Jersey, researchers found that feeling like a "definite minority in a group tends to blank out your intuitive ability in that group" (Ostrander, Schroeder, & Ostrander, 1979, p. 205). In contrast, the increased sense of belonging or attachment in the integrative thinking classroom may facilitate cognitive gains. Peer interaction is a prime vehicle for academic and cognitive growth in the integrative thinking environment.

In some sense, all students may fall victim to the minority effect in a classroom characterized by alienation and competition. Students in an exclusively competitive classroom become more rigid, dichotomous thinkers as a result of working in a win–lose, polarized academic environment (Kohn, 1986). Interestingly, our competitive individualistic environment also creates "rank conformity" and "dampens creativity" (Kohn, 1986, p. 130). In contrast, in an integrative thinking classroom, students routinely examine other perspectives thereby reducing the my-side bias that flaws most thinking, regardless of high levels of intelligence (Perkins, 1995).

When students "seek to find the value in each position or idea" (Berman, 1991, p. 15) they learn to engage in "synthesis thinking" (Berman, 1991, p. 15)— or integrative thinking (Johnson & Johnson, 1996). Rather than focusing on a polarized, quick, right or wrong response, they broaden their perspectives and begin to synthesize new solutions.

THE TOOLS OF ACADEMIC ACHIEVEMENT: THE TOOLS OF PEACE

Increased school attachment and prosocial orientation improve academic and prosocial behaviors. Cooperative conflict and constructive controversy fuel higher level reasoning as well. There are, however, several aspects of the conflict resolution process itself that should be examined individually for effect.

The first skill students learn in conflict resolution training is active listening. Many consider listening skills more important than oral communication (Davidson & Worsham, 1992). Most of us spend 8.4% of our time writing, 13.3% reading, 23% speaking and 55% listening (Davidson and Worsham, 1992). Listening is an essential academic and social skill, and "improvement in it also results in improved behaviors in speaking, reading, and learning" (Cawelti, 1995, p. 89). As children are asked to listen carefully, identify a purpose, and report it back, they are strengthening a host of other skills. The active listening and paraphrasing in the integrative thinking classroom increases students' listening comprehension (Heydenberk & Heydenberk, 1997a). The paraphrasing, role reversal, and perspective taking required in the conflict resolution process have been researched extensively. Johnson and Johnson (1991) found that students' reasoning is enhanced "by the combination of explaining one's knowledge and summarizing and paraphrasing the other persons' knowledge and perspective" (p. 299).

Paraphrasing may be the single most powerful academic tool we have for increasing comprehension. Researchers from the United States Army Learning Resources Center and the University of Maryland conducted a controlled study of fourth graders' comprehension after silent reading of a content area passage. Half of the students used notes and illustrated a model to represent their knowledge of the content they studied. The other half of the students "reinforced" the content "by teaching it to another student" (Jones, 1990, p. 5). This procedure involved a considerable amount of paraphrasing. The teaching group had higher scores, even several days after the study, than did the illustrating students on the day of the study. Some theorists believe teaching each other, a process which involves paraphrasing, increases memory and comprehension by up to four times as compared to the lecture format of learning (Jones, 1990, p. 5).

David Johnson's (1971) original review and summary of the research on role reversal first affirms the seminal work of Deutsch, indicating that in a competitive environment it is difficult to effectively resolve problems or conflict because "participants do not have a very complete or accurate understanding of their opponents' position or frame of reference." (p. 322). In a problem-solving situation, role reversal is "the most direct procedure" (Johnson, 1971, p. 322) and the most effective procedure "for increasing understanding" (Johnson, 1971, p. 322). It is important to note that engaging in role reversal or paraphrasing increases understanding, retention, and comprehension of all sides (Johnson & Johnson, 1979).

People who engage in role reversal are more disposed to negotiate a constructive resolution, but they remain as "committed . . . to their position" (Johnson, 1971, p. 324). Effective conflict resolution is, therefore, more often characterized by synthesizing a new solution than it is by giving in or compromising ideals or goals. In general, the Johnsons' research indicates that role reversal or paraphrasing changes the students' dispositions toward problem solving, not their ideals or principles. This "attitude change" (Johnson, 1971, p. 326) is essential to the synthesis of a constructive solution that honors both parties' perspectives. The role reversal increases "bias scanning" (Johnson, 1971, p. 327) in participants, causing increases in reflection and comprehension.

Perspective taking or role taking is a "form of social cognition intermediate between logical and moral thought" (Kohn, 1990, p. 101). Furthermore, "a certain level of cognitive development is requisite for being able to imaginatively take in the world from someone else's perspective, and this skill, in turn, has been shown to promote learning" (Kohn, 1990, p. 101). In addition to the "cognitive flexibility" (Kohn, 1990, p. 101) required to step "just outside one's usual way of thinking" (Kohn, 1990, p. 101) to consider an alternative perspective. This task also requires a sense of physical and physiological safety—an unthreatening and free environment (Kohn, 1990, p. 101).

Another proponent of role reversal, Richard Paul (1991), recommends a dialogical thinking environment in which students consider multiple perspectives. This dialogical (versus monological) environment causes students to actively reason and reflect on their own thoughts. Even the very young child working in an integrative thinking, cooperative group will engage in critical thinking. The student's discussion with his peers will cause them to provide an "elaboration of meaning . . . [and] perhaps the need to express ideas in exemplary parallel structures" from time to time (Davidson & Worsham, 1992, p. 3). Brainstorming with teachers or peers may call for "metaphor or analogical thought" (Sternberg, 1977). The elaboration and communication become vital tools for academic success.

More than fifty studies of cooperative learning teams reveal that "exchanges among teachers and learners are more frequent and specifically directed toward students' problems and interests" (Cawelti, 1995, p. 17). Students are less likely to get lost as this increased interaction tends to allow individual problems to "become clear" (Cawelti, 1995, p. 17), and students give and receive criticism without taking offense. Expressing ideas through oral communication forces students to reflect on and organize their ideas (Cawelti, 1995). In mathematics, using cognitively guided small team instruction and "allowing students to interact when solving problems and providing opportunities for students to develop and discuss their own solutions results in increased achievement"— achievement that is often "significantly improved" (Cawelti, 1995, p. 107). Studies of the cognitive benefits of giving explanations, discussing, paraphrasing, and elaborating materials in peer interactions show that students engage in more active learning, and show improved comprehension in anticipation of such interactions (Webb, 1985). In short, students who anticipate discussion and paraphrasing content, listen and attend more closely. Students who work with content in an integrative environment show improved content comprehension.

Csikszentmihalyi (1996) considers perspective taking one of the most important tools for increasing creative thinking. Csikszentmihalyi (1996) prescribes consideration of a problem "from many different perspectives" (p. 367) and avoiding "our first impulse to label problems by relying on tried and true prejudices" (p. 367). This reversal of perspective and tolerance of ambiguity increases cognitive flexibility.

Arthur Costa (1984) suggests that "evaluating with multiple criteria" (p. 60) and "paraphrasing" (p. 61) are among the most important tools for developing metacognition. Perkins and Salomon (1988) suggest that considering another's perspective requires and develops self-monitoring strategies. Because in virtually all contexts people tend to ignore the other side of the case—the side opposite their own—these metacognitive dispositions (reflecting and self-monitoring) are essential. Johnson and Johnson's (1992) research found that reversing perspectives and then reconceptualizing was the best possible tool for synthesizing a new solution to problems.

We have further indicators that paraphrasing is an essential academic tool. Whitman's (1988) work reveals that students who "learn materials for their own needs" (p. 5) use different, less effective cognitive processing than students who learn something with the expectation of teaching someone else. Costa and Liebmann (1997) report that shifting to multiple perspectives creates a cognitive flexibility they've termed "allocentricism" (p. 9) as opposed to egocentrism. Berman's (1991) review of interpersonal perspective taking found that with these skills "students could move from egocentric and impulse interpersonal negotiation strategies to mutual and collaborative strategies" (p. 13). Finally, at the brainstorming stage of conflict resolution, students engage in a synthesis thinking "that seeks to find the value in each position or idea" (Berman, 1991, p. 15). This is the essence of Johnson and Johnson's (1996, 1997) integrative negotiation. The related construct of integrative thinking is embedded throughout the CR-CT strategies.

Conflict resolution provides students with opportunities to practice the essential perspective-taking skills that correct "my-side bias" (Perkins, 1992). Karpov and Haywood (1998) suggest that Vygotsky's concept of cognitive mediation has been shown to be the "main mechanism of learning and development" (p. 27). The authors analyze Vygotsky's work to distinguish two major types of mediation: "metacognitive and cognitive" (Karpov & Haywood, 1998, p. 27). Cognitive mediation begins with the exploration of academic concepts in school-age children. To develop metacognitive skills in children, the authors recommended "cooperative, shared activity under mutual control" (Karpov & Haywood, 1998, p. 29). Through true integrative cooperative thinking this self-regulation and metacognition develops. The authors tell us that the effect of these activities on metacognition is "supported by experimental data" (Karpov & Haywood, 1998, p. 30). The ideal "environment for the development of children's self-regulation is one of collaborative problem-solving" (Kapov & Haywood, 1998, p. 30), as in the integrative thinking classroom.

Gilhooly, Keane, Logie, and Erdos (1990) offer a similar perspective. To help children increase metacognitive skills the authors suggest paired problem solving where students think aloud with a "listener-critic" (Gilhooly et al., 1990, p. 303) and then reverse roles. Although the authors recommend several types of activities for developing metacognitive skills all efforts rely on talk "in the context of social interaction as a means for promoting thinking" (Gilhooly et al., 1990, p. 307). Social interaction and social problem solving is a "recurrent theme" (Gilhooly et al., 1990, p. 307) in all the metacognitive development strategies.

Within this recurring theme it is easy to understand how increased metacognition and sense of responsibility are among the frequently reported results of a conflict resolution program. Several studies (Johnson et al., 1997; Zins & Forman, 1988) report that conflict resolution, integrative thinking, and perspective reversal skills create students who are empowered to reason and form prosocial bonds on their own. Other studies (Wittmer, Sterling, & Honig, 1994) report that when children study a comprehensive conflict resolution program, "even aggressive and shy children become more positively social within three months" (p. 252) and increased positive social functioning is associated with children's ability to "think of more strategies" (Wittmer, Sterling, & Honig, 1994, p. 152). All of these factors may help explain why some conflict resolution programs are associated with significant increases on measures of cognitive as well as social skills.

Conflict is such an effective learning tool and "conflict is so vital to development that some experienced teachers go out of their way to highlight or even create situations where kids must think or feel their way out" (Kohn, 1986, p. 74). Alfie Kohn (1986) also reminds us that in the case of conflict "the natural supply is abundant" (p. 74).

The cognitive and social skills of the integrative thinking environment are powerful tools for enhancing thinking and creating a school climate conducive to learning.

 CHAPTER **1**

Communication
and Comprehension

ACTIVE LISTENING

> *I touch the future. I teach.*
> —Christa McAuliffe

Our communication and comprehension chapter begins with activities to improve students' listening. Because the process is assumed to develop adequately naturally, it is given little curricular attention. This attitude persists despite decades of research indicating that listening comprises over 50 percent of our communication time and effective listening is central to school success. Fortunately, direct instruction in listening is effective. Fifty percent gains can be realized and listening improvement effects improvement "in speaking, reading, and learning" (Cawelti, 1996, p. 80). Furthermore, listening ability at the fifth-grade level is the best predictor of academic achievement in high school.

Students enjoy activities that improve listening; thus, listening instruction provides a way to engage students in the listening–reading–thinking activities essential for increased academic performance and conflict resolution.

Chapter 1 begins by creating awareness of the listening process and includes students' insights about their listening. Although listening strategies are introduced in the context of content areas, conflict scenarios, student journals, and portfolios are integrated to enhance their personal insights about listening.

INTRODUCTION TO THE CR-CT PORTFOLIO

Purpose

As students and their teachers begin using the CR-CT curriculum, they are encouraged to create a portfolio system. We begin with the Personal Portfolio from which we select pieces for our Progress Portfolio.

Procedure

- The students are introduced to the concept of the CR-CT Portfolio system. CR-CT stands for Conflict Resolution and Critical Thinking. The various activities in *A Powerful Peace: The Integrative Thinking Classroom* are designed to help us develop our conflict resolution and communication skills and to strengthen our critical thinking in various content areas at the same time. As we proceed, various activities will be included in our CR-CT Personal Portfolios. The CR-CT Personal Portfolio will encourage students to reflect on their work, review concepts, and sense changes in their communication patterns.

- The CR-CT Personal Portfolio may include writing samples, selected journal reflections, drawings, mind maps, listening charts, interviews, question logs, summary tables, character maps, biographical sketches, analogy activities, concept maps, decision-making materials, essays, toolbox tours, and more. At appropriate locations throughout the text, **Portfolio Picks** will appear. This is to identify activities which are appropriate for students to place in their portfolios.

- The CR-CT Progress Portfolio will be comprised of selected pieces from the CR-CT Personal Portfolio. These pieces will be chosen by the student and teacher at appropriate times to showcase the students' learning and progress for peers, parents, and others to observe.

- Students may have time to work on a preliminary design for their portfolio folder or box and begin to design a Table of Contents for their CR-CT Personal Portfolio.

SOUND SCAVENGERS

The opposite of talking isn't listening. The opposite of talking is waiting.
—Fran Lebowitz,
Social Studies (1977)

To help students distinguish between hearing and listening, we help them become aware of the many sounds they may hear but not actively listen to during the day.

CR-CT Skills Developed

Active Listening

Anticipation

Metacognition

Procedure

- Students work alone during 3 or 4 minutes of timed silence, during which time they record all of the sounds they hear in the classroom.
- Students read their lists in groups of 3 to 5 students. Each student checks off sounds listed by previous students and reads only sounds not mentioned so far.
- The recorder for each group reads the group's list to the class while the teacher compiles a master list on the board.
- The small groups reconvene to spend 5 minutes writing:
  a. A definition of hearing
  b. A definition of listening
- A new recorder reads each group's definition to the class as the teacher or student volunteer constructs a listening concept map on the board—"What Is Listening."

Extending Activities: Journal Writing and/or Discussion Questions

Do we screen our listening?

Do we listen to everything in our environment?

Do we hear everything or just what we pay attention to?

When am I a careful listener?

When do I have trouble listening?

STOP, LOOK, AND LISTEN

After we talk and listen to each other, we realize that we don't have a problem. It was a misunderstanding. We go through the rest of the steps to figure out how we can be more careful next time. Now we can listen to each other.

—High school student
(conflict manager)

In "Stop, Look, and Listen" we give students a chance to experience just how important it is to maintain eye contact with the speaker, not only to let them know we are paying attention but also to direct our attention and to aid our listening effort.

CR-CT Skills Developed

Active listening

Paraphrasing

Procedure

- Groups of 3 students are formed; one student in the group is selected as a listener.
- Each listener has a speaker standing back-to-back with the listener and reading script "A."
- Each listener has another speaker facing her and reading script "B."
- Both speakers/readers are instructed to use a moderate tone and pace when reading.
- The speaker facing the listener is instructed to actively engage the listener (changing body position, making eye contact often, and varying delivery rate).
- The listener is instructed to lean forward a bit and maintain eye contact with the speaker in front of her, but she must listen to the passage read behind her back.
- When the passages are finished the listener must summarize what the speaker behind her has read.
- If time permits, all may exchange roles until everyone has had a chance to be the listener.

Students should then be encouraged to comment on or discuss their conclusions.

Script 1-A

For the "Behind the Back" Speaker

For decades, Albert Einstein has remained the most quoted man in America. We came to know Albert Einstein for his contributions to our understanding of physics, but most of us will think of him first as a great humanitarian, passionately concerned about peace. One week before his death in 1955 he wrote, "There lies before us, if we choose, continued progress in happiness, knowledge, and wisdom. Shall we, instead, choose death because we cannot forget our quarrels? We appeal, as humans beings, to human beings—remember your humanity and forget the rest" (Calaprice, 1996, p. 130).

Despite the fact that Albert Einstein's theory of relativity changed our understanding of science and nature and marked Einstein as the greatest scientist of our time, most of us remember him first as a great humanitarian and outspoken pacifist. Einstein told us that "Concern for man himself must always constitute the check objective of all technical effort" (Calaprice, 1996, p. 173).

Script 1-B

For the "Facing the Listener" Speaker

Albert Einstein's favorite book was Gandhi's autobiography. He told a friend in a letter that it was his belief that "the problem of bringing peace to the world on a supranational basis will be solved only by employing Gandhi's method on a larger scale." To another friend he wrote that he could "identify" his "views nearly completely with those of Gandhi" (Calaprice, 1996, p. 116). Albert Einstein once told us that "in all cases where a reasonable solution of difficulties is possible, I favor honest cooperation and, if this is not possible under prevailing circumstance, Gandhi's method of peaceful resistance to evil."

Einstein met presidents, scientists, artists, and other remarkable people during his lifetime, but always considered Mahatma Gandhi as one of his greatest inspirations.

Script 2-A

For the "Behind the Back" Speaker

Mahatma Gandhi was born Mohanda Gandhi in 1869 near Bombay, India. He studied law at the University of London. After graduating from the University, Gandhi traveled to South Africa where he found all Hindus and many other people had a different and more difficult set of laws to follow than the British ruling class. Horrified by how unfair the system was to many innocent people, Gandhi organized a peaceful protest. He convinced many friends and followers to ignore the unfair laws, but he asked them not to fight. Their peaceful protest resulted in thousands of people being arrested.

As the jails filled, the British had to find ways to feed and support thousands of peaceful prisoners. They repealed their unfair laws. Although this was an extraordinary feat, it was just the beginning of Gandhi's inspiring crusade for peace and justice.

Script 2-B

For the "Facing the Listener" Speaker

Mahatma Gandhi was born Mohanda Gandhi in 1869 in Bombay, India. His followers and eventually all people came to call him Mahatma Gandhi which means the Great Soul. His journey to his role as a leader in peaceful protest began in South Africa where the people from India were often mistreated. He helped his people in South Africa and two decades later he returned to his native land—India. In India he again found the British in power, as he did in South Africa. He studied the economic problems of his people and slowly devised a plan. He taught people how to spin and weave their own cloth for clothes. As they learned they started businesses and bought clothes and other goods from each other. Gandhi fought injustice with peaceful activism—never with violence. He organized strikes, marches, boycotts, and civil disobedience and told his followers over and over that they were not ever to fight back. His vision has inspired people all over the world—from Rosa Parks and Martin Luther King to Albert Einstein.

Extending Activities: Journal Writing and/or Discussion

How did the "behind the back" speaker feel?

How did the listener feel?

How does active listening affect the speaker?

How can I use active listening skills in my life (work, school, home, friendships)?

CONTEXT CLUES

Context Clues is another CR-CT activity that helps increase students' awareness of the variety of ways they understand messages. This activity helps students understand why part of being an active listener is watching and paying attention to all the clues.

CR-CT Skills Developed

Inference

Active listening

Procedure

- The teacher asks students to watch for a minute and think about what is happening.
- The teacher opens and closes several drawers, shuffles papers, and looks through shelves and pockets before exhaling a huge sigh of disgust and covering his frowning, frustrated face with his hands while falling into a chair.
- After sitting for a moment, the teacher stands up and asks the class what they think was happening.
- Students share their theories and how they inferred that something was lost and the teacher was frustrated.
- Students are then asked to work in groups of 4 or 5 to design or write a short "script" that they can "act out" without words. No sign language or symbols may be used—only actions for communication.
- After a brief period (5 minutes) to prepare, each group takes a turn communicating by acting out their scene.
- The class guesses what the script is about and discusses clues, context, prediction, and body language.
- Students review what they've learned from the listening activities (Sound Scavengers; Stop, Look, and Listen; and Context Clues).
- When the students have listed the listening skills that have been introduced they begin to devise a definition of active listening that includes paying attention, eye contact, and context clues.

Extending Activities: Journal Writing and/or Discussion

How do I show that I am angry, happy, or excited without use of words?

How can I use body language to communicate better as a friend, listener, student?

SOUND OFF

This activity is a fun and effective method for introducing the concept of non-verbal communication. Teachers love it because it takes only a few minutes of their time. Students enjoy the homework as they begin to think about the complexity of communication.

Procedure

- Students are asked to write the name of their favorite television character on the top of a piece of paper.
- When all students have identified their chosen television personality, they are asked to write down on the top half of the same paper all of the nonverbal communication and gestures they think their favorite character typically uses.
- When the lists are complete and have been collected, students are assigned to watch their favorite show and record all the gestures and methods of nonverbal communication their favorite character uses. As students watch their show and note the character's body language, they should also try to determine the theme or what the show is about.
- Students bring their Sound Off homework into class and discuss their findings.

Extending Activities: Journal Writing and Discussion

What nonverbal communications do I use?

Am I aware of my gestures and what they say?

Do my gestures add to or distract from my verbal communications?

INFERENCE CARTOONS

Because students love to create and draw, our inference cartoons use an art activity to introduce students to the important concept of inference.

CR-CT Skills Developed

Inference

Main idea

Procedure

- Students are placed in groups of 4 to 6 to read one of several passages selected by the teacher (each group may be assigned different pages of a story).

- Students are instructed to draw boxes and fill them in when they finish reading. No words or symbols may be used—only events to tell the story they've read. Each student draws his own sequence. They decide as a group, after reviewing everyone's work, who will draw each box and what will go in the box.
- When finished, they switch cartoons with another group and write a story about the other group's cartoons.
- When everyone is finished, the groups who exchanged cartoons are given time to read their stories.
- The group given the cartoons reads the story they made up about their classmates' cartoons.
- The group who drew the cartoons reads the actual piece that the cartoons were drawn to illustrate.
- When all students' stories have been read the teacher defines inference: e.g., "using evidence, in this case visual, to draw conclusions without having something directly stated or told to you."

Extending Activities: Journal Writing and/or Discussion

Was there more than one way of "reading" the inference cartoons? How did asking questions help us understand what the story was about?

Portfolio Pick

TALES FROM THE TONES

Groups of students will use tone of voice, one of the context clues that active listeners can learn to observe, to show different emotions while reading the same scripts. Their classmates will infer different meanings and messages as the tone of voice changes.

CR-CT Skills Developed

Inference

Active listening

Communication

Procedure

Groups of 3 to 5 students review a short script and each group chooses 3 actors to effect each of the feelings. No body language is allowed; only tone of voice. After each reading, class members identify the emotion and discuss how the meaning is conveyed without words.

Script 1—Group 1

"Happy Birthday! Happy Birthday! How did you find out it was my birthday?"

Actor 1 shows surprise.

Actor 2 shows anger.

Actor 3 shows joy.

Script 2—Group 2

"Well, I often wondered what you were doing. I must admit I never thought of this!"

Actor 1 shows surprise.

Actor 2 shows anger.

Actor 3 shows joy.

Script 3—Group 3

"I'm glad she's gone. This will be the best thing for everyone here."

Actor 1 shows happiness.

Actor 2 shows sadness.

Actor 3 shows disgust or anger.

Script 4—Group 4

"You wouldn't believe what grade I got on that special report."

Actor 1 shows sadness.

Actor 2 shows surprise.

Actor 3 shows happiness.

Script 5—Group 5

"I'm glad she didn't invite me. I have a lot to do next weekend."

Actor 1 shows happiness.

Actor 2 shows anger.

Actor 3 shows indifference.

Script 6—Group 6

"Wait until you see it. It hasn't changed at all while you were gone."

Actor 1 shows frustration.

Actor 2 shows happiness.

Actor 3 shows shock.

Extending Activities: Journal Writing and/or Discussion

How does tone affect me as a listener?

How can tone affect my ability to communicate?

How can I use this at home or with friends?

LOOKING IN–LOOKING OUT JOURNALS

Howard Gardner's theory of multiple intelligences includes two types of personal intelligence: intrapersonal and interpersonal. Intrapersonal intelligence helps us understand ourselves—our needs, feelings, talents, habits, strengths, and weaknesses. Interpersonal intelligence helps us understand and interact with others. As an introduction to journaling, students explore the meaning and importance of intrapersonal and interpersonal intelligences by generating journal topics appropriate to both areas.

CR-CT Skills Developed

Metacognition

Communication

Procedure

A large version of our "journal page" is drawn on the board and labeled as shown:

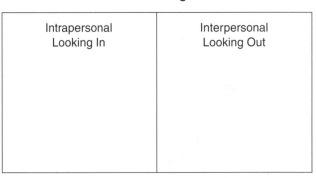

Journal Page

Intrapersonal Looking In	Interpersonal Looking Out

Students are introduced to intrapersonal (looking-in) and interpersonal (looking-out) intelligences.

The intrapersonal/looking in journal entries ask students to reflect on how an issue or activity is personally important to them. Students will generate intrapersonal journal starters which are copied on the board, such as:

This (concept, issue, conflict, context) reminds me of . . .

This is important to me because . . .

This makes me feel . . .

When this happens I wish . . .

I learned . . .

What interested me most was . . .

The interpersonal/looking out journal entries ask students to reflect on how an issue affects their friends, family or community members and their relationships with those people.

A favorite or current topic is chosen by the teacher and the students to write their first double journal entries using intrapersonal and interpersonal journal starters. Students may be asked to write entries in their LI/LO Journals once or twice a week or they may develop entries as homework assignment weekly.

Portfolio Pick

TIMING IS EVERYTHING

It seems rather incongruous that in a society of supersophisticated communication, we often suffer from a shortage of listeners.
—Erma Bombeck,
If Life Is a Bowl of Cherries, What Am I Doing in the Pits? (1971)

Although critical questioning is an essential component to active listening, active reading, critical thinking, and conflict resolution, it is also essential that it doesn't disturb or interrupt the speaker, as we will learn in this activity. There are times when it is appropriate to ask questions and other times when we should write down or simply note questions and wait until later to ask. We will develop an awareness of how timing questions depends on the speaker and the context.

CR-CT Skills Developed

Active listening

Analysis

Procedure

- The teacher reviews the essential importance of listening: what has been learned about listening and what has been posted in the classroom.
- The teacher asks a student volunteer to read the script (provided). The volunteer is quietly instructed to keep reading through all

interruptions. The teacher interrupts, as indicated on the script, as students record questions in their logs.

- The volunteer student reads the second half of the piece uninterrupted.

Student's Piece	Teacher's Piece
Ironically, Alfred Nobel, the * creator of the Nobel peace prize, was also the inventor of * dynamite. Born in Sweden in 1833, Alfred Nobel's father was a famous military engineer. Alfred's brothers, Robert and Ludwig, were successful oil men * and Alfred was a respected inventor.	*Wait until you hear this. *Isn't that ironic. *What a family! That must've been an interesting dinner table.
He experimented with explosives in his lab. * As he became more successful he opened a small work shop. * One day, during a terrible explosion, * all were killed. Grief stricken, Alfred Nobel's father died of a stroke three weeks later.	*Maybe he wasn't so smart after all. *Oh no, here it comes! *I just can't stand this part.
*	*I can't listen to this. From now on I'm just going to let you listen to the story.
There were more explosions from Nobel's work: a factory in Hamburg and a huge ship, as well as buildings in San Francisco and New York. Many countries banned these explosives. Nobel mixed his nitroglycerin with clay so that it could be safely transported.	
Nobel was a global citizen who spoke several languages. When he died he left millions of dollars for peace. The Nobel Prize is his legacy.	

- After the speaker is finished the class members may question the teacher about the piece and discuss which part was easier to understand, the interrupted or uninterrupted part.
- Students review their definitions of active listening from the CR-CT journal. They may refine their definitions. The final definition might be placed in students' CR-CT Portfolios.

Extending Activities: Journal Writing and/or Discussion

What was positive or negative about the presentation?

Which way would you rather present (interrupted or uninterrupted) if you were reading or speaking?

Which presentation was easier to understand?

Portfolio Pick

INTRODUCTION TO ACE PARAPHRASING

Students are introduced to the power of paraphrasing for increasing active listening, clarity, and comprehension by practising ACE Paraphrasing.

CR-CT Skills Developed

Active listening

Perspective taking

Metacognition

Procedure

- As the teacher writes "ACE Paraphrasing" on the board, students are asked to brainstorm or offer definitions of the term "paraphrasing."
- The parts of paraphrasing are then introduced:
  1. **Affirm:** To assert or state the main idea from the conversation or from a written passage. E.g., "So Socrates is considered by many to be the father of modern philosophy."
  2. **Clarify:** To ask any questions or raise any considerations about any supporting facts or inferences that seem confusing. E.g., "Were Plato and Aristotle also considered to be fathers of modern philosophy?"
  3. **Express:** To state in your own words the main idea and any important supporting facts as you understand them. E.g., "Socrates was considered to be one of the fathers of modern philosophy."
- Students then work in pairs asking each other an assigned question such as, "What was your favorite or most disliked topic studied in this class? Why?"
- One student takes notes as the other answers, and then uses ACE Paraphrasing techniques to paraphrase and clarify the answer.
- Each student then has an opportunity to paraphrase their partner's opinion to the class.

Extending Activities: Journal Writing and/or Discussion

Do I listen differently when I have to paraphrase? If so, how?

Do I think about my response when I listen, instead of thinking about the speaker's message?

Do great listeners concentrate on the speaker?

How does planning my response distract from my ability to listen?

In what areas of my life can I use paraphrasing?

METALISTENING

This ongoing strategy is designed to generate students' interest in listening as they explore their individual listening styles, identify their strong and weak listening habits, and practice listening to content-area topics. As they make progress in listening, students redefine their listening goals periodically, determining a new area of focus. Their progress charts become a part of their portfolios.

CR-CT Skills Developed

Active listening

Procedure

- The teacher locates 3 passages of approximately 200–500 words in length which are to be read to the class. This length will provide 2–5 minutes of listening time. Content-area topics are ideal. Passages may be found in textbooks, trade books, or in newspapers and magazines. Variety should be sought: One passage could be a boring weekly business report; another could be a controversial topic such as an editorial in support of teen curfews; another could be loaded with facts, and read in a monotone.
- The teacher introduces one of the passages and asks students to listen carefully as the passage is read to them.
- Students are asked to share how they listened to the passage. Specifics are sought such as: "I began to daydream because the topic was boring," "I listened to the details so they would help me guess the ending," and "I stared at the speaker's bowtie and lost track of what he was talking about."
- The teacher or designated student records students' responses on the board as students disclose their listening insights. They can be presented in two columns as "hot" and "cold" listening techniques.
- The teacher reads the other two passages at different times and the students are again asked to disclose their listening habits and techniques. The teacher should disclose his/her listening habits along with students to generate their interest and disclosure.
- After several passages are read and feedback is given, the teacher duplicates and distributes a list of positive and negative listening traits. The list may be arranged like the one following:

Hot	Cold
Looking away from distractions	Daydreaming
Taking brief notes	Thinking of the topic as boring
Setting goals before listening	Disagreeing with the speaker before response is appropriate
Asking questions (if allowed)	
Mentally reviewing while listening	Creating distractions
Not drawing conclusions ahead of time	Tolerating distractions
Believing all topics are worth listening to	Tuning out on hard material
Stopping daydreams as soon as they start	Trying to write too much
Trying to take the speaker's side if you disagree	Listening for facts only
	Listening for main point only
Making a mark on your paper every time you lose attention	Tuning out because of speaker's age
	Tuning out because of speaker's voice
Mentally recalling as soon as the speaker is finished	Tuning out because of speaker's dress

This list can be placed on the wall or bulletin board.

- Each student then identifies one of the faulty listening habits to work on over a period of about one month.
- Students plot their score and connect lines on a line graph such as the one given below:

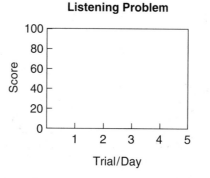

Listening Problem

- After each practice listening exercise the whole class can discuss their listening experiences and/or the specific-problem groups can meet to share their experience and add to their list of strategies.
- After approximately one month students identify a new listening problem to work on; new groups are formed around specific problems and the previous steps are repeated.
- The selection of passages to be read by the student can be assigned to the listening groups. These passages can be catalogued and incorporated into a classroom listening center for further use.

- Small groups of students are formed based on those who chose the same habit. They convene and brainstorm ways to correct their faulty habit. A recorder for each group transmits their ideas to the teacher, who makes a master list of ways to improve listening.

The teacher presents at least one listening occasion per week after which students rate their performance on the single habit they chose to work on. A scale like the one at the end of the chapter can be used and kept in students' portfolios.

Portfolio Pick

LISTENING TIP OF THE WEEK

> *Once we started to really listen to each other*
> *we realized that we were all on the same side.*
> —Elementary student
> (conflict manager)

This activity encourages mastery of listening strategies identified in earlier activities. It encourages students to work on listening within the context of the regular learning day.

CR-CT Skills Developed

Active listening

Procedure

- Each of the metalistening groups supply a listening tip of the week. They should be straightforward, concrete activities such as, "Focus on the speaker," "Don't be distracted by friends," and "Ask a question if you get lost."
- The listening tip should be displayed prominently in the classroom and should be referred to when listening occasions warrant.

THE LISTENER INTERVIEW

This activity invites students to look beyond themselves to determine what makes a good listener. To accomplish this, students investigate the listening styles of someone they respect and trust.

CR-CT Skills Developed

Active listening

Paraphrasing

Summarizing

Procedure

- Ask students to interview someone they trust and would be willing to share a problem with. Their goal is to discover the person's listening style. They can ask questions and/or use the Personal Listening Scale with the person being interviewed.
- The students can give brief talks to the class, celebrating the good listening traits of those whom they interviewed.
- As an alternative, students could write a paper based on the interview to incorporate the activity into their journals.

Listening Journal Starters

The following sentence stems might prove useful to encourage students to make listening entries in personal or content-area journals:

I listen best when . . .

When I'm excited about the topic . . .

People listen to me when . . .

I fake attention . . .

When topics bore me . . .

When I'm tired . . .

Daydreaming . . .

My mind wanders . . .

Good listeners make good friends because . . .

I think best when . . .

I wish people would listen to me when . . .

I listen to people who . . .

The speaker's voice . . .

When I don't understand something I listen to . . .

When I disagree with the speaker I . . .

If the speaker makes me angry I . . .

If I sit near the front of the class . . .

When people disagree with what I say . . .

I listen best in _____ class because . . .

I think my friends would say that my listening . . .

My greatest problem with listening is . . .

My friends call me a good listener because . . .

Paying attention is hard because . . .

If the speaker is angry I . . .

THE LISTENING GAUGE

This exercise provides students ongoing opportunities to evaluate their achievement in listening and to sharpen their metalistening abilities.

CR-CT Skills Developed

Active listening

Procedure

A large thermometer-like figure will be drawn and put on the wall to display how well the class listened each day (see example below). The "mercury" level should be determined before the close of each day, with the class providing rationale for the decision. Students should be encouraged to give specifics in support of their choices. They should be encouraged to review previous listening checklists.

Classroom Listening Gauge

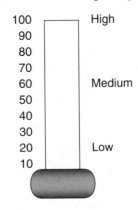

100	High
90	
80	
70	
60	Medium
50	
40	
30	
20	Low
10	

QUESTIONING FOR CLARITY

He who knows only his own side of the case, knows little of that.
—John Stuart Mill,
On Liberty (1859)

The "Questioning for Clarity" section of our Communication and Comprehension chapter begins with activities designed to stimulate student interest in questioning. The importance of questioning is illustrated by the belief of some theorists that the heart of critical thinking itself is disciplined questioning (Beyer, 1991, p. 93). The development of questioning strategies in the classroom helps students become "more purposeful in their thinking and behaving" (Costa, 1991, p. 202) and increases comprehension.

In addition to students learning to monitor their own comprehension, cooperative questioning increases co-learner's comprehension and metacognition (Karabenick, 1996). Furthermore, the use of classroom questioning strategies provides an ongoing forum for the teacher to access students' progress.

CLARIFICATION QUESTIONS

Clarification Questions direct students' attention to the importance of asking good questions. Clarification Questions function to increase understanding and help students to show interest as a listener.

CR-CT Skills Developed

Critical questioning

Clarifying

Procedure

- The class brainstorms reasons for asking questions.
- After responses are recorded, the teacher identifies two volunteer actors for each script below. The actors are asked to convey active or apathetic emotions when answering same script, as indicated below.

  Scenario 1
  ACTOR 1: "I can't wait for vacation. We've been planning this trip for years."
  ACTOR 2: *(apathetic)* "Oh, yeah."

  Scenario 2
  ACTOR 1: "I can't wait for vacation. We've been planning this trip for years."
  ACTOR 2: *(excited)* "Really? Where are you going?"

Students work in groups to generate their own scenarios of active and apathetic responses.

Questions directed to the class:

Which listener seems more interested?

Which listener would you rather talk to?

What kind of listener am I?

What could I do to be a better listener?

QUESTION CARD

Question Card is based on a teaching strategy that improves active listening and active reading, and helps students to develop their ability to identify the main idea and formulate questions (Hayes, 1992). Although we begin this activity with question cards, students will eventually develop their own question logs.

CR-CT Skills Developed

Active listening

Active reading

Critical questioning

Procedure

For the first few sessions of Question Card the teacher may make up index cards with questions about a main idea, supporting evidence, and implications. On separate cards the teacher may provide answers to those questions. The cards should be marked with a Q or an A to avoid confusion.

- After introducing the reading assignment the teacher asks students to skim the text. As students skim the text to get the gist of it, the teacher distributes question cards and separate answer cards to the students.
- After skimming the text the students who hold question cards are asked to read their question.
- Students with or without answer cards may attempt to answer the question.
- In the next step, students engage in the Question Card activity with blank cards and begin to use their own questions as they read. Students are asked to write "how" and "why" questions and any other questions that can't be answered by pointing to part of the text. When each student has written at least one question they share their questions and discuss answers in small groups or as a class.

Extending Activities: Journal Writing and/or Discussion

How does active listening help me answer questions?

How does active reading help me answer questions?

How can I use this with other subjects?

Do I pay attention more often when I'm asking and answering questions?

COOPERATIVE RE-QUEST

*Men are never so likely to settle a question
rightly as when they discuss it freely.*
—Lord Macaulay

Reciprocal questioning has been used for years as an effective tool for introducing inquiry and questioning skills and stimulating interest in content material (Hayes, 1992). Although we start out with the teacher modeling questioning with a few students, we then ask students to use reciprocal questioning in small groups. Students enjoy having a chance to ask teachers questions for a change, as well as hypothesizing without fear of being wrong. In this activity good questions are more important than correct or incorrect answers. An answer must be attempted when a question is asked.

CR-CT Skills Developed

Active listening

Prediction

Critical questioning

Clarifying

Procedure

- The teacher introduces a piece of literature or content reading assignment and tells the students that we are going to read "X" pages (specified portion of the piece), and then stop and ask questions.
- After reading, the teacher puts the piece down and asks for everyone to finish the section and then write down as many questions as possible.
- The teacher opens the questioning session by asking students to ask him questions about the part of the text they have already read.
- Teachers and students must make some attempt at a guess or prediction even if they don't have the answer. Rephrasing and reinspecting the text is allowed and encouraged.

- When the students have asked many questions, the teacher may then ask the students questions. Open-ended and prediction-type questions are encouraged (e.g., "How would your predictions have been different if the title was "Tony's Homecoming" instead of "Tony's Strange Trip"?).
- The reading and questioning cycle may be repeated as time permits.
- After doing Cooperative Re-quest as a class several times, students may be instructed to use this method on assigned reading in small groups. Each student must write down their questions and possible answers in a log for individual accountability.

Extending Activities: Journal Writing and/or Discussion

How can I use Re-Quest?

Can I use Re-Quest when I'm alone?

What would solitaire Re-Quest look like?

Do I wonder about things when I read something alone?

Does asking questions while I read make me pay attention to the piece I'm reading?

How is active reading like active listening?

Portfolio Pick

QUESTION MARK

Inspired by McTighe and Lyman's (Davidson & Worsham, 1992) question book-mark, this activity introduces students to a tool which enables them to actively question and write in their question logs as they read.

CR-CT Skills Developed

Identify main idea

Clarification

Questioning

Procedure

- Students are asked to list some of the basic questions they ask themselves when they begin reading a new assignment:

  What do we need to know to make sure we understand the piece—who, what, where, when, why, and how questions?

What do I already know?

What is the main idea?

How does this make me feel?

- Students may look through their logs and add their own favorite questions to the list.
- When each student has a list of their most important and interesting general questions the students are given plain paper or poster board to write their questions on and use as bookmarks while they read.
- Students may create different bookmarks for different genres and different subjects. A discussion of how different genres and different subjects inspire different questions may follow a comparison of students' bookmarks.

Extending Activities: Journal Writing and/or Discussion

How does asking a question make me look at things in a different way?

Can all questions be answered?

Is there one right answer for every question?

Are there right or wrong questions?

COOPERATIVE QUESTIONING

Teaching is the royal road to learning.
—J. West

Inspired by Kagan's Q-Dials (question dials) (Davidson and Worsham, 1992), this activity asks groups of students to generate questions and answers about content using two sets of question cards (color coded) that can be used for any content area.

CR-CT Skills Developed

Active listening

Active reading

Critical questioning

Analysis

Procedure

- Teacher or students have cards prepared (examples of cards are provided on the next page).

- In groups of 6, each student receives one blue card and one green card. Cards should be color coded, as shown.
- When students put two cards together, the cards generate questions about the content area being studied and the students then pose those questions to the class. For instance, what (blue card) resources might (green card) be in demand if current weather patterns continue? Who (blue card) did (green card) Caesar suspect of betraying him?
- Each group poses questions. Students have "wait time" to think and respond individually on paper.
- Teacher then asks for and records answers on the board.

Blue		Green	
Where and When?	Which?	Would?	Will?
What?	Who?	Can?	Might?
How?	Why?	Did?	Is?

Extending Activities: Journal Writing and/or Discussion

Is there more than one right answer for some questions?

How did other peoples' questions make you look at the information differently?

Which question was the most interesting to you?

PREDICTION DETECTIVES

The Prediction Detectives activity gives students a chance to review material and generate predictions and to validate the predictions they make.

CR-CT Skills Developed

Prediction

Critical questioning

Cooperation

Procedure

- The teacher groups students into pairs and instructs them to skim the new chapter material and write down several prediction questions.
- After generating several predictions, students read and then assess predictions and answer questions together.

Extending Activities: Journal Writing and/or Discussion

How did we predict based on facts?

What assumptions did we make to generate our predictions?

Were all of our assumptions completely right?

Were all of our predictions right?

How does predicting make you a reading detective?

INNER DIALOGUE AND QUIET QUESTIONING

There are many times when students should actively listen or actively read but they aren't able to speak or question aloud. For those times students will generate questions for the journals. Students may have difficulty maintaining attention and active engagement with material when they can't ask questions. In this activity we teach students to develop an inner dialogue, and to note any questions they may have.

CR-CT Skills Developed

Metacognition

Questioning

Clarifying

Procedure

- Students divide a page in half and mark the left half for Questions and the right half for Answers.
- The teacher asks students if they ever silently wonder what will happen next when a character in a book or movie is acting a certain way.
- Students have a chance to respond.
- The teacher labels that "quiet questioning" as part of our "inner dialogue"—when we wonder or reason silently.
- Students are asked to note any questions they may have when the teacher presents new material, for instance a poem or essay.

- Students are asked to write 3 questions that they would ask the author if she were in the room. This should be an individual activity.
- Students may share and compare questions at the end of the session.
- Students are asked to keep a piece of paper next to them as they listen in class or read. The students can note questions as they arise and answers when they are found. Any unanswered questions may be brought to the teacher or to class discussion.

Extending Activities: Journal Writing and/or Discussion

What conversations would you like to have with the author?

Would you get along with the author?

Why did the author write this piece?

What was the author feeling while writing this piece?

MAPPING UNDERSTANDING

In this section of the Communication and Comprehension chapter students learn to use maps and journals to help them check their comprehension, the essential first step in critical thinking. Maps and journals help students identify main ideas, paraphrase, explore multiple perspectives, and write summaries. The mind maps (graphic organizers) help students organize their thoughts and identify problem areas that require further clarification. David Hyerle's (1996) research has shown that mind maps may simplify content, aid comprehension, and "specifically facilitate dialogue, perspective taking, mediation of student thinking, metacognition, theory development, and self assessment" (p. 23). Paraphrasing is one of the most powerful tools students can learn for exploring points of view other than their own. Also, the abilities to listen empathetically and to understand others' points of view are among the "highest form of intelligent behavior" (Costa, p. 101, 1991). Researchers from the U.S. Army and the University of Maryland (Jones, 1990), as well as our own research in this area, show that paraphrasing or teaching another student are the most powerful comprehension tools we have.

When teachers and students listen empathetically to each other, paraphrase, and use "I" messages, comprehension improves and classroom and school community attachment is increased (Costa, 1991, p. 203; Hawkins, 1995). Increased attachment, according to the research on resilience (American Psychological Association, 1993; Hawkins, 1995) is perhaps the greatest gift a teacher can give to help students live productive, safe, and happy lives. Because of this, graphic organizers and mind maps are provided in this section to invite student reflection on their thinking, and cooperative paraphrasing activities abound to enhance students' comprehension.

START WITH ART

One way for us to explore, organize, and extend our understanding of a concept or a story is to create a mind map. This activity encourages students to create a visual representation of what they have listened to as an introduction to mind maps.

CR-CT Skills Developed

Main idea

Summarizing

Active listening

Analysis

Procedure

- The teacher reads the passage or introduces the passage entitled, "William Penn, Peaceful Pioneer," while students take notes about the important or interesting facts.
- Using their notes, students draw a picture of what they remember about the life of William Penn. The pictures provide a basis for concept maps or murals created by the students.

William Penn—Peaceful Pioneer

As I read about Penn I realized how much he did to establish a state with freedom of religion and freedom of speech. He thought differently and other people began to think differently because of him. He was very wealthy. He did not live the life of the rich. He dressed and lived simply. He looked up to people who had courage and big hearts. He spoke about this in many countries, and he was thrown in jail numerous times because of his beliefs.

The king of England owed Penn and his father a lot of money, but he didn't give Penn the money. He gave him a large plot of land in America, now the state of Pennsylvania, which means Penn's Woods. On this land he built a city called Philadelphia—the city of brotherly love. Penn's dream lives on today after over 250 years. He helped change the world through the people's minds and hearts, and through freedom and understanding.

Sample student work. Heydenberk, 4th grade.

MIS-MAP: MAIN IDEA SUMMARY MAP

MIS-MAPs help students summarize, paraphrase, and clarify the content or message presented. This is an effective tool for teachers to assess prior knowledge and identify interests and understanding.

CR-CT Skills Developed

Summarizing

Paraphrasing

Clarifying

Procedure

- The teacher introduces students to the activity and to the Main Idea Summary Map. Although there are many ways to arrange information (e.g., tree maps or flow charts) our students will start with the simple main idea hierarchy map (Hayes, 1992). This design places the main idea at the top with supporting facts and inferences below (as illustrated).

Greek Philosophy		
Define philosophy. Include contributions of the "fathers of philosophy."		
Plato	**Socrates**	**Aristotle**

- The hierarchy is drawn on the board.

- Students read about Greek philosophy (script provided).

- The teacher asks:
  What is the main idea?
  Who or what is this about?
  What are the main points the author makes about Greek philosophy?
  What evidence or examples does the author provide?

- Students fill in their MIS-MAPS as the teacher completes one on the board.

- Students write a summary based on their maps.

- Students compare their summaries in pairs or groups.

Extending Activities: Journal Writing and/or Discussion

Is it easier to understand and remember material after I draw a map?

Is it easier to write about material after I draw a map?

Is it easier to write a summary after I draw a map?

How can I map and summarize information about my life?

What event in my life can I map?

Script for the MIS-MAPS Activity

Philosophy is a Greek word that means "love of wisdom." The fathers of Greek philosophy, Plato, Aristotle, and Socrates, are perhaps the most famous of all philosophers. All three of these philosophers lived in Athens, Greece.

Plato's philosophy was that the goal of human beings should be physical and mental strength and perfection through courage, wisdom, and knowledge—a thoughtful sense of justice and balance in all things.

Aristotle was Plato's student. Although he is thought to be more practical and less idealistic in his philosophy than his famous teacher, Aristotle's method of deductive logic is often credited as the foundation for the formal logic of our time. Aristotle wrote extensively and made contributions in science, mathematics, and politics, as well.

Socrates was an idealistic philosopher who taught by asking questions. For Socrates, questions were more important than answers. Questioning was the way to knowledge and truth; knowledge and truth were the goals of a good life. Socrates is credited as the father of the Socratic discussion, in which questions lead to the truth.

Portfolio Pick

SUMMARY/PARAPHRASE PARTNERS

Students get another view of how to identify and summarize main ideas and a tool to help them do both. Summary/Paraphrase Partners helps students clarify their understanding of important concepts.

CR-CT Skills Developed

Main idea

Summarizing

Paraphrasing

Procedure

- The teacher asks students to read an assigned content piece.
- Students brainstorm all facts known from listening to the passage while the teacher writes them on the board.

- The teacher helps students to identify the main idea and the related facts from the list on the board.
- After students identify the essential supporting facts needed for a summary, the teacher erases all of the other information. The summary is compiled using a graphic organizer, such as a MIS-MAP.
- Students are asked to combine as many essential facts as possible to write a summary.
- Independently, students write a summary from the information left on the board.
- Students work in pairs and paraphrase their summaries to their partners. They write a single summary after listening to each other's summaries.
- Partners share their summaries with the class.

Extending Activities: Journal Writing and/or Discussion

How was my partner's original summary different from mine?

Is it possible to write a summary in 2 different ways and have both versions be right?

Portfolio Pick

STORY MAPS

Men would rather be starving and free than fed in bonds.
—Pearl Buck (1943)

Like MIS-MAPS, Story Maps can be used to help students identify the author's or speaker's main idea and supporting facts and inferences. This activity provides an interesting way to approach the understanding of causes and consequences. Students and teachers may also find story maps useful for clarifying and assessing understanding of important events and facts.

CR-CT Skills Developed

Active listening

Main idea

Procedure

- The teacher introduces story maps as another way to help us clarify our understanding. Story maps are timelines that can be used to help us understand and comprehend material presented in any content area.

- The teacher reads or introduces the story from our content area studies.
- Working together, the teacher and class put the story map on the board. First identify the main character, the conflict, the cause of the conflict, the main event, and the consequences, both immediate and long term.
- Students can work in groups to create their own maps of a favorite story.

Extending Activities: Journal Writing and/or Discussion

- Was there a conflict or a challenge in most of our favorite books?

MIRROR, MIRROR

Teachers and students work together in the Mirror, Mirror activity to create charts that will help students reflect on their own understanding and assess and strengthen their questioning and comprehension skills. Creating rubrics with students and having them identify and label their questioning and comprehension skills heightens students' awareness of their skills. Checking comprehension is the first step to increasing critical thinking.

CR-CT Skills Developed

Metacognition

Critical thinking

Procedure

The teacher has drawn a chart on the board entitled "Mirror, Mirror" with five spaces across in each row, as shown:

Mirror, Mirror				
Who	Where	What	How	Why

The students are introduced to the concept of creating a chart to help them understand the skills they use and the questions they must ask in order to reflect on their comprehension as they read a story.

- After reading any content piece or listening to a lecture students may be asked to fill out a Mirror, Mirror chart to check their comprehension.
- When all students have completed their Mirror, Mirror charts, they may compare and discuss answers in small groups or as a class.

RSVP: READ, SUMMARIZE, VERBALIZE, PARAPHRASE

Once a human being has arrived on this earth, communication is the largest single factor determining what kinds of relationships he makes with others and what happens to him in the world about him.
—Virginia Satir,
Peoplemaking (1972)

RSVP gives students a chance to read a passage, summarize their understanding, read it to a partner, and then actively listen as their partners paraphrase their summary. This cooperative exchange expands students' understanding of any content passage.

CR-CT Skills Developed

Active listening

Summarizing

Paraphrasing

Cooperation

Procedure

- Students work in pairs and read an assigned content/literature passage.
- While reading individually, students take notes, summarizing the passage.
- When both partners have finished, one paraphrases his summary to the other.
- The listening partner may ask clarifying questions before he paraphrases his partner's understanding of the main concepts and supporting evidence.
- Partners switch roles.
- Partners then compare how their summaries differ and how they agree and write a more comprehensive summary that combines the important points made by each partner.

Extending Activities

Do you summarize more clearly when you know you will be reading your summary?

Can you use paraphrasing at home or in other parts of your life to help you make sure that you understand someone?

SOCRATES SAYS

Socrates Says is the opposite of Simon Says—here we must question what we're doing rather than just follow along mindlessly. In fact, students must question every assumption and instruction of their group.

CR-CT Skills Developed

Metacognition

Communication

Cooperation

Active listening

Procedure

- Students may review what they've done in Mirror, Mirror or Cooperative Questioning activities, but this time rather than focusing on themselves, students focus on questioning the groups' understanding.
- They begin by responding to the questions, "Do we question for clarity when we're working in a group or do we tend to just go along with the group? Do we assume that others know what they're doing?"
- Socrates Says begins checking comprehension by asking the basic questions—who, where, when, what, how, and why—about a chosen content-area passage.
- Students write their responses to the questions, including any supporting facts or inferences, in their notebooks.
- Students begin by comparing answers, not just what they know, but also how they supported it.
- When the Socrates Says comprehension check is done, each student has to write at least one question pertaining to the same content passage to pose to the group.
- When all student-generated questions have been answered or discussed, the groups may add a second set of new questions raised by their discussion if time permits.

Extending Activities

- How does explaining your answer to your classmates affect your understanding?
- Did your classmates' answers change your understanding?

SUMMARY TABLE

Students are introduced to another graphic organizer that helps them summarize their understanding of important facts and inferences.

CR-CT Skills Developed

Distinguishing facts from inferences

Main idea

Summarizing

Critical questioning

Procedure

- The teacher draws a table on the board:

- Students read a content area passage individually.
- The teacher asks students to draw the table in their notebooks.
- Students write a summary of the passage on the "table top."
- Students work in pairs to generate questions about the passage and to answer them. They decide which questions were answered with clearly stated facts (marked with "F") and which were answered by inference (marked "I").
- Students then finish the summary table by writing the related facts and inferences to support the table. Once the "legs" on the table have been filled in with information related to the summary, students go back over each piece of supporting information and label it "F" or "I" for Fact or Inference.

Extending Activities

Is it easier to "support" your summary if you have more information (more "legs")?

Did you feel sure of your conclusions after asking questions or searching for evidence?

Have you ever inferred incorrectly because you didn't have enough information (about a friend or a sibling?)

Has anyone ever inferred incorrectly about something you did?

Portfolio Pick

CHARACTER MAPS

Instead of mapping a whole story and all the important events, the students will now focus on one character's experience, increasing their understanding of that character's perspective, challenges, conflicts, behavior, and the consequences of his or her behavior. Often, focusing on the experience of one character makes the content personally meaningful and increases comprehension of related materials.

CR-CT Skills Developed

Main idea

Distinguish fact from inference

Identifying conflicts

Identifying causes and consequences

Analysis

Procedure

- Students are told that they will be doing a character map of a character they've studied in history or literature.
- Students are instructed to work in groups of 3–5 to devise a map of that character's life or experience from a story or content area piece they have read or studied, including any challenges, conflicts, causes, and consequences.
- Groups share their maps with the teacher who draws a master map (combining all of their important points) on the board.

Extending Activities

What favorite characters would you like to map? Why?

Do most stories you can think of include a conflict or challenge?

How would your life map look if students drew it a hundred years from now?

Character Map

The Salk Story

1952. Just another year in American history, right? Not so. In 1952 Jonas Salk's polio vaccine was developed and later, in 1955, it was proven effective. Salk's many years of hard work for very little money had paid off. It was said to be the greatest event in American history since the end of World War I, but Salk's story doesn't end there. He was working on an AIDS vaccine, when he was 83 years old. Whether or not his AIDS vaccine works, Jonas Salk is still a great hero, and not just a hero—a dedicated, hard-working, persistent hero who is concerned about human suffering.

Story Timeline

1914	Salk was born
1926	Jonas Salk admitted to a New York high school for the gifted
1930s	Salk starts law classes in college
	Salk quits law study and begins study of medicine
	Jonas Salk begins to conduct research
1952	Salk discovers polio vaccine
1955	Polio vaccine proven effective
1990s	Salk working on AIDS vaccine

Sample student work: Heydenberk, 4th grade.

ME AND MY SHADOW

In Me and My Shadow each student draws a Venn diagram of how they are alike and different from a favorite character or a historical figure.

CR-CT Skill Developed

Analysis

Procedure

- Students are asked to list facts about the chosen character.
- Students are asked to list the related facts about themselves—when they were born, their gender, interests, and anything they wish to include.
- The teacher then asks students to draw a Venn diagram, labeled as shown, as he models his diagram on the board.

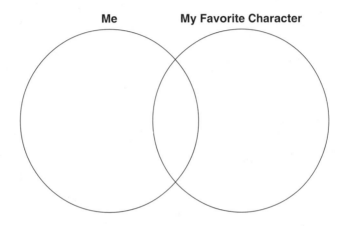

Me   **My Favorite Character**

- Students cut out or copy the facts and put them into the parts of the diagram to see what they have in common and how they differ from their favorite characters.

Extending Activities

Does what you have in common with your favorite character affect your feelings about him/her? How? Why?

Do the differences between you and your character affect your feelings about him/her? How? Why?

Portfolio Pick

MOCCASIN MILES

Do not judge a man until you have walked a mile in his moccasins.
—Native American saying

Students will use content passages from literature, science, history, social studies, or the news to teach each other the various perspectives in the passage being studied.

CR-CT Skills Developed

Active listening

Multiple perspectives

Summarizing

Paraphrasing

Communication

Cooperation

Procedure

- The teacher asks students to reflect on the Native American saying, "Do not judge a man until you've walked a mile in his moccasins."
- Students may recall times when someone has judged them without understanding their experiences and vice versa.
- Students read an article or a content passage with various possible perspectives on an issue (e.g., anything from "Little Red Riding Hood" to articles about environmental activism, depending on grade level and content issues).
- After reading, students are assigned to groups of 3–5 to research one of the perspectives (e.g., Little Red Riding Hood and the Grand-mother vs. the Wolf) presented in the reading.
- After each student has finished her own essay or notes on the assigned perspective, the students come together with other members of their group who have written from the same perspective to draft their summary presentation.
- When each group has learned all facets of their position, each student from that group is assigned to one person in each of the other groups to paraphrase or teach their perspective and learn from that student about the other perspective.
- Students are rotated until each student has taught one person in each group and listened to one person in each group.
- When everyone has taught their group's perspective and heard from a member of the other groups, the teacher lists the positions or perspectives on the board and chooses one student to provide a quick summary of each position or perspective.
- Students discuss how their perspective changed from (a) working with their group, to (b) hearing from other students with a different assigned perspective.

Extending Activities

How did you see your assigned perspective differently after thinking about it and presenting it?

Did more than one group have a reasonable perspective?

Did you understand the positions and concerns of each group?

Portfolio Pick

DIFFERENT LENSES

In Different Lenses student use metaphorical thinking to describe a variety of perspectives.

CR-CT Skills Developed

Active listening

Metaphorical thinking

Analysis

Communication

Procedure

- Facilitated by the teacher, students first define and give examples of metaphors (e.g., describing something by giving an example of a different object with some similar trait or attribute such as, "He is as solid as a rock").
- Students are then asked to work in groups to generate metaphors for the concept "cooperation" from the lenses or perspectives of a doctor, a builder, a musician, an athlete, a writer, a mathematician, or for any profession they choose. For example, a student might provide the following metaphorical statement for a doctor: "Cooperation is when the heart sends blood to the lungs to get the oxygen which keeps the body going." Another student may create a cooperation metaphor from an entomologist who describes an ant farm, or a mechanic who describes parts of an engine working together, or a plumber who describes water pumps, pipes, and fixtures working together.
- As each group presents their metaphor to the class, their classmates try to guess which lens they are looking through.
- When all groups have presented they may pick another concept from a content area for further practice.
- Students may illustrate their favorite metaphors (e.g. the "cooperation engine" or the "ant farm") and describe the metaphor.

Portfolio Pick

CONFLICT MAPS

Students draw story maps about a conflict that was recent or important in their lives. Students then consider alternate ways of handling that conflict that may have caused a better or worse consequence as a result.

CR-CT Skills Developed

Identifying conflicts

Identifying causes and consequences

Analysis

Communication

Cooperation

Procedure

- Students are asked to recall a conflict in their lives that they can discuss without hurting or embarrassing anyone.
- Students make a story map of their conflict while recalling the types of essential information.
- The conflict maps include what students consider to be the cause and effect of the conflict, including what leads to the conflict.
- Students then draw alternative conflict resolution maps with different resolutions and different consequences (e.g., the student walks away from the conflict or uses conflict resolution skills instead of arguing or fighting).
- Students identify interesting conflicts they would like to map, such as: Isaac had the flu and his mother was at work. Tony borrowed Isaac's new bike without asking. Tony left the bike unlocked in front of the grocery store and went in to get Isaac some juice and cough syrup. The bike was gone when Tony left the store.
- Students or the teacher identify conflicts to map from a content area, such as a difference of opinion on controlling resources (social studies) or analyzing data (math).

Extending Activities

What caused your conflict?

Was a misunderstanding or miscommunication involved?

Did drawing it help you to see it differently?

What could have happened to change the outcome?

Can you "map" consequences in your mind during a conflict?

THE "I" OF THE STORM

> *We possess nothing in the world—a mere chance can
> strip us of everything—except the power to say "I."*
> —Simone Weil

Finally students move from listening, summarizing, and paraphrasing to expressing themselves in meaningful, effective, non-threatening ways.

CR-CT Skills Developed

Communication

Analysis

Procedure

- The teacher writes the following statements on the board:
  - A. MS. JONES: "That tapping is driving me crazy. Don't you ever think about what other people are doing?"
  - B. MS. AMES: "I can't work well when you tap on my desk because I can't concentrate."
  - A. MRS. KENDER: "I am disappointed when you don't bring in your paper because I know you can write about this very well."
  - B. MS. PANE: "You're wasting my time when you don't do your work."
  - A. MS. SHEETS: "You can never get organized or be on time, can you?"
  - B. MS. KANE: "I feel like you don't care about my time when you don't show up because you said that you would be here. I was here waiting."
- Students are asked to pick the statement that they think they would be most likely to listen to and respond to in a positive way.
- Students are asked to describe how the "I" and "you" statements affect the listener differently.

Extending Activities

How can I use "I" messages at home?

How does the same message sound different when we use an "I message" instead of a "you message"?

THE THREE C's: THE SIMPLE "I" STATEMENT

A powerful communication tool, the Simple "I" Statement helps us to avoid blaming, angering, or alienating those we speak to by letting us point out our concerns and clarify the issues in a non-threatening manner.

CR-CT Skills Developed

Communication

Cooperation

Metacognition

Procedure

- Students review the following:
  "You pushed ahead of me in line" vs. "I think I was ahead of you."

- Students are asked to determine which statement is more effective. Then another is entertained:
  "You never pick up the phone or get out of your chair. I'm sick of it."

- Compare this to . . .
  "I'm tired of taking every call in the house. What do you think we can do?"

- Which statement is more effective as constructive communication?

- The teacher helps students analyze the statements: Simple "I" statements are often effective when students need to change, criticize, or clarify (the 3 C's) an idea or an action. Whenever one of the 3 C's is involved, a simple "I" (or the classical 3-part "I" introduced later) should be considered. It reduces the sense of criticism, accusation, and intolerance and instead begins constructive communication and clarification.

- Students work in groups to finish the simple "I" statements and several "you" statements after receiving the following constructive communication criteria:
  "I" statements are best used when we need to:
  1. criticize an idea or action
  2. clarify an idea or plan
  3. change an idea or plan
  Simple "I" and "you" statements are fine when we are making a positive or neutral comment or a command affirming or expressing appreciation for something or someone. "I" statements conform to the formula: I feel _____ about _____.

- Students are asked to complete the following list of the 3 C's:
  I'm confused about _____.
  I'm wondering if we should consider changing _____.
  I was hoping we might be able to _____.
  One thing I'm not comfortable about is _____.

- In small groups or in a whole class setting, students share completed "I" statements. They should be encouraged to form positive "I" statements in responding to others' choices.

- Students may create their own 3-C "I" statements or interchanging "I" and "you" statements and analyze them with the class.

MEETING MASLOW

Abraham Maslow's work on the hierarchy of human needs provides us with a model for understanding human needs, aspirations, and conflict. In the following activity, students are introduced to the model with which we will work throughout the CR-CT curriculum.

CR-CT Skills Developed

Analysis

Cooperation

Communication

Procedure

Students are introduced to the Maslow hierarchy. Some needs, such as physiological and safety needs, are primary or basic needs and must be met before anyone can be successful in attaining higher level needs.

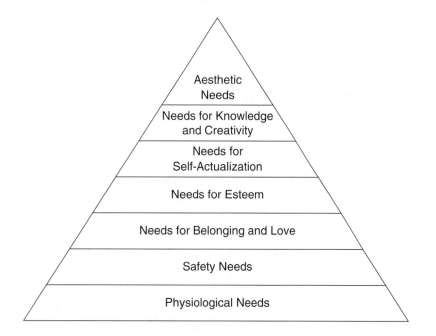

- Students are asked to offer examples of times when they couldn't concentrate or work or enjoy someone's company because hunger or fatigue intervened (physical needs).

- Students are asked to generate examples of the importance of meeting the basic needs. Could you sit down and read a magazine if the house were on fire? How is safety a basic or primary need?
- The teacher should explain the importance of establishing sense of safety, both physical and psychological, and the feeling of being part of a group (the need to belong). Once these basic needs are met, one can move on to the higher needs of self-actualization and acquisition of knowledge.
- Students are asked to brainstorm both physical and psychological characteristics of a safe environment. Once students have described the characteristics of a safe environment, they may brainstorm ways to make a classroom feel safe.

ME MAP–WE MAP

The Me/We Map helps students analyze some of the basic needs that all people have in common and some of the interesting and diverse ways in which we met these needs. The Me/We Map activity helps us strengthen our sense of community as students expand their understanding of themselves and others.

CR-CT Skills Developed

Communication

Analysis

Cooperation

Procedure

- The teacher reviews the basic idea of Maslow's hierarchy of human needs (see page 69).
- Students draw their own hierarchy and note how they meet their own needs as the teacher shares her model on the board.
- Students help design a Metamap on the board listing all the ways people they had studied in content areas have met the needs listed (e.g., different types of food, shelter, ways of feeling safe).

Extending Activities

Do we all have the same basic needs?

Do we all meet them differently?

How would this activity be different if we all gave the same answer for every need?

What are the most interesting ways people meet needs?

How would life be different if we were all exactly the same?

DO YOU SEE WHAT I SEE?

In this activity students enjoy drawing while they expand their understanding of perspective.

CR-CT Skill Developed

Understanding of perspective

Procedure

- The teacher sets up 2 identical textbooks on the desk in front of the class at right angles to each other.

- Students are asked to take out a piece of paper and draw the books as they see them, from each student's unique perspective.

- When they are done the teacher asks them to share their sketches as she asks:
  "Are these 2 books different?"
  "Why do they appear different in your sketches?"

- "Does anyone know what perspective means?" (Perspective: a point of view.)

- Students work in groups to identify examples of how people may have a different view or perspective on issues just as they may have a different perspective on a physical object.

Extending Activities

How do things look different from different perspectives?

How do situations or other points of view "look different" from a distance?

When might two identical situations look different to you from a distance?

Have you ever changed your perspective or changed your mind about something? How? Why?

THE UNITED STATES CONSTITUTION

Democracy is the form of government in which the free are rulers.
—Aristotle

We begin developing our class constitution by reviewing the history of the United States Constitution. Although most of our students have studied this remarkable document to some degree, we make this brief historical review available before introducing the classroom constitution.

CR-CT Skills Developed

Analysis

Communication

Cooperation

Procedure

- The teacher and students review the history of the United States constitution:

In the spring of 1787 the framers of the American Constitution met in Philadelphia to begin their arduous task. By 1789 our new president and congress took office under the new American constitution. The members of the constitutional convention were inspired by many great thinkers, including philosophers such as John Locke who spoke and wrote about individual rights and freedom.

These Americans were driven by a sense of mission—a belief that America had a "manifest Destiny"—to create and protect personal freedom and inspire personal responsibility. This was to be, as John Adams wrote, a mission to create the wisest and happiest government that human wisdom could contrive. The goal was a federal democracy where many ordinary citizens would have a voice—a representative democracy. Democracy is a word derived from two Greek roots: *demos,* which means people, and *kratos,* which means authority.

Although the constitution did not rectify all injustices and woes during this era, it stood as a remarkable achievement, providing a broad vision of a free society which values human freedom and holds high expectations for its citizens to uphold liberty.

Soon the Bill of Rights provided ten amendments to the Constitution to further guarantee that "no one be deprived of life, liberty, or prosperity without due process of law" and that Americans have freedom of religion, speech, and assembly, among other rights. These rights and freedoms carry with them the responsibility for the citizens to be informed and to make thoughtful choices. For all Americans to have their rights, they must each assume the implicit responsibility of enjoying their rights while respecting those of their fellow citizens.

Education opens the door to the American dream. CURTISSA ODI, COFOUNDER, S.T.A.R. (STUDENTS THAT ARE READY) ACADEMY, BETHLEHEM, PA. PHOTO: ROBERTA HEYDENBERK.

- Students may reflect on governments that have restricted human freedoms by controlling what people read, the music they listen to, and which movies they watch. Some countries have required that all typewriters be registered in order to control what people read and write.
- Students are asked to write essays describing how they would feel about living in a place where the government controlled what students could write and say, what music students could listen to, which movies they could watch, and who students could meet and spend time with in their private lives.
- If time permits, groups of students may research freedom and the lack thereof in various countries and cultures through time.

Extending Activities: Response Journals

What freedoms do we take for granted?

What does freedom to speak and think mean?

Why is intellectual freedom important?

Portfolio Pick

LIFE, LIBERTY, AND THE PURSUIT OF HAPPINESS

Lean liberty is better than fat slavery.
—Thomas Fuller

We begin by considering what have been termed our "inalienable rights": life, liberty, and the pursuit of happiness. As a class we then decide what life, liberty, and the pursuit of happiness mean in the classroom and how we can provide and protect these rights.

CR-CT Skills Developed

Active listening

Cooperation

Communication

Divergent thinking

Procedure

- The teacher introduces our inalienable rights: "life, liberty, and the pursuit of happiness," and writes them on the board.

- The teacher introduces the concept that the right to life in a classroom includes the right to physical safety—to be free of threat to our physical well-being.
  The right to liberty demands, in return, the determination to make responsible choices and informed decisions.
  The right to pursue happiness indicates that we have the right to psychological safety—the right to be free of ridicule and psychological oppression.

- Begin with an exploration of the right to life (safety and security) with the class.
  As a general definition develops, students are asked to relate these rights to behaviors in the classroom. To students the right to safety might mean no bullying, no punching, and no weapons in school. Students are given time to brainstorm about a sense of safety in the classroom.
  Similarly, the right of liberty and the pursuit of happiness might be described by students as no threats, no teasing, and no put-downs. Students may work in groups to brainstorm responses to these rights.

- Students are asked how it would feel to be in an environment that dictated their thoughts, their career choices, their goals, and their life choices. Are liberty and the pursuit of happiness important parts of freedom? Students may write essays about their students' rights.

Extending Activities: Response Journals

How can we protect our rights?

How can we protect people's rights to be physically safe?

Who are freedom fighters in our country?

What rights have different groups fought for in America or elsewhere in the world?

What rights did the early settlers from Europe value?

Portfolio Pick

THE TWISTER: A BACKDOOR INTRODUCTION TO THE CLASSROOM CONSTITUTION

> *We stopped trying to take away their power, and*
> *instead we redirect it. Now that power is a resource.*
> —Middle school principal,
> talking about conflict managers

It is often much easier for us to list what we shouldn't do than what we should do, particularly when we are grappling with abstract concepts like liberty, rights, and freedom. For that reason, we begin working on our classroom constitution by developing a picture of what a democratic classroom *doesn't* look like.

Procedure

- The teacher introduces the concept of the classroom constitution, a document that helps to protect the students' rights to physical and psychological or social safety, and, in return, demands responsible, thoughtful decision making. In the classroom students have the right to feel safe, the right to work together, and the right to learn.
- Beginning with a twister (a backward brainstorm) students brainstorm how *not* to create a safe classroom. A tape recorder might be used to list students' responses.
- Once students have brainstormed what *not* to do, the twister is reversed, item by item, to describe a safe classroom.

RIGHTS AND RESPONSIBILITIES: A SKILL STORM

Liberty can no more exist without virtue and independence,
than the body can live and move without a soul.
—John Adams

We have established a general idea of how our classroom environment should be characterized. In this skill storm, we brainstorm the skills we can use to uphold our classroom constitution, protect our rights, and encourage our responsible behavior.

CR-CT Skills Developed

Metacognition

Communication

Cooperation

Procedure

- Students are asked to cite the behaviors we brainstormed in the twister activity. They could be put in positive and negative columns. For instance:

Twister	Safe Classroom
put-downs	no put-downs
name-calling	no name-calling
interruptions	no interruptions

- Students are asked to consider the related rights and responsibilities: For instance, "If we all have a right to be safe and to learn, what are the related responsibilities? How are conflicts resolved? How is criticism expressed?"

- The teacher introduces the idea of developing an action plan—a list of skills that students can use to keep the classroom rights intact.

- With the teacher's help, students are asked to develop a skill storm—to brainstorm all the communication and cooperation behaviors and skills that enhance communication and cooperation, and reduce conflict. These are the communication skills that help keep the peace while respecting everyone's rights. Some of the entries might be:
Active listening
Using "I" statements
Paraphrase
Clarify
Sharing work in group situations
Respecting others

- When the skill storm is complete, the class develops a Rights and Responsibilities chart (see the example). The Rights and Responsibilities chart should be posted prominently in class; it should be refined and expanded as the classroom constitution develops for the class.

THE CLASSROOM CONSTITUTION

> *I believe in my children. Once they have the skills, they do the right thing. Now that they know they have a choice, they make the right choice. They believe in themselves.*
> —Classroom teacher

After reviewing what we've learned about the constitution and about communication and cooperation, we look at the various responsibilities involved in group work (e.g., offering ideas, encouraging others, recording activities). We determine which rights we should include to help us feel productive and safe, and which responsibilities we should include to protect those rights (e.g., taking turns, active listening, eye contact, no put-downs). We brainstorm lists of rights (e.g., to learn, to feel safe) and related responsibilities (e.g., how to relate to each other with respect, to be fair, and to do our share to help others in group work). We will add to this list as the year progresses. Students now have ways to develop a comprehensive classroom constitution.

CR-CT Skills Developed

Cooperation

Communication

Divergent thinking

Convergent thinking

Procedure

- Initially the teacher has all the students work together to develop the basic list of rights for the classroom constitution. Some of the outcomes might be:
The right to be physically safe
The right to be psychologically safe
The right to freedom of speech (to express opinions)
The right to respect
The right to due process (conflict resolution)
The right to learn

- Students may brainstorm related rights as the discussion proceeds, for instance:
  The right to have personal property respected
  The right to be heard (active listening)

- When the list is complete, students from groups to draft various sections of the Constitution.

- Students are instructed to develop both sides of their issue, listing the rights and the responsibilities that ensure those rights. Whenever possible, students should try to state a responsibility as a positive action: "Use conflict resolution table in a conflict" vs. "Don't get angry." Groups may be assigned to consider the rights and responsibilities related to respecting each other, respecting property, and creating physical safety.

- When sufficient time has been given to the initial draft, each group presents their section of rights and responsibilities to the class for review.

- The various groups should have time to discuss the students' contributions to the constitution, ask questions, and make suggestions.

- Groups may return to the drawing on the board if necessary to work on the various sections of the constitution.

The final version of the constitution can be decorated and posted in the room. Each student may have a smaller version for their journal or portfolio.

Rights	Responsibilities
Right to learn	No interrupting cooperative work
Right to be safe	Use conflict resolution table for conflicts
Right to liberty	Active listening
	Conflict-positive communication

INTRODUCTION TO RESTITUTION

Despite the best-laid plans and careful construction of a constitution, all classrooms face challenges and mistakes. Restitution fosters self-discipline, empathy, and self-understanding for the disciplined student, and often offers a deeper sense of justice to those who were offended.

CR-CT Skills Developed

Metacognition

Divergent thinking

Cooperation

Analysis of main point

Procedure

- The teacher introduces the "Restitution Amendment" to our constitution by first defining restitution: Restitution is a word that means restoring—giving something back to its rightful owner or restoring something to its original condition. Restitution means making something right after a wrong.
- Students are asked to help generate examples of restitution versus getting even or doing nothing.

Restitution vs. Retribution

Scenario	Restitution	Retribution
Someone spills juice on a new carpet.	The person who spilled the juice cleans it up and removes the stain.	The person who spilled the juice is called names and sent away.
Jerry spreads a rumor that you cheated on a test.	You resolve the conflict and Jerry tells everyone that he made a mistake and you never cheated.	You spread a rumor that Jerry is flunking out of school and stealing.

- The students analyze the scenarios. Getting even does punish the offender, but it doesn't make it right for the victim. Students are asked: "Which scenario is better for the victim?" "Which is better for the student who makes a mistake?" "Does the offender learn from restitution?" "Which system reflects and strengthens our rights and responsibilities?"
- The teacher explains that although not all disputes and mistakes can be handled with restitution, many can be constructively resolved this way and the restitution chart is displayed.
- Students are asked to work in groups to generate a list of class problems and a restitution suggestion list. Restitution is characterized as a solution that makes it right for the person who was affected by the mistake and helps the person who made the mistake learn a new way of interacting or handling the situation. Students should understand that each problem is handled as it occurs and this is just an idea list to help us understand restitution.

WEAVING STRAW INTO GOLD

*We are not to expect to be transported
from despotism to liberty in a feather bed.*
—Thomas Jefferson

The first step in introducing reasoned restitution to the classroom is to first transform our anger into questions—to shift from punishment to self-control and problem-solving.

CR-CT Skills Developed

Metacognition

Critical questioning

Analysis

Communication

Cooperation

Divergent thinking

Procedure

Our goal is to effect the following:

From assigning blame to . . . problem solving

From negative thinking to . . . positive actions

From focusing on the person to . . . focusing on the problem

From focusing on their mistake or misunderstanding to . . . asserting your needs and understanding

Students are asked to identify which of the following sentences was spoken by a student who has restitution skills:

Scenario 1:   "She's an idiot! She never does anything right. I miss the bus whenever I wait for her."
Or . . .
"She's late a lot. I've got to tell her that I can't wait for her anymore unless we change something."

The first expression assigns blame; the second asserts the problem.

Scenario 2:   "I don't want him to constantly joke about me anymore. I can't stand it.
Or . . .
"I'm tired of all of these jokes. I don't think they are funny anymore. Can we skip them and move on?"

The first statement is negative; the second is changed to positive and offers a solution.

Scenario 3:   "You think you're better than everyone. You're wrong! You're not better than anyone. In fact, you're a dweeb and everyone hates you!"
Or . . .
"I'm tired of having everything I do compared to everything you do. We're different people. Can we stop competing about every little thing and have fun?"

The first statement focuses on the person; the second focuses on the problem.

Scenario 4:   "You really blew it. You didn't do anything you said you would do. You lied about all of it."
Or . . .
"I'm frustrated when I get stuck with all the work. Can you get yours done or let me work with someone else?"

The first statement focuses on their misdeed; the second concerns your needs.

After students analyze the scenarios, we review Restitution Responses:

From   *To*
From assigning blame . . . to problem solving
From negative thinking . . . to positive actions
From focusing on the person . . . to focusing on the problem
From focusing on their mistake or misunderstanding . . . to asserting your needs and understanding

---

After students correctly identify the restitution statement, they work in groups to write a blame/personal attack statement and revise it to a restitution problem-solving statement.

FROM SORRY TO SOLUTION

The love of liberty is the love of others; the love of power is the love of ourselves.
—William Hazlitt

Here students are introduced to a Restitution Rubric. We develop a rubric that characterizes the most essential aspects of constructive restitution policy. When a student has made a mistake that the teacher feels they may be able to resolve by themselves or with the offended student, the student may offer suggestions toward making restitution and check those suggestions against the Restitution Rubric.

CR-CT Skills Developed

Metacognition

Communication

Divergent thinking

Convergent thinking

Procedure

- Students review the Restitution Rubric which includes all of the essential elements of a successful restitution. Although not every restitution situation satisfies all of these criteria, we should still consider all of these suggestions when devising a plan.

The Restitution Rubric: **RESTORE**

R = Reflects our rights and responsibilities as stated in our Constitution.

E = Exhibits understanding of the problem and the rules or rights violated. (Talia's property rights were violated.)

S = Satisfies the needs of the victim. (Talia borrows Jean's bike until hers is repaired.)

T = Takes focus from people and puts it on the problem. (From "Jean is an idiot!" to . . ."We have a missing bike.")

O = Other party's perspective. (Talia worked hard to earn her bike, and she's hurt that I lost it.)

R = Relevant to the nature of the problem. (Replaces the stolen bike.)

E = Examines new ways of interacting or handling the situation if it comes up again. ("Next time I'll make sure . . ."; "I'll ask before I borrow anything again"; "I'll make sure I have the bike lock if I borrow . . .")

TOOLBOX TOUR

Before leaving Chapter 1, students create a Toolbox Tour and describe their new tools and how to use them.

CR-CT Skills Developed

Synthesizing

Critical thinking

Procedure

Students review the communication, comprehension, and critical thinking tools they have used in Chapter 1 and create a list for their table of contents (to be used in the CR-CT Portfolio).

After listing their essential tools, students review each by writing a brief description about how each tool is used, including any notes about individual student's projects.

Portfolio Pick

Active Listening

Listening awareness	Clear communication
Paying attention to context	"I" messages
Body language to maintain attention	Tone awareness
No interruptions	Graphic organizers
Inference	Venn diagrams
Main idea and supporting facts	Summaries
Summarizing	Timelines
Paraphrasing	Charts
Multiple perspectives	Restitution
Understanding rights and related responsibilities	

CHAPTER 2

Creative and Critical Thinking

QUANTUM QUESTIONS

Chapter 2 introduces students to the power of creative questioning through the stories of famous flops that were turned around by asking better questions. The questions we ask direct our focus and attention and therefore our lives. The activities in Chapter 2 help students discover how the quality of the questions we ask determines the quality of the answers we receive.

We then consider creative questions by examining the lives and characteristic curiosity of great thinkers. Studies of many geniuses have found that great thinkers have studied and modeled other great thinkers. In Chapter 2, "Quantum Questions," we learn how to enhance every student's creativity and curiosity.

FANTASTIC FLOPS

Only he who does nothing makes a mistake.
—French proverb.

Fantastic Flops introduces students to the creative power of questions to transform a "flop" to a "fantastic!"

CR-CT Skills Developed

Metacognition

Critical questioning

Communication

Cooperation

Procedure

The teacher presents and discusses one or more of the following histories in a class situation (Jones, 1991; 1996)

1. Louis Pasteur was using chickens to study the bacteria that cause cholera. When his work was interrupted for several weeks, many of the cholera samples he was growing became weakened. Instead of discarding the weakened cultures, he asked himself what would happen to chickens injected with the weakened culture. The chickens did not get cholera, as was anticipated. When injected later with fresh, strong cholera these chickens did not become sick. They were immunized by the weakened culture.

2. Alexander Fleming was a bacteriologist in England. He left a bacteria sample by an open window one night, where it was contaminated and ruined. Instead of throwing it away, he observed that the strange new mold killed the staph germs. He realized that the mold might be able to stop deadly infections. He took it to a lab where he and his colleagues studied it and discovered penicillin. They all won the Nobel prize.

3. Edward Benedictus was a French chemist who was clumsy one day and knocked over a glass flask in his lab. When it fell, it shattered into rounded pieces which remained in the shape of the original flask. Benedict asked himself what was different about this glass flask. The answer was that liquid plastic had been stored in the flask at one time. Safety glass was invented.

4. George de Mestral was a Swiss engineer who came home from a walk one day with burs stuck to his pant legs. He asked himself how burs were able to fasten so firmly to fabric and fur. He studied how the small hooks grabbed any hair or fabric. After eight years of trying to develop a similar nylon hook, he invented Velcro.

5. Levi Strauss was a businessman in New York who left for California to sell dry goods—particularly fabric for tents and wagons—during the Gold Rush. As business slowed Mr. Levi was left with a store full of heavy denim tent fabric. He noticed that the gold prospectors needed strong pants. He had a tailor cut his tent fabric into "Levis." Thus, jeans were invented.

6. Spencer Silver was hired by 3M Company to make an extremely strong adhesive. As Silver worked toward that goal he developed, instead, a weak adhesive. The adhesive stuck to most surfaces for as long as it was left there and then pulled away easily without leaving any adhesive behind. Silver asked himself what else this adhesive could be used for. Silver asked a good question and Post-it® notes were invented.

7. The employees of a candy store in Philadelphia were making caramels. They made a mistake and the caramels became dark and hardened. The store owner screamed "Fudge!" This was an expression for

a stupid mistake. Instead of throwing the bad lot of caramel in the trash, the store owner asked a good question: "I wonder what this tastes like?" and fudge was created.

8. Ruth Wakefield was making chocolate cookies one day when she realized she was out of baker's chocolate. She crushed semi-sweet chocolate pieces and threw them in the batter instead. The pieces of chocolate did not melt as she expected. She asked herself how this mistake tasted and the original chocolate chip cookie was invented.

9. Hundreds of years ago the camera obscura was a box with a hole that artists used to capture an image of an object which they could then trace. A man in France was using silver-covered copper plates, trying to pick up an image of an object through the camera obscura box. He found faint outlines and images on the silver plates. He tried everything he could think of to get a clearer picture, but nothing worked.

   One day he put his plates away in a chemical cupboard without first washing them. Clear images appeared overnight on the plates. He asked himself what accident or phenomenon could have caused this. Every day he put the plates in the cupboard and took a single chemical out. When all the chemicals had been removed the plate still developed a clear image. But he had not identified the chemical that caused the photographic image. Then he noticed that mercury had spilled on a shelf. The fumes had produced the first photograph.

10. Perch LeBaron Spencer was working with a microwave-producing machine for the Raytheon Company. When Percy became hungry he reached for a chocolate bar in his pocket, only to find it melted and cooked. What did Percy ask himself? Did he ask, "How can I get something to eat?" Perhaps. What other question did he ask? The microwave oven was soon invented!

11. During the 1904 World's Fair, Mr. Hamwi was selling thin Persian waffles at a food stand. Another food stand was selling ice cream to fairgoers. It was so hot that the ice cream stand soon ran out of cups to serve their customers. What did the two vendors ask themselves and each other? The ice cream cone was invented.

12. When Martin Luther King became frustrated with injustice and racism, what question did he ask himself: How can I get even, or How can I change this situation for the better for all people? How did that question change the outcome of his efforts?

   • Students work in groups to create quantum question lists considering the pivotal effect and power of questions in the lives presented above or in any other biography they may wish to research.
   • When lists are complete, students compare each others' quantum questions and discuss how these "flops" were transformed to "fantastics."

INTERVIEWING EINSTEIN

Studies of the world's greatest thinkers show that many of them were high achievers and also were inspired by those who came before them—often meeting with or studying the lives of the great thinkers in their chosen field. In Interviewing Einstein students analyze the lives, conflicts, challenges, and triumphs that shape the lives of great thinkers. Students then identify the thinking dispositions and characteristics of these great thinkers and leaders.

CR-CT Skills Developed

Analysis of multiple perspectives

Communication

Critical questioning

Procedure

- Students are asked to write down the names of three people they have studied in school whom they admire.
- Students share their lists and give a reason for each choice.
- The names of some of those chosen are put on the board along with the related behaviors, characteristics, and thinking dispositions or habits that the class identifies: Lincoln, for example, could be identified as visionary, smart, persistent, compassionate, and caring. Martin Luther King could be identified as compassionate, faithful, determined, brave, peaceful, visionary, and a great speaker.

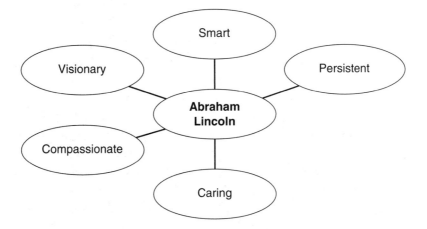

- Students then identify the characteristics of great thinkers on a chart to be added to as we consider other biographies.

Characteristics of Great Thinkers

Lincoln: Visionary, smart, persistent, compassionate, and caring

King: Compassionate, faithful, determined, brave, peaceful, visionary, a great speaker

---

- Students may either be assigned to biographies related to a content area or may choose one of their own to study.

Students write a biography of their chosen character and a brief analysis of that person's thinking characteristics.

Failed in business, 1831

Defeated for legislature, 1832

Again failed in business, 1833

Elected to legislature, 1834

Defeated for Speaker, 1838

Defeated for elector, 1840

Defeated for Congress, 1843

Elected to Congress, 1846

Defeated for Congress, 1848

Defeated for Senate, 1855

Defeated for vice-president, 1858

Defeated for Senate, 1858

Elected president of the United States, 1860   (Costa, 1991)

Abraham Lincoln

"4 Score and 7 Years Ago . . ."

When little Abe was born on that cold February day there was nothing different about him, he was just a normal baby. Nobody realized that he would help change America forever.

Abe had many obstacles thrown at him. The Lincolns moved many times, and Abe often went without enough food or warm clothes. A disease took Mrs. Lincoln.

Abe's stepmother realized how much he loved to learn and made sure that each night Abe had time to read books. Where did he get them? Books were very scarce in the wilderness and Abe would do almost anything to get his hands on one—including walking 20 miles to the library and walking 20 miles to return the book. Sometimes a book would be destroyed and Abe would have to work to pay it off, usually for many days of long hours.

Soon, the Lincolns had moved to the new "Green State" of Illinois. Abe's hard work was known for miles around. Once he split 1,000 rails to earn a pair of jeans. When Abe turned 21 he moved out of the house. Abe and a friend started a store and Abe began to make speeches so people would elect him to the state capitol. They did. More than anything, Lincoln wanted to study law and become a lawyer. One day he was in the store when a stranger came in the store selling barrels of old stuff. He had no use for it but he decided to buy it to help the man. At the bottom of the barrel lay a dusty old book. He brushed it off and realized it was the book he needed to study law. He spent most of his time studying the book. The local school master helped him. Abe's store went in debt and he lost all of his money. Meanwhile, Ann Rutledge who Abe was about to marry became ill and died. Lincoln went out to the capitol, sad and poor. He asked the store owner to lend him some bedding. The store owner, Joshua Speed, offered to share his house and his own bed. From then on, Lincoln and Speed were best friends. Abe became a well known lawyer. Lincoln soon married a lady named Miss Todd. Meanwhile there was a great controversy between the north and the south over slavery issues. The northern states thought slavery was wrong and therefore wanted to abolish it. But for the southerners, slavery was a way of life and they wanted it to continue.

"Let each state decide for itself," said Douglas. This alarmed Lincoln. He said, "All men are created equal. There must be freedom in all America because a house divided against itself cannot stand." Lincoln had been poor and bankrupt. He had run for office and lost many times, but Abe did not stop working for what he believed in. People came from all over to see Abe and Douglas. Although Douglas was elected senator of Illinois, Lincoln's greatness was known nation wide. People began to think that Abe Lincoln might not be the one for president. But then late one evening Lincoln got the word that he had been elected president. So the Lincolns bid farewell to peaceful Illinois and hello to Washington, D.C. But Lincoln was only president of the northern states, the southern states had rebelled and replaced the stars and stripes with a new flag. Lincoln realized he had nothing to do but call war. So, with sadness in his heart, he declared war. Lincoln would do all he could to help the wounded out on the battlefield. After the Battle of Gettysburg, Lincoln made his famous Gettysburg Address in memory of those who had died for equal rights. Soon he had written the Emancipation Proclamation to stop slavery. The southerners fought and fought until they could fight no more and finally gave in. The Civil War had ended. Once again, America was one nation, under God, and the slaves were free.

Characteristics

persistent   optimistic

determined   fair-minded

compassionate   disciplined

Sample student work. Heydenberk, 5th grade.

THE GRASS IS ALWAYS GREENER ON THE OTHER SIDE

Getting a perspective from another field is often essential for understanding or problem-solving. Many doctors have taken art classes for help in visualizing the internal structures of the human body. Scientists have been known to gain inspiration and understanding from a child or a painting. Some great creators like Leonardo da Vinci have brought a diverse body of knowledge and perspective to bear on any problem or project. Students will benefit from the multiple lenses developed in this exercise.

CR-CT Skills Developed

Analysis of perspectives

Communication

Cooperation

Metacognition

Procedure

- Students work in groups to identify different thinking styles and habits used in different fields. The following examples might be examined in a whole class setting before students consider the remainder in small group settings.
  An artist might visualize a problem or an issue being studied.
  A scientist might analyze the problem using cause-effect reasoning or the scientific method.
  A doctor might study structure and function of systems or parts.
  A police officer might look for laws and limits pertaining to the subject.
  A teacher might be inclined to explain something in multiple ways.
  A fireman might be concerned with potential dangers.
  A librarian might approach a subject by organizing resources and gathering as much information as possible.
  A mathematician might attempt to maximize or minimize parts of a problem or divide the problem into subjects.
  A garbage collector might try to sort the junk from what can be useful.

- The small groups are asked to generate potential responses to the following:
  What would an archeologist do?
  What would a chef do?
  What would an architect do?
  What would a dancer do?
  How would they approach this problem?
  How would they define this problem?
  What questions might they ask?

- Groups are formed to brainstorm thinking styles for several of the scenarios selected.

- Student groups design and illustrate *thinker's toolboxes* for each of their chosen fields. For example, for an artist, students might put imagination, color, perspective, memories, and emotions in their toolboxes. A doctor might use different tools, such as medical tests.

- When each group has finished their *thinker's toolbox*, they may have a chance to present it to the class and ask the students to guess what field the toolbox belongs to.

Portfolio Pick

THE BRAINSTORMING BANQUET

> *I understand that we have problems. We don't have the time we need, we don't have the money we need. Our kids have problems, too—lots of problems. But they also have us, and that's a lot. For some of them, it means everything.*
> —Elementary school principal,
> talking to teachers and parents

Students are introduced to the art of integrative brainstorming through the ancient fable of the banquet, wherein life or death depends upon creative thinking and cooperation.

CR-CT Skills Developed

Divergent thinking

Metacognition

Integrative thinking

Procedure

- The teacher introduces the banquet fable:

    There are 2 identical banquets, each in a large, beautiful room with high ceilings, beautiful artwork, exotic plants, and stained glass windows. In each room is a huge fireplace, a large, plush oriental rug, and a large dining table. The guests are served a 7-course meal. However, the guests all have long wooden spoons tied to their hands. The spoons' handles are too long and no one can put any of the food into their mouths. At one banquet the guests are all fighting, hitting each other with the long spoons, and starving. At the other banquet table they are all eating and laughing and having a fine time. What is the difference?

    The answer is that the guests at the successful banquet have cooperated and fed each other, solving the problem of the long-handled spoons. They have found a win–win solution.

- Students worked in small groups to identify problems that require integrative thinking and cooperation to effect solutions (e.g., anything from crime and environmental issues to studying for exams or cleaning up the baseball field behind the school).
- Students work in small groups to create win-win, integrative solutions. An integrative solution is one that is considered to meet the needs of all involved versus a win-lose, or forced, solution.

Students may draw, define, or write an example of an integrative (win-win) solution vs. a distributive (win-lose) solution to a problem, illustrating or elucidating the different outcomes.

Portfolio Pick

TIME MACHINE

Diamonds are only chunks of coal that stuck to their jobs.
—M. R. Smith

Time Machine offers students and teachers another tool for expanding understanding by considering new perspectives. We have considered multiple perspectives and thinking styles or characteristics through the lenses of people in a variety of disciplines. In Time Machine we consider the perspectives of people in different cultures at different times.

CR-CT Skills Developed

Analysis of perspective

Communication

Cooperation

Procedure

- Students are asked how life was different when their parents or grandparents were students.
- After sharing stories students are asked how different people think about things differently during different times in history. For instance, there have been times in history when very young people had jobs and even families to support and age 30 was considered old age. There have been times when an eccentric or artistic young girl would have been considered a witch, or perhaps a goddess. Students reflect on: "How would you be different if you had been born in those times?"

- Students work in groups to research the lives of people in different times or cultures (e.g., "Europe/Asia through Time" or "Ancient Heroes throughout the World," depending on the curriculum or needs of the class).
- When the groups complete their research reports and murals or illustrations they may invite classmates to use the Time Machine to tour their assigned culture.
- After sharing their research and reporting their finding to the class in a presentation, students should take questions from the "tourists"— their classmates (e.g., "At what age did children go to school in Ancient Greece? Did they go to school at all?").
- Questions that the Time Machine can't answer can be discussed and researched later, if possible.

Time Machine—Eleanor Roosevelt at the Turn of the Century

Only a handful of people accomplished what Ms. Roosevelt did. She paved the way for women in politics. Eleanor Roosevelt was born in New York City, October 11, 1884. Her mother died when she was eight. She went to live with her Grandmother.

She married Franklin Delano Roosevelt. In 1910 he ran for the New York State Senate and won. Eleanor began to enjoy being a politician's wife. She went to business school and joined the League of Women Voters. She drafted bills, made policies, and organized for the group.

When Franklin was running for vice-president, Eleanor helped with the campaign. This was the first election where women would be allowed to vote. Even though they worked very hard they lost that term. Eleanor set up Women's Democratic Clubs and started a newspaper called Women's Democratic news.

She worked on her public speaking and began to give speeches. She became known as a woman with a very respected point of view. She loved what she was doing and was very good at it even though "politics was a man's game." When Eleanor was a young woman she was not allowed to vote. She wanted a more just system. Eleanor began to fight for children's and women's rights. After a lot of hard work, Franklin won the presidency.

She helped everyone who needed her help: African Americans, the unemployed, the hungry, the homeless, the coal miners, and the veterans. She published a book that was a collection of her speeches and articles. It was titled "It's Up to a Woman." She started NYA, a program that helped high-school and college students stay in school and get proper training for jobs. One of the great things about the program was that it included African American students. She often visited African American communities and schools, campaigning for voter rights. When she went to meetings, she was upset about the fact that she was being unlawful to sit on the "black side" and not on the "white side." Of course she couldn't break the law and so she sat in the middle of the aisle.

On April 12, 1945, in his fourth term, Franklin D. Roosevelt died. Many people believed this was the end for Eleanor too. They all were wrong.

The president Harry Truman looked to Eleanor for guidance which helped her learn she could not just stop her work. She had to go on and she did. In November of 1962 the world lost a wonderful person, but the path she blazed and the things she started live on.

Questions:

How were voting rights different in Eleanor Roosevelt's time?

What else was different in the early 1900s?

Sample student paper. Schaeffer, 6th grade, 1999.

THE RIGHT QUESTION

> *If we would have new knowledge, we must get a whole new world of questions.*
> —Susanne K. Langer

So much time is spent looking for the right answer that students often forget that the right question is often more important. This activity introduces the importance of concentrating on the right question when dealing with a problem.

CR-CT Skills Developed

Critical questioning

Divergent thinking

Convergent thinking

Communication

Cooperation

Procedure

- The importance of asking the right question is introduced to the whole class using one of the scenarios included.
- Consider the following quote: "The quality of life is determined by the quality of the questions you ask yourself."
- Students are then asked to consider what happens if you ask the wrong question.
- If someone usually asks themselves, "How do I get even?" (a win–lose question) rather than "How can we solve this?" (a win–win question), how does the difference in questions affect the way he or she thinks and acts?
- Students work in groups to write win–win and win–lose questions to share with the class.

THE INVENTION QUESTION

In order to expand our appreciation and understanding of critical questioning, we move beyond social problem solving in this activity. In the Invention Question we attempt to look into the inventor's mind and ask ourselves what questions inspired our favorite inventions.

CR-CT Skills Developed

Critical questions

Divergent thinking

Communication

Cooperation

Procedure

Students begin by reviewing scenarios 1 and 2 and discussing how the questions Dr. King and Edward Jenner asked themselves affect our lives.

Scenarios for the Right Question

No. 1

Computer pioneers Dr. Mauchly and Dr. Eckert werre undoubtedly inspired by the earlier work of Charles Babbage and Ada Lovelace, who invented a machine that could add and subtract numbers, and the work of Dr. Atanasoff, who invented a machine that performed more complex calculations. Dr. Mauchly and Dr. Eckert asked themselves how this machine could be made differently and what else it could do. Because of their questions, the ENIAC, considered by many to be the world's first computer, was invented.

No. 2

In England, Edward Jenner, the scientist who invented the vaccine for smallpox, asked a different question. Everyone asked how to help the afflicted and how to help people avoid smallpox. Jenner instead studied those who did not get sick and asked why. He found that milk maids who were exposed to cowpox, a weaker strain of smallpox disease, were immune to smallpox. The smallpox vaccine was invented.

- In small groups, students brainstorm the questions an inventor has to ask in order to invent.

- Students are asked to list some of their favorite inventions, such as:
Bicycle	Television
Car	Air bags
Compact disks	Ice cream cone
Movies	

What question did the inventor likely ask before inventing one of the above? What did people use before the inventor asked the question? How did the inventor improve our lives?

- Students may then generate a list of questions to make them think creatively about any problem. Some student examples are:
  How could this be done?
  Why is this done this way?
  Is this the only way this could be done?
  Can we make it bigger, smaller, or from different materials?
  How can we make this better?
  What is good about this?
  How can we make this fun?
  How else can this be used?
  How could this problem be made worse (e.g., as in the "Twister" activities introduced earlier)?

- When a student is faced with a problem or a conflict, what questions might he ask? For instance,
  "How can I teach this person a lesson?"
  "How can I make them sorry?"
  "How can I get even?"
  "How can I make this person understand my position?"
  "How can we work this out?"
  "How can we make this better?"
  "How could this be done?"
  "Why is this done this way?"
  "Is this the only way this could be done?"
  "How else could this be used?"
  "How else could this help people?"

Ada Lovelace: Computer Pioneer

How could one girl suffer from severe headaches and become paralyzed, and still be able to invent a commonly used machine in the modern day? She was an amazing girl named Ada Lovelace.

When Ada became an adult, she went to a dinner party. Little did she know that the dinner party would change her life forever. Ada overheard an inventor named Charles Babbage talking about a machine he invented that could add and subtract numbers correctly.

Ada grew more and more interested in Charles's machine. She became his partner in inventing the machine. Ada and Charles worked on improving it and Ada wrote papers about it for inventors' groups.

After Charles and Ada died, other inventors improved their machine. In the 1950s the machine was as big as a room. It could do many more things than add and subtract numbers correctly. That's when the machine finally got its name, the computer: a complex machine that can accept information. Ada wasn't kidding when she said "No one knows yet the power left undeveloped in that wiry system of mine."

Questions Ada Lovelace asked:

How can we let other inventors know about this machine?

How else can we use this machine?

Sample student paper. M. H. Cappella, 5th grade.

Young people create murals, banners, and sets to illustrate the conflicts in their lives. PHOTO: NANCY DAVIS, DIRECTOR, CITY AT PEACE, SANTA BARBARA, CA.

CREATOGRAPHY

Students examine how the choices a person makes affects their lives and may affect history, as well. Favorite historical figures are chosen and studied by students, who try to determine what question the person asked him- or herself and what choices they made. Students then examine other paths the person could have taken and the consequences of asking a different question.

CR-CT Skills Developed

Critical questioning

Analysis

Divergent thinking

Cause-effect reasoning

Communication

Procedure

- Depending on content area needs, students develop a biography of a character from literature, history, or social studies, or use a biography they have previously developed.

- Students are instructed to find the character's interests and concerns and the important or pivotal moments in the character's life.

- Students should consider what questions the character asked himself during the important times or various crises in the character's life. For example: Students could imagine the questions that Pickett, the Confederate general at Gettysburg, asked himself before ordering the legendary charge that took the lives of many soldiers.

- Students can then pose alternate questions and reflect on how these might have changed the course of history. For example, what if Martin Luther King asked, "How can I get even?" instead of "How can we peacefully protest and make things more just?" How would his march on Washington be remembered if he had asked a different question?

- After students complete the biographies, they create a list of the concerns and questions that they feel affected their character's life, in list form or as an essay.

"Mr. Beethoven, They're Applauding"

Upon hearing the works of Mozart, Ludwig Van Beethoven's father was determined to raise his child as a prodigy. As a result, young Ludwig would spend sixteen to eighteen hours a day at the piano. When he would fall asleep, he was awakened by his father beating him. As Beethoven grew older his father grew more impatient for his son's success. The older he was the less impressive his skill, and he would no longer be a prodigy, though he was writing music and giving concerts at the age of seven. His father frequently changed Ludwig's birth certificate. At the age of twelve he was alleged to be nine. Beethoven never knew his age. Historians estimate the year of his birth to be around 1770. Years later his father gave up on being the father of a genius and abandoned the family.

In need of money, Ludwig began to give musical lessons. His students said that he was highly sensitive and moody with bad manners and a temper to match. His friends would agree, but they saw a side of Ludwig that was warm, generous, and caring. He dedicated numerous pieces to them. Around the age of twenty-seven Beethoven started to lose his hearing. He began to push away his students and the people he loved the most. His world became cold and empty and, worst of all, silent. By the time he was twenty-nine he could no longer hear his own work.

Beethoven continued to compose. One of his last masterpieces was his ninth symphony. It was his final masterpiece performed for the public. He sat in the front of the hall, near the orchestra. As the music played he tapped his foot and nodded his head, never letting on that he couldn't hear anything. The last song approached: *The Ode to Joy*. It was performed with such perfection and beauty that the audience was awed after it had ended. Then their shock died and they rose from their seats and roared "Bravo" and "Encore"; and the applause was deafening. It was a moment of pure respect and glory for the composer, yet, Ludwig Van Beethoven didn't turn to accept their applause. He sat in his special seat and pretended to listen to what was going on around him. A violinist tapped him on the shoulder. "Mr. Beethoven, they're applauding." The audience with tears in their eyes knew that all the horrible rumors they had heard were true. Beethoven had achieved, he was a genius, but he couldn't reap what he had sown. He could not hear the music or the applause.

Beethoven's story is impressive, because he began to fight a battle that is going on to this day. Stereotypes are a cause of hate and problems in our society today. Beethoven broke the stereotype that deaf people cannot write music. And he fought the battle without violence and without harming anyone. He went along peacefully. So when his work proved to the people that their misconceptions were wrong, he'd set an example.

Even after becoming deaf, Mr. Beethoven asked himself how he could continue to be productive and creative rather than giving up.

Sample student paper. Raver Pray, 9th grade.

Portfolio Pick

QUESTION BRIDGE

> *It is better to ask some of the questions than to know all the answers.*
> —James Thurber

"Question Bridge" helps students to get into the habit of asking themselves questions that can make their learning more productive and memorable. Most students are more interested in a subject when they can describe why it matters, what else they can learn by mastering the material, and how they can use it in their lives. The associations they make will sharpen their focus and increase memory.

CR-CT Skills Developed

Critical questioning

Communication

Inductive-deductive thinking

Procedure

- A corner of the chalkboard, a poster board, bulletin board, or sheet of paper folded in half lengthwise are used. One side is labeled; the other side is left blank.

- Across the top is written: "Why Energy?" or "Why African Cultures?"

- Students generate questions that will make content area studies more relevant; they build bridges to their lives. Examples are:
Why do we study_____?
Why is it important?
What are the most interesting facts?
What are the strangest?
What is most confusing about _____?
What does it have to do with our lives?
What else can this help us understand?
What else does this remind us of?

- Students can add questions or answers to the board; multiple answers are encouraged.

- Once per week (or whenever the teacher deems appropriate) some of the questions and answers are reviewed and discussed by the class. The goal is to bridge understanding between the content studied and the students' lives, interests, and concerns.

- Students may be asked to compose an essay about their most compelling question or related answer or keep a log of interesting questions and answers about the unit.

Portfolio Pick

CONCRETE AND CONCEPT QUESTIONS

Computers are useless. They can only give you answers.
—Pablo Picasso

Students learn the difference between literal (concrete) and open-ended (concept) questions. Both types of questions are important to the learner. However, one type without the other leaves students with a shallow understanding of their studies. Both question types are introduced in a simple, memorable way for students to incorporate.

CR-CT Skills Developed

Classification

Analysis

Communication

Critical questioning

Divergent thinking

Convergent thinking

Procedure

The teacher writes CONCRETE QUESTIONS and CONCEPT QUESTIONS on the board, explaining that concrete questions are essential—like pouring a concrete foundation for a house. Concrete questions are usually questions with one short, correct answer; they often address who, what, why, where, or when. For example: "Ben Franklin started a school in what major city?" "Philadelphia" would be the correct answer. More interesting concept questions can be entertained after we have the "foundation"—after we have answered the concrete questions.

Concept questions are questions that require some conceptual or deeper understanding of the subject. For example: "Why did Franklin want to start his own school when there were others in Philadelphia?" "What knowledge did Ben Franklin think his students would need and why?"

- The teacher asks students why each type of question is important. Would our understanding be complete if we did not know the "who" or "where" answers? Would our understanding be complete if we did not know how or why something occurred? How do both types of questions increase our understanding?

- Students read a content area passage and write three concrete and three concept questions to share with the class:
  Concrete: "What year was Lincoln made president?"
  Concept: "What inspired Lincoln to write the Gettysburg Address?"

BRAIN BOOSTERS

Brain Booster cards offer teachers and students an interesting way for students to stay actively engaged in monitoring their own understanding. The Brain Booster cards are on a table or the teacher's desk. Students may ask to choose one or the teacher can pull one out and pose the question to the class to stimulate interest.

CR-CT Skills Developed

Critical questioning

Communication

Analysis

Procedure

- Students may help create question cards for any subject area with the teacher's assistance. Examples are:
  What happened before this time that caused these events?
  What do you predict will happen because of these events?
  Would you like to live in this place or time? Why?
  What would be the most exciting part of living in this time or place?
  What would you miss most living in this place or time?
  Who would you like to be friends with in this place or time?
  How would your life be different if this event happened today in your community?
  Who would you like to talk with from this time or place?
  What was a young person's biggest challenge in these times?
  What were the main conflicts in the story, place, or time?
  How would you feel about . . . ?
  What advice would you give to a friend during this time/event?

For extra credit, students may answer controversial or compelling questions in essay form, journal format, or reports.

Portfolio Pick

GOAL AND QUESTION POWER: Q.P.

A goal is just a dream with a deadline.
—William Hartwell

Students are introduced to the power of asking important questions every day to help them reach their goals and stay focused on what is important.

CR-CT Skills Developed

Analysis

Divergent thinking

Prediction

Critical questioning

Communication

Procedure

- Students review how the questions people ask themselves determine the direction of their understanding, behavior, and life. They begin by using examples from content area studies. For example: Inventors researched in content areas or Creatography activities.

- Famous examples may be given to begin the discussion. For instance, What if M. Ghandi asked himself how he could get even, instead of how he could work for justice? How would his life be different? How would India be different? How would the world be different?

  What if you are in a dangerous situation with an angry stranger? Do you ask yourself, "How do I tell this guy he is a jerk?" or "How do I get out of this situation safely?" How would each question affect the outcome?

  What if a stranger in a car pulls up in front of your school and asks you to come over and give directions? Do you question the safety of that decision?

- We ask questions all of the time in our lives, although we are often not aware that we are doing it. For instance, whenever we cross a street we stop ourselves and silently ask if a car is coming.

- Students should be asked to think of examples and share them with the class.

- Every decision implies a question—e.g., whether to watch TV or finish an assignment.

- In this session we look at our questions and make sure we ask the right question when we make a decision. We can decide not to take this important part of thinking for granted. It makes us better thinkers and, consequently, smarter and safer human beings.

- Students need to think about their goals, beginning with the basic goals of being successful, healthy, and a good person (friend, son, daughter, or student). What questions do we have to ask ourselves and what decisions help support the pursuit of these goals?

- Students brainstorm their goals for school, home, and life. Have any steps been taken toward goal "A" or "B" today? If not, are there any steps that can be taken? Periodically students may review goals A and B to make sure they are still relevant.

- Students individually draft a Question Power (QP) Chart which can be used as a reference throughout the year.

- Whenever students seem stuck and unable to solve a conflict or an academic challenge, they can raise their QP by first checking the QP chart and then brainstorming new questions. Question Power charts can be revised periodically. Students must ask themselves if their questions motivate them in a positive way, toward their major life goals.

QUANTUM QUESTION

If you want a better answer, you've got to ask a better question.
—Anonymous

Quantum Question is designed to introduce students to brainstorming as a problem-solving technique. The technique is designed to use on chronic or habitual problems. A sense of curiosity develops in students when they discover what a powerful and effective problem solver Quantum Question and critical questioning can provide. In many cases, students have been so focused on finding the right solution that finding the right question has often been ignored completely.

CR-CT Skills Developed

Critical thinking

Analyzing main idea

Cooperation

Communication

Procedure

- The teacher explains that we often engage in the same behavior even though we do not want the same results. Often we will look in the same place for a missing object—under cushions on the couch or under a bed or in a desk drawer—even when we know that we already checked these places. Students can share stories to corroborate the point.

- Again, using the metaphor of an electron taking a quantum leap to a new orbit in an atom, we are going to design our Quantum Questions that help us write a new, more positive outcome. Students identify a problem which they may habitually encounter from the list below or from the classroom suggestions. For instance:
  Lack of time
  Unfinished assignments
  Arguments
  Fights with classmate
  Fights with siblings
  Being late
  Not having time to read
  Not having time to practice an instrument
  Not having time to write to grandparents
  Forgetting things you said you would do

- As a class we attempt to identify any useless, destructive, or negative questions we ask ourselves when we have a bad habit or recurring problem:

Why am I always late?
Why can't I ever get this right?
Who is going to win on picking out the TV show we watch tonight?
Why don't I have enough time to get this done?
Why am I always too tired to . . . ?
Why do I always avoid getting things done?
Why do people always give me a hard time about . . . ?
Why can't I be better at . . . ?
Why can't I be as smart as . . . ?

- Since our brains will search for an answer to any question we pose, we rewrite negative questions to incorporate a more positive, proactive, problem-solving answer. Our first question, "Why am I always late?" can take a quantum leap to a more positive question: "How can I change my schedule to make it easier for me to be on time?"

- Students brainstorm answers to the positive questions. Typical responses might be:
Take the phone off the hook
No TV during homework
Leave earlier
Combine activities
Reduce number of activities

- Students look at the next question, "Why can't I ever get this right?" This may take a quantum leap to "How can I get this right more often?" which in turn may lead to, "What do I do differently when I get this right?"

  "Who is going to win on picking out the TV show we watch tonight?" may take a quantum leap to "How can we work out the TV schedule so that we both see what we want and we don't fight every night?"

  "Why don't I ever have enough time to get this done?" may take a quantum leap to "How can I rearrange my schedule to get this done more efficiently?"

  "Why am I always too tired to . . . ?" may take a quantum leap to "How can I get this done?"

  "Why do I always avoid getting things done?" may take a quantum leap to "How can I make it fun, easy, and fast to get things done?"

  "Why do people always give me a hard time about . . . ?" may take a quantum leap to "How can I act and react differently so that I don't get in as many arguments about . . . ?"

- Students design a chart of negative questions and Quantum Questions which they have designed. Characteristics of Quantum Questions are that they focus on the problem (not the person) and they ask a positive (solution-oriented) question.

- Students brainstorm their own questions and add them to their portfolios.

Portfolio Pick

CARPE DIEM—USING QUANTUM QUESTIONS EVERY DAY

Hitch your wagon to a star.
—Ralph Waldo Emerson

Because our basic foundation goals of being safe, behaving in a smart fashion, and being a good person are quite general, and the Question Power concept is important, we add a Question Power journal to our portfolios. This journal may be one of the most powerful personal success and safety tools a student ever uses.

CR-CT Skills Developed

Critical questioning

Analysis of perspective

Divergent thinking

Convergent thinking

Procedure

- Introduce Carpe Diem (seize the day) to students.

- Using the metaphor of an electron taking a quantum leap to a new orbit in an atom, we will take a quantum leap to a new solution and a new level of understanding using Quantum Questions every day.

- The teacher introduces Quantum Question Power Journals. Students will design questions to help them make good use of every day and move toward important goals. Always begin with what the student feels good about to get in a Quantum Question mood.

- Students are asked to list what they feel good about, what they care about, what they enjoy, in what areas they excel, and what major goals they may have.

- The teacher provides an example for students to model:
"I want to be a good teacher"
"I want to be a good spouse"
"I want to be a good parent"

The teacher's questions are. . . ,
"How can I be a good teacher?"
"How can I spend some time with my family?"
"How can I stay healthy?"

The teacher's answers may be: "I will cook dinner with my children and my spouse and take a walk with them tonight."

"What's good about my situation?"
"What are the problems?"
"How can I make it better?"

- You can add to your Quantum Question Journal or review the same questions every day.

- It is important to review the goals and questions and to write in the journal every day, if possible.

Journals may also be useful when students have important decisions to make.

- It is important when making a decision to ask if that decision makes sense for your foundation goals: being safe, smart, and successful. How we define "successful" will differ from individual to individual: One person may wish to be an artist, another may wish to coach soccer. The questions students ask themselves should reflect their goals and their criteria for success, as well as how to create the most positive outcome. For instance, "How can I continue to get great grades in math?" "How can I get along better with my sister?" "How can I find the time to play the harmonica?"

- Students can begin to design their Question Journals. They may be integrated into their CR-CT portfolios. Regular time intervals should be established in which students update their journals. During update times some group sharing of questions will help expand their knowledge and maintain interest in the process.

Portfolio Pick

BIOSCAPE

Bioscape uses artwork to depict a biography of a favorite person or character who has been researched by the class or individual students. In Bioscape we examine some of the choices made by the people we have studied, such as Eleanor Roosevelt, Helen Keller, or Albert Einstein. In this activity, students make a mural which highlights the challenges and choices the characters we have studied have made.

CR-CT Skills Developed

Classification

Comprehension

Communication

Sequencing

Critical questioning

Procedure

- The teacher introduces Bioscapes as an extension of the critical question activities. In Bioscape each group is asked to create a mural of their character's life, focusing on challenges, failures, triumphs, and critical incidents which helped or discouraged the individual. Murals may be created from art supplies, magazines, photos, and anything else the group finds appropriate. Captions such as "Lincoln failed in his congressional race . . ." are encouraged. Bioscapes might employ chronological event maps to elucidate events in the life of the individual.
- Prominent display of the murals encourages the students' efforts.
- The school art teacher could be helpful with this activity.

Portfolio Pick

ANALOGIES

Chapter 2, Section 2, was inspired by recent research on the Connecting with Analogies model of analogy instruction (Greenwood, Huff-Benkowski, 1998). This analogy instruction is effective with elementary school students and beyond—increasing comprehension, content interest, and critical and creative thinking. Analogical thinking is necessary for most transfer of knowledge and understanding. Comparisons of similarities and differences between concepts, systems, or events is central to our cognitive processes (Cropley & Dehn, 1996). Students find the Connecting with Analogies model engaging and the process provides an invaluable assessment tool for the teacher, too.

INTRODUCTION TO ANALOGIES

The Connecting with Analogies (CWA) model developed by Dr. Scott Greenwood and Dr. Kelly Huff-Benkowski emphasizes reasoning and has been shown in studies to be the most effective method of introducing the concept of analogy. Analogies are an engaging method for increasing critical thinking and comprehension of content area material.

CR-CT Skills Developed

Active listening

Consideration of multiple perspectives

Analogical thinking

Cooperation

Divergent thinking

Procedure

- The teacher draws and labels two types of footwear on the board: sneakers and skates.
- Students are then asked how they are different. How do their uses differ?
- Students are asked to help write a sentence beginning with "Sneakers are to . . ." They are encouraged to explore relationships, such as "sneakers are to runners," "walkers," or "basketball players."
- Students are then asked to reflect on the relationship with skates. They are given a sentence starter such as: "Sneakers are to runners as skates are to . . ."
- Students finish the sentence.
- The teacher labels the sentence as an analogy. Students are now asked to help create examples of analogies using content area words/vocabulary such as the following:

Snow is to white as grass is to _____.

Wave is to ocean as ripple is to _____.

Dime is to silver as penny is to _____.

Fawn is to deer as cub is to _____.

Nose is to smell as tongue is to _____.

Peel is to apple as shell is to _____.

Surgeon is to operating room as teacher is to _____.

- Students are asked to explain their reasoning.
- The teacher then reverses the order of several of the analogy stems:
Skates are to skaters as sneakers are to runners.
20 degrees is to ice as 212 degrees is to steam.
Grass is to green as snow is to white.
Clam is to shell as apple is to peel.
Teacher is to classroom as surgeon is to operating room.

- For each analogy the students analyze the analogy to see if it still makes sense.
- Working in groups, students are asked to define analogy and to compare their answers.

Portfolio Pick

ANALOGIES: COMMON CHARACTERISTICS

In this activity we analyze how different things or events may share a common characteristic (a central theme in analogical thinking) by adding one to the given list and then eliminating an item that doesn't share the identified characteristic. This may be developed as a useful and fun tool for assessing students' understanding of themes and concepts in content areas.

CR-CT Skills Developed

Consideration of multiple perspectives

Analogical thinking

Cooperation

Active listening

Paraphrasing

Procedure

- The teacher writes four words on the board, three of which are related and one of which is unrelated. Examples are:
  boots, sneakers, slippers, hat
  evergreen, spruce, pine, daisy
  stamen, petal, leaf, bone
  convection, conduction, radiation, refrigeration
  coal, oil, natural gas, wheat
  liquid, solid, gas, wood
  Aristotle, Ulysses, Greece, Rome
  Wordsworth, Dante, Shakespeare, Einstein

- Students write the one they would eliminate on a piece of paper and their reason for their choice. Whole class discussion is used to reveal responses and to compare reasons for choices of elimination.

- Students can then create their own "add-one" analogies individually or in small groups. Examples might be:
  leaf, branch, roots, _____
  green, red, blue, _____

ANALOGY ATTRIBUTES

In Analogy Attributes students continue to design three-part classification groups for classmates to analyze and complete. Students are asked to decide on a central attribute that characterizes the three-part list. The students add to the list, themselves.

CR-CT Skills Developed

Classifying

Paraphrasing

Summarizing

Cooperation

Main idea

Procedure

- Students begin by designing three-part analogy lists for their classmates to finish, such as:
  Jupiter, Saturn, Neptune, _____

- In the first stage of CWA students are asked to identify the central, relevant attributes which characterize all of the items in their list (a). Students then generate an example of another item that could be included in the list (b).

- Divergent answers are accepted and encouraged if students can explain their reasoning (e.g.: Jupiter, Saturn, Neptune, and Uranus are all the largest planets in our solar system. Jupiter, Saturn, Neptune, and Venus are all planets).

- Examples are:
  Saturn, Jupiter, Neptune, . . .
      a) planets
      b) Venus
  Conduction, convection, radiation, . . .
      a) heat transfer
      b) precipitation
  Gravity, electromagnetism, strong force, . . .
      a) fundamental forces
      b) weak nuclear force
  Tornado, hurricane, monsoon, . . .
      a) weather   a) weather threats
              or
      b) clear sky   b) flood
  Rose, daisy, orchid, . . .
      a) plants   a) flowering plants
              or
      b) oak tree   b) impatiens

Molecule, atom, proton, . . .
　　a) parts of matter
　　b) electron
Remember to discuss and develop reasoning for multiple right answers.

CONNECTION SENTENCES

Students examine analogies and construct sentences explaining the relationship between items in the analogy stems they've created. This is an effective method of reviewing content vocabulary and critical concepts while teaching critical thinking skills to students.

CR-CT Skills Developed

Analysis

Analogical thinking

Cooperation

Procedure

- The teacher first models this activity by writing familiar analogies on the board and by describing aloud the relationship within the stem and then between parts. For instance, in the analogy whale is to mammal as snake is to _____, the teacher explains the relationship between the whale and the mammal group.

- Students are asked to find the relationship in the second part of the analogy using the logic used in the first part. For example, if a whale is a mammal, then a snake is a member of what group?

- After students recognize the snake as a reptile, they are asked to complete their analogies and write a connective sentence to explain the relationships within the analogies, e.g., "A whale is part of the mammal family just as the snake is part of the reptile family." Other examples of connectives are:
You wear sneakers to play basketball just as you wear skates when you go skating.
Water turns to ice when the temperature is below 32 degrees just as water turns to steam when the temperature goes over 212 degrees.

- Using content area vocabulary and concepts, students then construct their own analogies and connection sentences, alone or in small groups if some students find the task difficult.

THE ABC ACTIVITY: ANALOGY BRAINSTORM CONCEPTS

This is an engaging and useful activity to use in any content area once students become comfortable with analogies. Students have an opportunity to interact with content concepts and vocabulary and teachers have a unique opportunity to assess students' understanding of the analogy process and their grasp of content area materials.

CR-CT Skills Developed

Analogical thinking

Classification

Divergent thinking

Creative thinking

Cooperation

Procedure

- At the appropriate time during a content area unit the teacher asks students to brainstorm any important words related to the subject. For instance, for the subject Greece, the following terms might be generated:

  Greece, Aristotle, Parthenon, Zeus, Gods, war, Socrates, Alexander, grapes, wine, Mediterranean, Plato, democracy, questioning, astronomy, language, alphabet, Hercules, thought, constellations, island, Cyclops, and Romans.

- Students are then asked to work in small groups to create three parts of four-part analogies for classmates to solve using the brainstorming concept/vocabulary list with any relevant additions. For example, grapes are to wine as olives are to (oil).

THE CAUSE–EFFECT ANALOGY MAP

A #2 pencil and a dream can take you anywhere.
—Joyce Meyers

This activity is designed to introduce students to an ongoing exercise that uses universal concepts as a thematic springboard for creating analogies. Concepts such as cause–effect help students anchor content to higher level concepts for more meaningful understanding.

CR-CT Skills Developed

Analogical thinking

Divergent thinking

Classification

Analysis of features of concepts

Procedure

- The teacher draws the words "cause–effect" in a circle on the board.

- Students brainstorm all of the cause–effect relationships they have recently encountered in a chosen subject to complete the map. In science the following list might occur:
  pesticides—pollution
  lack of rain—drought
  pollution—diminished ozone
  compost—rich soil

CRITICAL CONCEPT MAPS

Although the integration of the curriculum has been found to make students' educational experience more coherent and meaningful, it is often nearly impossible to coordinate such integration with all of the diverse content demands in a school. Critical concept integration offers us another integration tool focusing on broad, timeless, abstract concepts as they endure in all disciplines through time. Universal concepts such as cause and effect, continuity and change, or conflict and cooperation can draw students thinking to a higher level and make coherent studies across content areas and through time. Using analogical thinking we begin by looking at different units of study with an eye for some enduring themes related to these critical concepts.

CR-CT Skills Developed

Analysis

Divergent thinking

Communication

Cooperation

Procedure

- The teacher chooses a critical concept word related to a content area or from the list below and writes the word on the board.
- Students are asked to silently brainstorm and write related words at their desks.
- After the appropriate think time students share their examples and generate new examples which are written on the board. For the term

communities, for instance, the following terms might be generated: ant farms, our town, ecosystems, flocks of birds, New York City, Athens, interrelatedness, independence, families.

Students may draw a critical concept brainstorm map with the critical concept term in the center and the related words and examples in the map.

Critical Concept Resource List

Defined by Lynn Erickson (1995) the most compelling critical concepts for integrating thinking above the disciplines are concepts characterized as broad and abstract, universal and timeless. Some examples are:

interaction	communities	commonality
culture	communication	cause–effect
cycles	human needs	conflict
families	interrelatedness	cooperation
power	interdependence	continuity
change	diversity	change

All of the above terms can be applied to a subject theme. For instance, continuity and change in technology shows us how our technology changes to meet the same basic human needs.

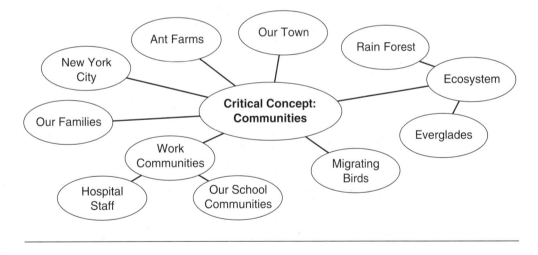

CRITICAL CONCEPT FEATURE MATRIX

Before introducing the students to critical concept maps and critical concept integration, students often benefit from having an opportunity to develop a critical concept feature matrix to ensure their understanding of the concept that will integrate their units.

CR-CT Skills Developed

Classification

Analysis of features of a concept

Cooperation

Communication

Procedure

- The teacher writes the concept under consideration on the board and asks students to define the concept; they should refine their definition. For the term *culture* the dialogue between students and the teacher might be similar to this:

    STUDENTS: Culture is a group of people living in a community.

    TEACHER: How is that different from community?

    STUDENTS: Culture has to do with the laws and rituals and beliefs.

- When students have brainstormed a definition, the teacher refines the definition. The class makes sure that they are satisfied that their definition is appropriate.
- Students then develop a feature matrix with the defining features and examples of their critical concept. For instance, *culture* could be defined as, "The concepts, habits, skills, arts, instruments, beliefs, or a given people in a given period; a civilization" (Webster, 1957). A feature matrix for culture would look the one below:

Culture

Civilization	Habits	Skills	Arts	Beliefs
Greece	debate	math astronomy medicine	statuary architecture columns	worship of gods

Portfolio Pick

BRAINSTORMING

This section of Chapter 2 includes instruction and activities in creative brainstorming. Creating brainstorming maps increases content retention, comprehension and develops metacognitive awareness as students have a chance to reflect on what they know (Hyerle, 1996). As students graphically show their thinking, their thinking and understanding increase. Students create connections, link or chunk information around an idea or concept, and eventually create and explore new connections.

INTRODUCTION TO CREATIVE BRAINSTORMING

In other parts of the book we have used a variation of brainstorming and maps to help us check our work or increase our understanding of concepts, stories, or problems. Those connection maps organized relevant facts, attributes and sequences. In creative brainstorming, however, the rules are very different.

CR-CT Skills Developed

Divergent thinking

Analysis of multiple perspectives

Communication

Procedure

- First, the rules and goals for creative brainstorming are introduced:
  Our goal is to generate as many ideas as possible—the greater the number, the better for our purposes.
  All ideas are accepted; there are no right or wrong ideas.
  Ideas are not judged at this juncture—no put-downs, corrections, or criticisms.

- Students then practice creative brainstorming, using one of the questions below:
  How many ways can you make new friends?
  How many ways can you teach something to a classmate or sibling?
  How many ways can you have fun with a friend that costs no money?

- The teacher allows students to give ideas for three minutes; students' ideas are written on the board after the brainstorming session.

HITCHHIKER'S GUIDE TO THE UNIVERSE

Imagination is the highest kite one can fly.
—Lauren Bacall

This activity represents one of the rare moments when hitchhiking is recommended! Once individuals have honed their individual understanding, this activity provides practice for an important part of group brainstorming.

This type of brainstorming should be called "hitchhiking" so that students are always aware whether they should be working individually or with the group.

CR-CT Skills Developed

Analysis

Cooperation

Communication

Divergent thinking

Procedure

- Students are told that "hitchhiking" is when a group works together to explore and expand each others' ideas while brainstorming.
- Asked for examples, students may share ways that a friend, parent, or classmate helped them solve a problem or understand something that had previously been confusing.
- The rules are the same as for other brainstorming sessions but this time the students will work as a group to develop the ideas of each person in the group.
- The teacher begins by asking students to brainstorm a simile, metaphor, or analogy for a content-area concept. E.g., *molecular bonds:* like a hug; like a planet with a moon.
- Each person writes down one or more thoughts in their notebook.
- When the end of "think time" is called, the group members share their thoughts and begin developing their chosen idea until everyone's work has been discussed and fully developed. Each student's vocabulary/idea word may be developed into a brainstorm map.
- When each student's idea and brainstorm map has been developed, students may be invited to share how their perceptions changed from listening to the ideas of their peers in their cooperative groups.

BRAIN FRAME

You are a product of your own brainstorm.
—Rosemary Konner Steinbaum

Students are now asked to do an individual brainstorm. Because one well-intended, bright, out-going student can easily control the direction of a group brainstorming activity, it is important that students use and practice skills individually, as well. This particular activity serves to pique students' interest in brainstorming while giving them skill practice opportunities.

CR-CT Skills Developed

Divergent thinking

Creative recall

Associations

Risk taking

Procedure

- After reviewing the rules for creative brainstorming, students are told that they will work individually to create a personal brainstorm, including dreams, goals, or subjects of high interest for brainstorming.
- Each student will use colored pencils, markers, or pens to draw themselves in the center of the page (artistic ability is discounted: anything from a stick figure to the person's initials are fine). A border should be placed around their figure or initials.
- When told to begin, students draw lines from the central figure out to words that represent the student's interest, talents, skills, hobbies, hopes, and dreams.

    The following prompt should be helpful: "If you could be anything, do anything, or go anywhere, what would it be?"

Portfolio Pick

THE CREATIVITY TWISTER

In a new twist, students are asked to brainstorm on how to *stop* creativity, culminating in a list of brainstorming rules which can be posted or placed in student portfolios.

CR-CT Skills Developed

Divergent thinking

Communication

Cooperation

Analysis of main idea

Metacognition

Procedure

- Students are introduced to the Creativity Twister and are asked to write down everything they can think of that would crush a creative effort. When lists are complete a master list is compiled on the board or on a transparency.

- The teacher discusses behaviors in a group and students rank them as "creativity coach" or "creativity crusher." Examples are:
  Put-downs and negative comments
  Judging ideas while we brainstorm
  Weighing pros and cons
  Disgusted looks or smirks directed at the speaker
  Comparing your ideas to the ideas of others
  Looking for the easiest or first right answer
  Acting disinterested
  Not understanding the problem or goal
  Having the group controlled by one or two individuals

- When the students have generated lots of ideas and considered others' ideas, the brainstorming rules chart is voted on and the essential elements are listed on a posted chart; students should write the elements in their notebooks, too.

- One or two students are chosen to comprise the "Put-Down Patrol" which serves to remind students of the rules during brainstorming activities. Membership on the Put-Down Patrol should change frequently.

- The Put-Down Patroller goes to the board when a rule is being broken and quietly writes the rule to remind the class of rules without singling out individual students. Examples are:
  No put-downs, please
  No pros and cons
  No comparisons
  Everyone involved, please

BRAINWRITING AND BRAINBOARDING

When I examine myself and my methods of thought, I come close to the conclusion that the gift of fantasy (imagination) has meant more to me than my talent.
—Albert Einstein

This activity encourages fluency in brainstorming for even the most reluctant student. Some research has shown that the most creative ideas are generated when individuals practice brainwriting alone before they brainstorm as a group.

CR-CT Skills Developed

Divergent thinking

Procedure

- Students are asked to take out lots of paper and a pen for brain-writing. Brainwriting is a silent individual activity similar to brainstorming, with some of the same rules. However, in brainwriting, students are not allowed to stop writing during the allotted time, even if they have nothing to say.
- When a content question, subject, idea, or problem is posed by the teacher, the students must begin writing, even if they write, "I have nothing to write yet, but I am hoping that will change."
- Once students are adept at brainwriting they can create a brain board: Their best ideas are written on an index card which is tacked on a bulletin board. These cards should all focus on a central theme. Similar student ideas may be arranged into clusters on the class brain board.

METAMORPHING AND SIMILE SOLUTIONS

Students use this activity to generate creative conceptualizations of an object, concept, entity, or problem under consideration. Using similes and metaphors often awakens the imaginative state necessary to begin brainstorming. Students are forced to consider all aspects of the subject they are studying.

CR-CT Skills Developed

Analogical thinking

Divergent thinking

Communication

Procedure

- First, students review the activity vocabulary: *morph* means change; *simile* means as or similar to something else.

- Students close their eyes, open a dictionary, and point to words, which they then write on three index cards. (For each of three cards, teachers may have cards already prepared with their favorite words from a content area or story.)

- When all students have finished, the cards are collected and redistributed—three to each student.

- Each student has to create at least one simile for one of the words and describe on the card how the assigned content word is like the randomly chosen word.

    Example: mammal (content word); *soap* (randomly chosen word)

    Explanation: A dolphin is faster than a bar of wet soap flying out of the bathtub.

    Example: pollution (content word); *sponge* (randomly chosen word)

    Explanation: Fossil fuel pollution is soaking up the ozone layer like a sponge.

- Students compare their best (or wildest or most difficult) similes and put the best or most interesting on the board.

Portfolio Pick

MAGNIFICENT METAPHORS AND STUNNING SIMILES

Like Metamorphing and Simile Solutions, this activity helps the student begin brainstorming. This is a useful activity for beginning dialogue in either problem solving or creative writing.

CR-CT Skills Developed

Analogical thinking

Divergent thinking

Communication

Cooperation

Procedure

- In a group brainstorm students generate approximately thirty related vocabulary words in a content area under study. For instance, the word *Egypt* in social studies may generate the words *pyramid, pharaoh, hieroglyphics,* and *mummification.*

- Each student is assigned to write one of the vocabulary words on an index card followed by *is like* to create a simile.

    Examples: Science may generate words such as:

    A liver is like . . .

    A heart is like . . .

- When the cards are collected and shuffled each student receives a new card.

- Students develop their simile and then take turns writing the part of the simile that they have created on the board.

    Examples: "A liver is like a sponge" becomes ". . . is like a sponge."
    "Cholesterol is like candle wax in a straw" becomes ". . . is like candle wax in a straw."

- Classmates then begin guessing which of the vocabulary words the student is describing with their simile.

TANTALIZING TWISTERS

This activity is a useful twist for either generating involvement and interest in subject matter or getting students engaged in a problem they are hesitant to approach. Tantalizing Twisters are good for concrete, everyday problems such as how to write an essay as well as for global issues such as how to save the rain forest—issues which appear difficult or overwhelming.

Procedure

- We begin with a problem that students are hesitant to approach or find overwhelming. The problem is rephrased with the word "not" and written in the center of the board—"How *not* to . . ." (save the environment, stay healthy, write an effective essay, pass a math test).

    Students will often offer responses more easily when asked to approach the rephrased, "twister" version of a difficult problem.
    Example: How *not* to get along.

    Come to school in a bad mood
    Don't listen to the whole problem
    Interrupt
    Insult
    Jump to conclusions

- Using this list, students then generate reversals to see if any "How To" vs. "How *Not* To" ideas are implied.
    Examples: Come to school rested and with a good attitude
    Listen to others
    Don't interrupt
    No name calling
    Withhold judgment until you understand everything

Portfolio Pick

SYNTHESTORMING

Synthestorming introduces students to the concept of incorporating several right answers when problem solving. Synthesis and integrative thinking eventually become automatic in the CR-CT classroom. However, years of distributive thinking and dichotomous thinking trends are not quickly overcome. Students become skilled integrative thinkers as their opportunities to practice these activities increase.

CR-CT Skills Developed

Synthesis

Communication

Cooperation

Integrative thinking

Procedure

- Students are asked to individually use any brainstorming tool they choose to brainstorm solutions to a social or content area problem. Some examples are:
  What is the best definition of an ecosystem?
  How can we reduce trash in our school in the next two years?
  What is the fastest way to solve the math word problem?
  How can we make the outside of the school more attractive?
  What is the most effective method of studying ancient cultures?

- Students write their responses to such questions.

- Student responses are written on the board and discussed.

- The class selects three favorite answers or solutions and attempts to synthesize a solution that encompasses the essential elements of all the choices given.

METAQUEST

This important academic tool teaches students to reflect on their own critical questions and how those questions determine all of the answers they get in their academic pursuits.

CR-CT Skills Developed

Metacognition

Critical questioning

Procedure

- Reviewing the term metacognition, the teacher tells students that *meta* is a Greek word root that means above. Metacognition means to stand over or look over our cognition—our thinking. In this activity we check our thinking by first checking the questions we're asking.
- The teacher explains the Metaquest Checklist.
- Before the students begin any major project or make any major decisions they check their Metaquest Checklist. To make this task easier and more automatic, begin with the sample rubric below.

Metaquest Checklist

Do we understand every aspect of the problem—who, what, why, where, and when?
Have we considered all perspectives?
Do we understand causes of the problem?
Are there any other questions we can ask?
Are there any other solutions we can consider?
Are we asking the most powerful questions for effective problem solving?
Have we envisioned the most positive outcomes?

- Students are encouraged to review the Metaquest Checklist and discuss the answers with their cooperative team or before beginning a project.

TOOLBOX TOUR

Before leaving Chapter 2, students create another Toolbox Tour and describe their new tools and how to use them.

CR-CT Skills Developed

Summarizing

Divergent thinking

Procedure

- Students review the critical and creative thinking tools they've used from Chapter 2 and create a list for their table of contents (to be used in the CR-CT Portfolio).

After listing their essential tools, students review each by writing a brief description about how each tool is used, including any notes about the individual student's projects (e.g., Bioscape).

Portfolio Pick

_____

Tool Box Tour

Question Power

Quantum Question

Creative Questioning

   Consideration of multiple perspectives

   Integrative thinking

   Analogical thinking

   Metaphorical thinking

   Brainstorming, including

      brain writing

      brain boarding

      twisters

      synthestorming

Portfolio Pick

_____

CHAPTER 3

Integrative Solutions

POTHOLES, BRAIN BLUNDERS, AND SOLUTION SNAGS

> *Toleration . . . is the greatest gift of the mind; it requires the same*
> *effort of the brain that it takes to balance oneself on a bicycle.*
> —Helen Keller

In the first section of this chapter we examine some of the classic potholes or errors in reasoning. After identifying and creating our own examples of risky reasoning, students develop a checklist to help them recognize these problems when they occur. Regardless of intelligence and level of education, most of us will show "my-side bias" (Perkins, 1995, p. 278) when analyzing an argument. Simply put, "people [tend to] focus overwhelmingly on evidence favoring their learning and neglect evidence on the other side of the case" (Perkins, 1995, p. 278). After examining several forms of risky reasoning we are made aware that we should be more reflective in our decision making.

WRONG EXIT

Some of us prematurely reach conclusions on issues before giving full consideration to the problem at hand. Strangely, the more uncomfortable or bumpy the road, or complicated and important the problem, the more likely we are to jump to conclusions for the sake of comfort. The ability to tolerate ambiguity while searching for the truth is one of the most central elements to effective thinking.

CR-CT Skills Developed

Metacognition

Analysis

Evaluation

Procedure

- The teacher reads the scenario below:
  Scenario: A nearby farm installed an elaborate irrigation system to water its fields. Soon after the school well went dry.
  Wrong Exit Response: The farmer used all of the water.

- Students are asked what happened. The teacher then reads other possible causes for the problems with the school well.
  Other Considerations:
  Did the farmer install the system because of a drought?
  Did the same dry spell cause the school well to dry up?
  Did the recent school expansion cause both problems?

- Students work in groups to develop alternate hypotheses to explain the scenario.

- Students define the thinking flaw, *jumping to conclusions,* in their CR-CT journals portfolios.

- Developing a clear thinking checklist, students add the attributes that *prevent* jumping to conclusions (e.g., checking to make sure that all facts are included, searching for alternate explanations, evaluating the evidence and asking questions).

ASLEEP AT THE WHEEL: EXAMINING UNSTATED ASSUMPTIONS

> *No point in asking Greenfield what he was up to; he had pulled up his mental drawbridge and there was no way over the moat.*
> —L. Kallen

It's easy to assume that because we've never had an accident, we won't have one now, and therefore we don't need to use a seat belt; or because we've never seen anyone else on this road its okay to cut the curve short and go into the other lane. This kind of thinking is one of the major causes of accidents . . . in life, and in thinking, as well.

CR-CT Skills Developed

Metacognition

Analysis

Communication

Active listening

Cooperation

Procedure

- The teacher reads the introduction above and asks, "How does being lulled to sleep by a few examples affect the outcome?"

- "Why do we assume that we've managed this before, and therefore it won't happen in the future?"

- Lazy reasoning, easy reasoning (jumping to conclusions), and no reasoning (asleep at the wheel) can be dangerous. Students should generate examples of faulty reasoning strategies.

   Students should explore the assumptions in the following expressions. Assumptions may be right or wrong. The important thing is that we recognize them as assumptions, not facts.

   "Have you stopped bullying your sister yet?"
   Assumption: you bully your sister

   "There are three keys to controlling behavior so that human beings won't become violent."
   Assumption: All human beings are naturally violent.

   "Irrigation would make it possible to grow crops there."
   Assumption: It is impossible to grow crops without irrigation.

   "The way to get this job done is to hire Oak Lane Painters."
   Assumption: Only Oak Lane Painters can get the job done.

   "The way to lose unwanted pounds is to take TNT pills."
   Assumption: The only way to lose weight is to use pills.

- Students should recognize and discuss the faulty assumptions after the following statements:

   "My neighbor doesn't wear a bike helmet and he's never been hurt, so I don't need a helmet."

   "My uncle smokes and he's okay, so smoking isn't that dangerous."

   "I didn't study for the first quiz and I passed. I guess I don't have to study for this one."

   "I ran this red light before and nobody hit me. Why should I stop this time? I'm in a hurry."

- Students may generate their own examples. Students should consider the possible consequences of making faulty assumptions, like those listed above.

Portfolio Pick

STRETCHED TO THE BREAKING POINT

We have seen how useful metaphors and analogies are for problem-solving and creativity. However, when an analogy fits one set of traits or one problem, it shouldn't be assumed that the analogy can be stretched to fit all aspects of a problem under consideration. A logical relationship is a useful tool; it is not a truth.

CR-CT Skills Developed

Analytical thinking

Metacognition

Cooperation

Communication

Procedure

- The teacher reviews definitions of analogies with students and solicits examples of analogies:

    When an analogy or metaphor is a useful tool for one part of a problem, it can mistakenly be assumed that it fits other aspects of a problem.

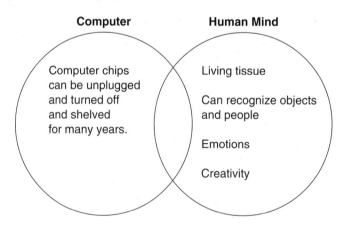

The following examples may be prove useful:

"The family reunion was so memorable it is permanently stored on my hard drive."
Does the analogical reasoning hold up?

"I love my aunt like my computer loves software."
Does the analogical reasoning hold up?
What's wrong?
What might a stronger analogy be?
How might we design a stronger analogy?

- Students are asked to find both strong and flawed analogies in their world. They should be encouraged to integrate this task with their content-area subjects. Some examples are:

  How is the brain like a flower?
  The brain rests on a stem, like a spinal cord that flowers at the top.

  How is the brain like a sponge?
  A sponge absorbs water like the mind absorbs information.
  or
  A sponge is damp; the brain needs cerebral fluid to stay healthy.

- Students work in groups to generate their own analogies in a content area. Each content concept (e.g., rainforest, architecture, algebra, mammals, protons . . . whatever is relevant) should have three analogies created by each group; one analogy should be intentionally weak.

- Students can present each groups' analogies to the class to be rated as best fit, good fit, or stretched to the breaking point.

Portfolio Pick

MENTAL FLOSS—REASONING AND RELEVANCE

> *A problem is a chance for you to do your best.*
> —Duke Ellington

Some arguments require us to wade through a mess of statements, desperately looking for anything that is relevant to the problem. If the information, however interesting, has nothing to do with the point or decision, it should be recognized as irrelevant to the decision at hand and the search for relevance should continue.

CR-CT Skills Developed

Analysis

Evaluation

Procedure

- The teacher introduces an argument between two students who both wish to be elected to serve on the staff of *Mediator News*, a student-run newsletter that addresses the peer mediation program in the school district.

Michele's reasoning: "I should serve on *Mediator News* because Sara was the prom queen. I am a great mediator and a good writer, too. Sara is too busy with athletics to do a good job."

Teacher's questions:
Which reasons should influence our choice?
Which reasons should be disregarded?
Which reasons are relevant?
The class should define *relevant* to ensure ability to answer correctly.

- Using Mental Floss, students mark *R* (relevant) or *I* (irrelevant) on statements in the following argument. (The use of *R* for related and *U* for unrelated may be easier for younger students to grasp.) The issue: choice of blue and gold as the school colors.
  Blue and gold were the school colors at my last school and we won every soccer game at that school
  Students like the colors blue and gold
  Band uniforms are blue and gold, so we would save money

- Student choices of *R* or *I* should be discussed to ensure that the meanings of the words "relevant" and "irrelevant" are understood and to evaluate their ability to choose valid reasons to support the argument.

- Students can then work individually or in small groups using the Mental Floss strategy on content-area topics, school issues, or current events. Controversial topics found in local newspapers are especially inviting to students. The addition of fluoride to a community water supply is an example of an issue which often provides examples of relevant and irrelevant support. Such topics also provide avenues to merge content areas (in this case, social studies, science and language arts).

- Since the process of finding good examples for Mental Floss demands evaluation of evidence, students should be assigned the task of locating samples for various subjects or content areas. Small groups could be formed for this purpose—e.g., the science groups and the social studies groups—to locate confounding or controversial newspaper articles.

- A simple contest could be formed among the groups to find the best and/or worst supporting statements for various positions or issues (e.g., saving the rainforest, adding fluoride to water supply, building a larger middle school, use of disposable diapers). This contest can be extended over a period of time, on a weekly basis.

Extending Activities: Response Journals

What examples of irrelevant arguments have I noticed in my personal life since evaluating (e.g., a sibling wanting a new bike because a neighbor got a new bike)?

Portfolio Pick

POLAR BEAR

A closed mind is a dying mind.
—Edna Ferber

The polar bear can be a dangerous animal if he is not treated with respect. Likewise, polar thinking can get you in trouble if you don't see it coming. Polar, or polarized, thinking is either/or dichotomous thinking which oversimplifies issues. Polar thinking often has a negative effect on problem solving. In conflict resolution, we might call it win/lose thinking, such as:

"If you don't agree with me . . ."

"If you don't do it my way . . ."

. . . and other statements that imply one right answer without consideration of obvious alternative.

CR-CT Skills Developed

Analysis

Integrative thinking

Procedure

- The teacher reads to the class or has them read individually a piece from a local newspaper or other source which will likely arouse polarized thinking. Examples might be:
School board proposes student activity fees
Senator Goodman advocates raising driving age
The Parent-Teacher organization discusses school uniforms
Mandatory community service may be required for graduation
School to shorten recess times to raise achievement scores
School to assign seats in the lunchroom

- Students can brainstorm supporting evidence. A recorder places each piece of evidence under Pro or Con on the board. Usually students will polarize or give only the evidence which supports their feeling about the issue. When students have exhausted their evidence, bring attention to the balance of entries in the Pro and Con categories. Ask students to think of evidence which counters their belief about the topic.

  1. Elm Street has a dangerous, narrow bridge that people approach too fast and crash into.

     Proposed solutions:
     We can close down Elm Street or . . .
     We can resign ourselves to the fact that we have a death trap in town

The teacher asks students to identify Polar Bear reasoning on this problem. What other possible solutions might exist, such as: change the bridge, change the speed limit, install flashing lights, increase police patrol?

2. Student achievement test scores are low.

Proposed solutions:
Give students a weekly test to check progress
Give up and admit failure

Students are asked to identify Polar reasoning, and to provide other viable solutions or explanations related to declining test scores.

OVERSIMPLIFICATION

A close relation of the Polar Bear, Oversimplification also leaves out vital information. Therefore, informed decisions can't be made on issues.

CR-CT Skills Developed

Metacognition

Analysis

Procedure

- The teacher introduces Oversimplification through examples such as the ones below:

Example 1:

A. Jerry got into a fight with his brother yesterday, so we now know that conflict resolution doesn't work.

This should be compared to . . .

B. Jerry and his brother had a fight yesterday, so we know that conflict resolution doesn't cure all problems overnight.

Example 2:

A. If we didn't have air pollution we'd all be healthy.

This should be compared to . . .

B. If we could clean up air pollution our health would improve or be protected.

Example 3:

A. If we could stop kids from watching TV we could eliminate all problems with violence.

This should be compared to . . .

    B. TV violence is related to violent behavior in some cases.

        Students should recognize the following traits of oversimplification:

        Oversimplification leaves out evidence about an issue

        Oversimplification is often done to persuade the reader

        Oversimplification prevents informed decision making

- Students might be asked to find examples of oversimplification. Good sources are commercials from radio and TV, and issues reported in newspapers. This search could be combined with the Polar Bear search.

- Students may pick a current issue and write oversimplification statements. For example:
  If we enforced a 6 P.M. curfew all crime would stop.
  If we all took aerobics class three times a week we wouldn't have health problems.

Portfolio Pick

MIRAGE: MISTAKING EVIDENCE AS PROOF

Observations and evidence are essential for making judgments, but once again good judgments can be easily derailed, in this case by presenting pieces of evidence as proof.

CR-CT Skills Developed

Metacognition

Analysis

Evaluation

Procedure

- The teacher can introduce Mirage by using the following account:

  Several computers were recently stolen from the school's computer lab. The police came into the school this morning and found two boys in the hallway carrying one of the computers that had been reported as stolen. Can you guess what the police did then?

What if the boys found the computer in the alley behind the school and were in the process of returning it?

When the police dusted the computer for fingerprints, they found only the boys' prints. What does this tell us? Did the boys steal the computer? Did the thieves wear gloves?

What if we discovered that both boys were away at a game with classmates when the school break-in occurred? How does the addition of that information affect our thinking?

- The teacher focuses on how evidence can be mistaken as proof. How does the incident change with the addition of new evidence? Here is another example:

> Ramone recently moved with his mother to a new community. Because he was anxious about making new friends, Ramone was happy to be invited to the birthday party for Al, a boy he met in the neighborhood. The parents who sponsored the party discovered that three ten-dollar bills and some change were missing from an upstairs drawer. The following pieces of evidence were considered:
>
> Al's old friends have been in the house many times and nothing has been missing before.
> Most of Al's friends are on the honor role; they aren't problem kids.
> Ramone seemed suspiciously quiet at the party.
> Ramone was seen coming downstairs at the party; he was alone at the time.
> Ramone left the party early.
>
> Further investigation revealed that Ramone had problems at the school he previously attended.
>
> Al's parents felt that Ramone took the money and shared their belief with neighbors. Ramone was shunned by some kids because of the accusation.

Did Ramone steal the money?
Did Al's parents have sufficient evidence to accuse Ramone? Why or why not?

What really happened? Consider the following evidence:
Ramone was quiet because he feared ridicule of his English, which he learned as a second language.
Ramone was seen coming downstairs after using the upstairs bathroom.
Ramone left the party early to baby-sit his younger brother when his mother left for work.
Ramone was retained one year due to extensive absences due to illness and second language learning.

Now what do you think happened?
Here is what really happened:

Al's older brother, who was in town only for the day, hurriedly took the money to buy some last-minute things for the party. In the pre-party confusion, Al's mother could not remember giving him permission to take the money.

- Students should reflect on the issue of evidence being mistaken as proof. What are the possible consequence about mistakes?

- Students are encouraged to share examples from news or from personal experience of incidents when new evidence changed their understanding.

FOOLISH FISHING OR WHEN TO THROW IT BACK

Foolish Fishing represents a common problem in reasoning, whether done consciously or unconsciously. This occurs when one fishes for only the evidence which supports a preconceived wish. What happens to the conflicting evidence? It is thrown back or ignored. This use and abuse of evidence may result in some "Fishy" conclusions.

CR-CT Skills Developed

Metacognition

Analysis of evidence

Inferential reasoning

Procedure

- The teacher might use the following example to introduce Foolish Fishing:

   A diet food company shows a commercial on TV with five people who lost 50 pounds each by using their products.

   Does this represent an *average* weight loss?

   Everyone is on my back to quit smoking. Why should I quit when I know Fritz Wenger smoked nonfiltered cigarettes until he died in his 90s?

   My grandfather doesn't want me to get a motorcycle because he thinks they are dangerous. I tell him motorcycles are safe because they are more maneuverable, allowing you to get out of tight spots.

   Is Foolish Fishing going on here? Explain. What do the statistics tell us about the safety of motorcycles? Cigarettes? Fad diets?

My mother thinks it is a mistake for me to quit school and get a job. This isn't true because my uncle Ralph quit at age sixteen and now owns a small trucking company. Uncle Ralph makes more money than my mother who is a registered nurse.

Is this Foolish Fishing? Do most high school drop-outs make more money than graduates?

- Students should be encouraged to identify other cases of Foolish Fishing in commercials, newspapers, or in discussions with friends. They can then be shared in class or displayed on a bulletin board.

Portfolio Pick

HITCHIKING ON THE BANDWAGON

No matter how much we explore motives, or lack of motives, we are what we do.
—Janet G. Woititz

The bandwagon was originally a large, high ornate wagon that came through town in a parade with a band playing on top. The bandwagon generated a lot of emotion and excitement and a crowd of interested followers. Often other people would gather around just because a large group had formed. The Bandwagon effect is when a person allows the majority to think for them. People use Bandwagon when they try to persuade someone to do something they're not sure about or think is wrong. A few expressions peculiar to Bandwagon are: "Don't think about it," "Don't worry about it," and "Everyone is doing it."

CR-CT Skills Developed

Analysis

Metacognition

Communication

Procedure

- The teacher might use the following example to introduce Bandwagon:

Alex is upset with his parents because they insist that the money Alex makes from his summer jobs be placed in a college fund. Alex sees his friends going to movies, buying clothes, dating, and doing other things which he can't afford. In an effort to loosen the purse strings, Alex tells his parents, "All my friends have new sneakers," "Most of my friends go out every night," and "Nobody waits for movies to come out on TV."

- Ask students to identify what appeal Alex is using on his parents.

- Ask students to identify risks associated with using Bandwagon reasoning.

- Have students write responses to the following situations:

  1. You want to get your own car when you earn your driver's license. Write down what arguments you would use to convince your parents that this would be a good idea.
  2. You want to buy a pair of the latest pants. Write down what evidence you would use to convince your mother that this idea has merit.
  3. The dance is rapidly approaching and some of your friends want you to stay overnight with them and have a party. Write down what appeals you would use to seek permission to go to the party.
  4. You want the latest computer game. It will cost more than your allowance. Write down what appeals you would use to get money and permission.

- Students can examine others' answers in small groups.

- The whole class can compare responses and a recorder can place them on the board in Bandwagon or Other categories.

- Students can share occasions when friends have tried using Bandwagon reasoning on them and how they responded or how they wish they had responded.

Extending Activities: Response Journals

How many times have I done something I didn't like or didn't think was a good idea just because everyone else was doing it?

SPHINX THINKS MATRIX

> *Anger and worry are the enemies of clear thought.*
> —Madeleine Brent

The ancient Egyptian symbol, the Sphinx, is used here to symbolize a silent, calm, thoughtful response to issues. Both reason and emotion play parts in decision making. Faulty decisions are often traced to heightened emotions and impulsive reactions, especially when the issue is close to the heart. In the Sphinx Thinks Matrix we identify the *appeal to emotion* argument.

CR-CT Skills Developed

Metacognition

Emotion-logic balance

Procedure

The teacher introduces the *appeal to emotion* argument.

> "Just as simplification may be an essential element in aiding understanding, oversimplification may threaten understanding. The same may be true of understanding emotions. It is essential to listen to both facts and feelings to completely understand another's perspective or the nature of a problem. However, when there is an unreasonable appeal to emotions, we must stop to consider the reasoning behind the emotions before we can make a valid decision."

Consider the following appeals:

> What would we ask ourselves if we read an article about a public figure that called a man or woman an abuser, a person with no respect for others or understanding of humanity, completely devoid of heart and soul, a person that should strike fear into the hearts of all decent people? What reasoning or facts support this assessment?

> What if we found out that this man had just broken off a business partnership with the writer because of the writer's unscrupulous behavior?

> What if we discovered that the man had just been released from prison for a series of brutal crimes?

> How would different facts affect our understanding of their emotional appeal?

> Can we understand this and respond reasonably without the facts?

There is nothing wrong with understanding someone's emotional reaction to a situation, but it is important to establish the reasoning behind the appeal to emotion.

The Sphinx Thinks Matrix will be used to judge several scenarios to assess appeal to emotion and appeal to reason.

Sphinx Thinks Matrix

Appeal 1	Appeal to Emotion	Appeal to Reason
You should vote for Tom for president because he just lost a really big soccer game and he's very depressed.	1 2 3 4 ⑤	① 2 3 4 5
Appeal 2	1 2 3 4 5	1 2 3 4 5
Appeal 3	1 2 3 4 5	1 2 3 4 5
Appeal 4	1 2 3 4 5	1 2 3 4 5

GROUP THINK OR GROUP SINK

In order to foster creativity and community, individuals must learn to get along with others. However, it is important that students voice questions or objections, as well. Group Think or Group Sink supports creative questioning without putting individuals on the spot.

CR-CT Skills Developed

Analysis

Metacognition

Communication

Critical questioning

Procedure

- The teacher conveys the following to students to introduce the activity:

When we work together we respect each others' ideas and affirm emotions. However, in order to be an effective team we must learn to question our decisions and choices, as well.

- Using a content area project students have Think/Sink cards. These can be simple notecards.
- Before content-area cooperative group decisions are made, each member must respond to their Think/Sink card. They should write two to three things which should be discussed before decision making and two to three concerns about issues that could sink the project.
- The teacher should encourage use of this activity during on-going content-area occasions.

Extending Activities: Response Journals

Would it be smart or useful for me to use think/sink questions in making decisions in my personal life?

THE NON SEQUITUR: SLIPPERY SLOPES ON THE ROAD TO REASON

Incomplete reasoning or the non sequitur (the Latin term that indicates that the logical conclusion does not follow reasoning) can be examined and informally diagrammed to facilitate increased understanding in the Slippery Slopes activity.

CR-CT Skills Developed

Evaluation

Analysis

Metacognition

Procedure

- The teacher presents the following scenarios for the students to examine:

  Students who miss a great deal of school are at risk for poor grades. Sandy does not miss any school, so Sandy is assured of good grades.

- The following questions should be posed:
  Is this logical?
  Is anything wrong?
  Do we need more information on the topic?
  Are all students who have good attendance good students?

Can we identify several reasons (other than attendance) why students do poorly in school?

> All boys at ABC School wear green socks. Person D has green socks. Is person D a boy?

Is this logical and complete?
What if all girls wear green socks, too?
Do we have enough information?

> All boys at ABC School wear green socks. All girls at ABC School wear yellow socks. Person D has green socks. Is person D a boy?

Is the above logical? Yes. Why?

> All students who have good attendance at ABC School are assured passing grades. Sandy has good attendance. Sandy is assured of passing grades.

There are times when a conclusion may follow (e.g., Person D may be a boy; Sandy may get good grades). But we can't assume it must follow (Person D may be a girl and Sandy may be getting poor grades.)
In the following example the conclusion must follow:

> All boys at ABC School wear green socks and all girls at ABC School wear yellow socks. Person D has green socks. Person D must be a boy because we had enough information to be sure of the logical conclusion.

- Students judge the following scenarios to see if the logic is on solid ground (the conclusion must follow) or if the argument is illogical.

Scenario No. 1: Students at Hope Elementary School enjoy playing soccer. Justin goes to Hope Elementary School. *Therefore,* Justin is on the soccer team. (Students discuss why this is a Slippery Slope; they give reasons for their positions.)

Scenario No. 2: Devin's favorite color is blue. Devin is a student at Solebury Girls School. *Therefore,* all of the students at the Solebury Girls School prefer blue, too. (Students find the Slippery Slope and explain their responses.)

Scenario No. 3: Carlos is bilingual, and he loves to dance. Carly is bilingual. *Therefore,* Carly loves to dance, too. (Students identify the Slippery Slope and defend their reasoning.)

Scenario No. 4: All students who attend Slippery Slope Middle School live in Slippery Slope County. Randi attends Slippery Slope Middle School. *Therefore,* Randi lives in Slippery Slope County. (Students identify the logic and defend their reasoning.)

Scenario No. 5: All students on the Hope High basketball team must maintain an A or B average. Tim is on the Hope High School basketball team. *Therefore,* Tim has an A or B average. (Students identify the logic and defend their reasoning.)

Finally, students work in groups to write and present Solid Ground logic and Slippery Slope problems and present them πto their classmates.

POTHOLES ON THE ROAD TO REASON

Some arguments or assertions are flat-out wrong, not merely weak or incomplete. In the Potholes activity we identify faulty arguments and identify their causes.

CR-CT Skills Developed

Analysis

Evaluation

Active listening

Communication

Cooperation

Procedure

- The teacher asks students to examine the following statements:
I am a peacemaker. I get violent only when I'm angry.
I'm so hot. May I borrow your sweater until I get warmed up?
I'm a vegetarian. I eat red meat only on weekends and weekdays.

- The teacher introduces the concepts of:
1. Contradiction: Two positions that oppose each other.
2. Inconsistencies: Two positions that are illogical or incompatible with each other.

- Students identify and analyze potholes in the statements below and respond individually:
I'm a good student. I flunked only half of my courses.
I have great attendance. I've been in school almost half of the time.
I'm a good friend. I cheat and lie only when I want to.
I'm a good driver. I've had only two accidents this year.

- For the following statements, reverse the order by having students add information which create potholes:
The weather was great . . .
The party was fun . . .
The book was boring . . .

The movie was interesting . . .

- Students work in groups to create their own potholes in reasoning.

- If time permits, students work in groups to patch the potholes; for example, "I'm so cold. May I borrow your sweater until I get warmed up?"

CRITERIA BY DESIGN

In the second section of Chapter 3 we ask students to design their own decision making tools. As we make several tools available, students review and articulate their own non-negotiable criteria (e.g., the Safe and Smart foundation criteria for any good decision) and develop specific criteria for the decision making task at hand.

Students are then introduced to academic controversy, one of the most powerful tools for increasing understanding and intelligent decision making. At a time when students are making crucial decisions—decisions that may affect their careers, their communities, and their very lives—this metacognitive awareness is an invaluable gift.

THE SUN AND THE MOON

The Sun and the Moon introduces students to the concept of divergent and convergent thinking modes. The students have used divergent strategies in brainstorming solutions. Now students switch to a convergent mode, applying criteria to a choice. The focus is now on finding the correct answer through detailed analysis rather than creating many possibilities.

CR-CT Skills Developed

Analysis

Metacognition

Cognitive flexibility

Communication

Procedure

- The teacher draws two large circles on the board.
- The teacher then asks: "When we brainstorm, where does the central idea go?" and "Where do the supporting ideas go?" The students will respond that the central idea belongs in the center and the supporting ideas go around the center.

Award-winning Youth Vision mediator Simonna Woodson and teacher-mentor Mary Allen. INDIANAPOLIS, IN, SCHOOL DISTRICT. PHOTO: ROBERTA HEYDENBERK.

- The teacher draws arrows radiating outward from the sun circle on the board. The sun metaphor is used to define divergent thinking. If we know the "sun," we can follow the "rays" to supporting ideas.
- The teacher draws arrows pointing inward on the moon circle on the board. The moon metaphor is used to introduce convergent thinking. The moon reflects the light from the sun. If we know the supporting ideas, we can move toward the central idea.
- Most tasks involve several types of thinking and problem solving. Many problems require brainstorming or divergent thinking, followed by analysis or convergent thinking to choose a creative solution.
- We will now analyze single choices using criteria we develop— looking closely to find a good fit to a specific problem.

  Students analyze the following problem solving tasks to decide if they require convergent or divergent thinking:

  Problem No. 1: We need to find a way to fund a student trip to Washington, D.C. (divergent).
  Problem No. 2: We need to decide which of the two feasible designs we should choose for the new auditorium (convergent).
  Problem No. 3: We need to develop criteria by which to judge essays in the upcoming contest (convergent and divergent).
  Problem No. 4: We need to buy shoes for the hiking trip (converging of choices).

- If time permits, students may work in groups to analyze content area or real life problems and related problem-solving or thinking modes.

CREATING CRITERIA: SAFE, SMART, AND SUCCESSFUL

Although Creating Criteria will be different for every task or problem a student tackles, there are some considerations that provide a good foundation for any personal decision making. Students will begin by designing criteria for personal decision making. They will then expand their designs to meet specific challenges.

CR-CT Skills Developed

Prioritizing

Categorization

Main idea

Cooperation

Procedure

- Students are introduced to the word criterion as a standard or test by which one can make a better decision.
- Reviewing the Maslow hierarchy and our basic human needs we begin designing criteria: *Safe, Smart, and Successful*. Students can help generate a list of standards by which decisions could be measured—beginning with the Safe, Smart, and Successful foundation criteria.
- Questions to generate student discussion may include:
  Should we consider the effect our decision or resulting action will have on our health, the health of others, our safety, the safety of others?
  Should the decision reflect our principles and a respect for our family, friends, and community?
  Could this action negatively impact my safety or the safety of anyone else?
  Could this action negatively impact anyone's esteem?
  Does this decision risk hurting anyone?
  What are the possible "costs" (psychological, physical, and material) of this decision?
  Is the "cost" justified?
  Have we considered all possible consequences?
  Have we experienced any weaknesses in reasoning?
  Have we scanned pitfalls? potholes? slippery slopes?
  Have we considered alternative solutions?
- Students brainstorm safe, smart, successful criteria for the personal decisions and choices they make in everyday life. Foundation criteria for personal decisions should include:
  1. Is it safe for myself and others, and
  2. Is it smart (productive, the best approach, worth the time or expense)?

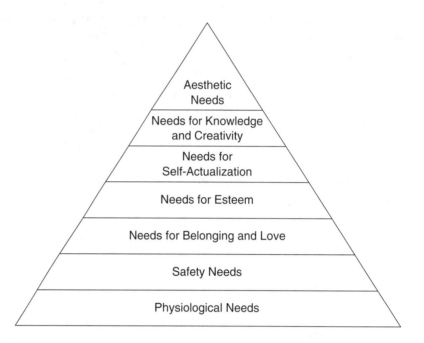

Students should prioritize the list.

- Students should be reminded that most adolescent fatalities result from poor decision making. Most accidents, homicides, and suicides can be prevented by using safe, successful, and smart decision making and problem solving. Students are then asked to develop a personal list of their safe, successful, and smart decision making questions for their portfolio.

- If time permits, students may work in groups to write role plays. Role plays should include typical or critical decision-making junctures (for example, being offered a ride from a stranger) and students' spontaneous use of safe, smart, and successful criteria.

Portfolio Pick

PICKING PRIORITIES

The price of greatness is responsibility.
—Winston Churchill

Picking Priorities gives students the opportunity to consider the important fact that not all ideas are of equal importance. To begin, we will brainstorm a list of the types of activities we might engage in over a weekend and then prioritize the list.

CR-CT Skill Development

Prioritizing

Categorizing

Main idea

Communication

Cooperation

Procedure

- Students are asked to define the word *priority*. Terms such as order of importance, rank, and rating should be mentioned and added to the list.

- Students are asked to set priorities in the following: They should number each action to establish a sequence. This is a good example to use with the whole class:

    If your house is on fire and it is 11:00 A.M., it is important to:
    Get lunch ready
    Clean your room
    Check phone messages
    Write a letter to a friend
    Water the plants
    Brush your teeth
    Scream "Fire!" and get out of the house

    The obvious answer is to leave the burning building. Students are then asked to discuss how priorities develop—how the most urgent or important issues are chosen as priorities.
    Students are then given a few minutes to jot down activities they do on weekends. The following are typical: call a friend, water plants, feed pets, shower, walk with the family, engage in a hobby, watch TV, listen to music, write a letter, cook, eat, dress, shop, see a movie, play computer games. When the lists are complete, students prioritize the list making #1 the most important priority.

- Not everyone will have the same list of personal priorities (letter writing, shopping, for instance) *but* their lists of practical priorities will be similar. This is a good time to review Safe, Smart, and Successful goals.

- Students are asked to separate their personal and practical priorities. For instance, eating and sleeping are practices we share. Taking time to listen to a favorite piece of music is a personal priority.

- Students then prioritize personal goals and compare differences (for example, exercise may be more important to a star athlete, while practicing or listening to music may be more important to someone who plays in a band) and similarities (for example, core priorities such as eating, sleeping, staying safe, and spending time with friends and family).

CRITERIA DESIGN

Criteria Design expands the concept of developing criteria to an academic challenge issue. Students consider which aspects of a project should be judged and which criteria are to be prioritized.

CR-CT Skills Developed

Prioritizing

Main idea

Cooperation

Divergent thinking

Convergent thinking

- Students begin development of a matrix for another decision design—a criteria rubric for evaluating Science Fair Entries. It might look similar to this:

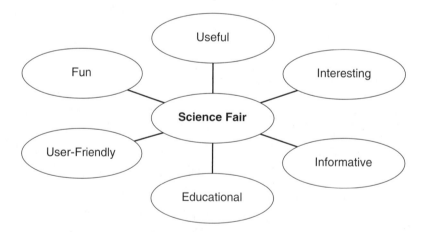

- Once students have determined which aspects of the project should be judged, they work in groups to prioritize their criteria (e.g., is "informative" more important than "user friendly"?).
- Students may compare criteria design matrices when the lists are complete.
- Another exercise might be "How would we rate a favorite book?"
- Students brainstorm related characteristics to begin a criteria checklist which might include: plot, setting, illustrations, boring parts, figurative language, humor, foreshadowing, flashbacks.

- From this emerging list, students then prioritize or rank the criteria they developed for judging a book.
- The teacher asks students to prioritize the list, beginning with "pair comparison" questions such as: "Is the title more important than the plot?", "Is the setting as important as the plot?", and "Have we established this order so far: plot, setting, and title?"
- This pair-comparison ranking continues until the criteria list is completed.
- Students may eliminate or add criteria as the ranking progresses.
- Students may then rate a book using the top three or four criteria they established.
- Students then rank the top three or four criteria for importance and ask whether plot and characters are equally important. If they are not, the students may want to consider each criteria separately. It is usually simpler to consider the three or four essential criteria, keeping the others on a separate list to be considered when students have narrowed their choices on the most important criteria.
- After some practice, students may be asked to work in groups to create a Criteria Design Matrix for an assignment or project.

Criteria Design Matrix

The Top 5 Books	Plot	Character Development	Personal Relevance

Portfolio Pick

CAUSE-EFFECT MAPS

We review simple cause-effect story maps using content-area studies to diagram how actions or choices effected consequences.

CR-CT Skills Developed

Foresight

Cause-effect analysis

Communication

Cooperation

Procedure

- The teacher draws a simple cause-effect map on the board, using content-area examples:
  Extended drought—lost crops and famine
  Cultural clash—mediation and peaceful resolution or war and conflict
  DDT exposure—reduction of bird population
  Fossil fuel shortage—investigation of alternative energy

- Students devise examples of cause-effect charts or maps in a content area of interest.

- The teacher works with the students to generate other content area cause-effect maps.

BOUNCE OR BREAK BLUES

Failure was sometimes more interesting than
success because it raised more questions.
—B. Stevens

Because of the simplicity of some of the strategies presented, our decision-making process may seem oversimplified. Some choices may be high risk and, therefore, deserve additional attention. The Bounce or Break Blues activity will help students identify the risks and consequences in decision making.

CR-CT Skills Developed

Analysis

Evaluation

Communication

Procedure

- Students are asked to interpret and discuss the following quote: "The harder they fall, the higher they bounce."

- Students are asked what meaning this may have in their lives and how they've learned from various mistakes.

- Students are asked to recall historical figures who have made comebacks after defeats (for example, the Lincoln biography in Chapter 2) and people they know who have rebounded successfully.

- Students are asked to consider, "What other choices might we bounce back from?" Examples might be:
  Getting second place in a contest
  Missing an appointment
  Losing a pet
  Getting a low grade
  Losing your allowance
  A close friend moving away

In Bounce or Break Blues we also give choices a risk factor rating—a break rating. For instance, getting into a car with a driver who has been drinking is a break choice. Why? Are there possible consequences that are irreversible or from which we can't recover? Any choice that endangers the well-being of anyone is a break choice. Any choice that does not measure up to our safe, smart, or successful criteria must be carefully analyzed.

Students generate a list of bounce and break choices. This could be done in graphic form such as the one below:

Bounce or Break

Bounce	Break

Place each of the following in either the Bounce or Break columns:

Taking a ride from a stranger

Entering a contest to win a quilt

Trying out for the track team

Getting in a car with someone who has been drinking alcohol

Skipping a study session before a test

Trying out a new recipe

Students should be encouraged to add their own examples.

Portfolio Pick

THE PROS/CONS QUESTIONS (PCQ)

This matrix is another invaluable tool for assessing choices. This format makes it easier to assess choices, highlight risk areas, and formulate useful questions, because authentic problem solving is never a truly linear process. Before choosing a solution it is important to consider questions about any choices.

CR-CT Skills Developed

Analysis

Evaluation

Synthesis

Communication

Cooperation

Pros/Cons Questions

Choices	Pros	Cons	?	!
CHOICE 1 Burn all solid waste	Less waste in landfills	Toxic fumes	Can solid waste be separated to avoid fumes?	Some burning plastics give off deadly toxic fumes
CHOICE 2				
CHOICE 3				

Procedure

- This activity is ideal for use after the Bounce or Break Blues activity. The exclamation point column is for any high-risk (break, not bounce) consequence or any high-risk concerns that threaten the foundation criteria developed earlier: Safe, Smart, and Successful. Because those concerns are not simple "cons" they should be highlighted and considered separately. If the concerns in the "!" column can't be eliminated, the choice itself may be eliminated.

- After brainstorming solutions to an identified problem (e.g., energy costs, overcrowding, solid waste, civil war) students list the pros, cons, and questions they may have in the matrix.

- Students are encouraged to note any useful questions. For instance, in order to consider efforts to raise funds to benefit the environment— such as recycling aluminum cans—students may need to investigate their state's laws. To raise funds and benefit the environment by recycling paper students may need to find a market for recycled paper. To choose a research topic students may need to review the resources to make sure they have enough information to develop into a viable project.

- Any questions or concerns students have about choices should be noted in the matrix.

- Finally, students should assess the matrix to decide if any parts of our best choices can be combined to design a *Super Solution*—a synthesis of more than one choice.

Portfolio Pick

WISHBONE THINKING

Wishbone Thinking introduces students to integrative (win–win) or synthesis thinking in the decision making process. When one simple choice is not clear or sufficient, or when more than one choice is being considered, an expanded understanding of the problem and the solution may help.

CR-CT Skills Developed

Integrative thinking

Divergent thinking

Synthesis

Procedure

- The teacher shares the following story with the class:

    A brother and sister are having Thanksgiving dinner together. During the dinner the brother states his need for money to go to camp. As the dinner progresses, the sister tells of her need for money for her new piano. Their rich uncle tells the brother and sister that whoever gets the largest part of the turkey's wishbone will receive all the money they need for their wish.

The brother and sister were required to write down the amount of money they wished for and the purpose for which it was needed.

How can the brother and sister be assured that they both will win? What should the brother and sister do? Students pose possible solutions to the problem.

- The teacher introduces integrative thinking: thinking wherein win–win solutions are sought instead of the usual win–lose thinking. In other words, what solutions are possible to allow both people or groups to gain something in the end?

- Students should pose possible integrative thinking solutions to the above issue. For instance, both siblings could write down the amount of money that would pay for both camp and the piano.

- Students may wish to share occasions wherein they successfully engaged in integrative or win–win thinking. What was the issue? What was the solution?

SUPER SOLUTIONS: THE SYNTHESIS SHIFT

The class works on combining sets of solutions or choices from a PCQ Matrix, going from analysis to synthesis. This activity may force the shift from analysis to synthesis by asking students to combine the best aspect of two randomly selected choices into a newly created Super Solution. Results may be more humorous than practical, however. It is important to explore the possibilities in order to synthesize a super solution.

CR-CT Skills Developed

Evaluation

Synthesis

Communication

Cooperation

Procedure

- Problems which hold several solutions are presented on the board along with top choices or solutions.

Pros/Cons Questions

Choices	Pros	Cons	?	!
CHOICE 1 Recycle cans				
CHOICE 2 Recycle paper				
CHOICE 3 Grow and sell flowers				
CHOICE 4 Car wash				
CHOICE 5 Sell newspapers				

- Although students will work in groups, individuals will first work alone brainstorming a synthesis of the two solutions assigned to their group. Students may add their own ideas or solutions to the two choices they receive. Any creative solutions that combine the choices assigned will be accepted.
- When individuals finish their synthesis brainstorming the groups work together to create a master map combining as many ideas as possible.
- For instance: Recycling Super Solution (student example)

  Students receive two Earth Day project choices: (1) recycling aluminum cans and (2) a paper recycling project. Students decide on recycling cans to collect money to buy paper-making equipment because there is no easy market for recycled paper. Working with the science and art teachers, students recycle their newspaper to make homemade stationery sets which they sell as a fund-raising item.

PROTECTION: A PREVENTION PLAN

Students are asked to develop a proactive prevention plan as a last step when solving a problem.

CR-CT Skills Developed

Analysis

Synthesis

Cooperation

Communication

Evaluation

Procedure

- Whenever a problem has been worked through or resolved, students are asked to list in their journals what they learned from the challenge and what, if anything, could be done to prevent a similar problem from occurring in the future. A couple of prevention plans might be:
  Trained mediators in study halls and on the playground could prevent violence.
  Additional fans and more insulation could reduce fossil fuel consumption in the school building.

- An environmental club, the Green Shopper, could publish a list of recycled products using materials so students could "shop green." An energy analysis could identify problems in buildings in an effort to reduce costs (e.g., areas that need insulation).

Challenge	Problem Prevention Plan

INTRODUCING CONTROVERSY

> *I am not afraid the book will be controversial,*
> *I am afraid it will not be controversial.*
> —Flannery O'Connor

Students are asked to: (1) reflect on various arguments pertaining to a controversial subject; (2) evaluate arguments; and (3) practice focusing critically on a perspective rather than on the presenters of such argument. All of these skills are essential for conflict-positive communication as well as for effective academic problem analysis.

CR-CT Skills Developed

Analysis

Evaluation

Communication

Cooperation

Active listening

Procedure

- The teacher chooses a content or current-event subject to be considered and analyzed.
- If the subject at hand is sufficiently familiar, students are asked to share their opinions on the controversial issue before reading and perhaps even write the opinion in several statements. A summary of opinions may be written on the board.
- Students may be asked to bring in books and other materials on the subject.
- Students read one piece about the issue and then review their opinions. Does this author agree with any, some, or all of the statements on the board or in their notebooks? If not, does the author have a new point of view? How have our opinions changed?
- Students then read an article which poses an opposite opinion.
- Students compare the article to the statements on the board and to the opinions of the first author.
- Students are asked to list valid points that each author offered and how they compared to the original list.

ACADEMIC CONTROVERSY

Academic controversy gives students an opportunity to use their conflict-positive communication skills to design an argument for and against an academic issue.

Students practice active listening, questioning for clarity, and evaluation of reasoning.

CR-CT Skills Developed

Active listening

Analysis

Critical questioning

Communication

Cooperation

Procedure

- In groups no larger than four, students are asked to research and design a presentation position on a controversial issue during a class period.
- Each group is given one of the opposing positions to present and defend.
- Groups are asked to use active listening strategies, take notes, and ask questions during opposing presentations.
- After each group has presented they defend their position and question any reasoning weaknesses they find in the other groups' presentation, being careful to attack the issues, not the presenters. They request evidence and information from opposing position groups in order to evaluate and critique their arguments.
- When each presentation and rebuttal is complete the groups reverse perspectives. Each group now defends the position they initially opposed, using all the information they have gathered.
- Finally, all students from opposing groups become one larger group and design a joint, integrated (win–win) position using the best reasoning about which they have reached consensus.
- The integrative positions should be presented to the class by each group.

TOOLBOX TOUR

In this Toolbox Tour, students review the reasoning tools that they've studied and describe them.

CR-CT Skills Developed

Metacognition

Summarizing

Procedure

- Students review the reasoning and decision-making tools they've studied in Chapter 3 (see Toolbox Tour, below).
- Students create a list of these tools and activities for their CR-CT Portfolios.
- After listing the essential tools, students describe each thinking and reasoning "pitfall" or "pothole" and elaborate through description and/or example on those they found most interesting, challenging, or useful.

Toolbox Tour

Dealing with ambiguity	Convergent/Divergent thinking
Examining assumptions	Sorting evidence
Metaphors as tools in problem-solving	Prioritizing lists
Oversimplification	Suspending judgment
Mistaking evidence as proof	Cause–Effect reasoning
Avoiding bandwagon	Controversy and reasoning
Avoiding Group Think or Group Sink	Evaluating risks in decision making
Dealing with emotions	Safe, Smart, and Successful criteria
Non sequiturs	

PART TWO

Conflict-Positive Communication and Cooperation

CONFLICT RESOLUTION: THE PROMISE OF PREVENTION

---

*Attachment is the opposite of alienation, but it is much more than that.
It's why we care. It's why we're all here—working together.*

—High school principal

One of the most important outcomes of a conflict resolution program is positive change in the school or classroom climate, the very arena which inspires most conflict resolutions programs. A sense of social and psychological safety is a requisite for students to develop school attachment and engage in higher order thinking (Sylwester, 1995). Educators and psychologists have long felt that a sense of safety is essential for any educational setting. Years before magnetic resonance brain imaging, Abraham Maslow "grasped the dilemma . . . that human motivation consists of a hierarchy" (Restak, 1995, p. 108). Our biological needs, including physical safety, should be met before we can ascend to self-esteem and creative and critical thinking. Our "higher needs mediated by the frontal lobes are fulfilled only after the satisfaction of more basic biological needs" (Restak, 1994, p. 108). Fortunately, conflict resolution curricula can help abate some of the physical and psychological threats to students' learning.

However, physical safety in school is not assured for many students, a condition which imposes deleterious effects on students' learning and the teachers whose role it is to help them. Every day thousands of students bring guns to school, or skip classes because of fear for their safety; dozens of students are hurt, and over 6,000 teachers are threatened (Bloom, 1997). In a recent survey, 25 percent of suburban high school students "endorsed shooting someone" if they had "stolen something from you" and the majority of 1,700 middle-school students considered rape an acceptable treatment for girls "under certain conditions" (Bloom 1997, p. 198). All too frequently, the news brings us examples of these threats to life and learning from all sectors of our country—urban, suburban, and rural—and from all socioeconomic groups.

The growth of interest in conflict resolution programs is understandable with adolescents disproportionately represented as both victims and violent offenders in America. Every year thousands of people die as the result of violence and another two million are injured (Mercy, 1993). Our "overall homicide rate for young males in the United States is between 4 and 73 times higher than the homicide rate for young males in any other industrialized nation" (Prothrow-Stith, 1991, p. 14).

"Weapons possession alone does not drive up a nation's homicide" (Prothrow-Stith, 1991, p. 15) rate, however. Dr. Prothrow-Stith reminds us of countries like Switzerland, where all adult males under fifty comprise the military and are required to bear arms, yet "few Swiss use handguns or other weapons to kill each other" (Prothrow-Stith, 1991, p. 15). The problem is not a simple one. Understanding which environmental influences affect our children is essential.

Although most young aggressors begin with bullying and antisocial school behavior, "they certainly don't see the impact of their own behavior on others" (Marano, 1995, p. 68). The victims' scars may last for decades and adversely affect them, both academically and psychologically (Marano, 1995). The aggressive child's "emotions may be preempting their cognition, or . . . distorting their cognition" (Marano, 1995, p. 68). When these angry or aggressive students are young they "have intelligence levels equal to those of their peers. But by age 19 their aggressive behavior gets in the way of developing intellectual skills" (Marano, 1995, p. 69). This anger or aggressive behavior and lack of self-regulation "is a marker of every negative outcome there is"(Marano, 1995, p. 69).

The effect of aggressive behavior on the classroom environment is significant. For three decades studies continue to show that the majority of surveyed teachers feel that aggressive students undermine learning for others and most feel that academic achievement would improve dramatically if the problem were remedied. Three quarters of the public surveyed agrees. The research shows that "a set of social skills commonly lacking in people prone to violent and aggressive behavior [include poor] impulse control, problem solving, and anger management" (Committee for Children, 1997, p. 1). Victims and bystanders of aggressive and angry students often lack assertive communication skills, as well (Marano, 1995). Conflict resolution program evaluations show that programs which address these issues not only reduce aggression and violence in communities and their schools, but also provide "life-long decision making skills" (U.S. Dept. of Justice, 1997, p. 55), and enhance the self-esteem of students.

Fortunately, conflict resolution programs provide hope in reclaiming the sanctuary provided by our schools. The Center for Law Related Education (Bodine, 1996) found that most conflict resolution programs reduce the time that teachers spent on conflicts, improve school climate, and improve problem-solving skills and self-control among students. There have been increases in peaceful problem-solving and a significant reduction in violence within the most violent gangs after conflict resolution training (Sherman et al., 1997). More significant reductions in destructive behavior are generally the case in school settings (Johnson & Johnson, 1996).

Now, with thousands of conflict resolution programs in place, we know that such mediation promotes responsible, pro-social behavior, "improved communication, problem-solving, and critical thinking" (Van Steenbergen, 1994, p. 22).

Improved academic performance is a particularly significant gain when conflict resolution skills are integrated into a content area, improving both conflict resolution skills (integrative thinking) and content comprehension (Johnson & Johnson, 1994). Conflict resolution programs improve students' social and emotional skill development (National Institute of Dispute Resolution, 1997). Johnson and Johnson's (1995b, 1996) decades of research show that integrative thinking skills are almost non-existent prior to conflict resolution training, yet are often used spontaneously afterward.

Studies of conflict resolution programs often include measures of positive changes in the classroom or school climate (Koch, 1988; Lam 1989). There are several studies which show that after implementation of effective conflict resolution programs students' ability to problem solve and cooperate improves dramatically and the "cooperative spirit goes beyond the classroom" (Steinberg, 1991, p. 5).

The gains in cooperative skills are significant for two reasons. First, in America our "children are often so highly and inappropriately competitive that they lose the opportunity to win prizes that require even minimal cooperation" (Phinney & Rotheram, 1987, p. 208). Effects may go beyond the social significance of increased cooperation when we consider that "currently, there is no type of task on which cooperative efforts are less effective than competitive or individualistic efforts" (Johnson & Johnson, 1985, p. 114) academically. And, second, students in cooperative conflict resolution environments "hold fewer negative stereotypes" (Lantieri & Patti, 1996, p. 26). This is not a simple effect. This anti-bias effect improves integrative thinking for the biased student and may also thwart any minority effect for any recipient of such bias. Steele and Aronson's (1995) work has shown that mere awareness of a negative stereotype will impair minority students' academic performance. In the integrative thinking classroom students have opportunities to move beyond their biases. Without such opportunities students who discriminate and those whom they discriminate against will have diminished or stunted cognitive and emotional growth. Without a cooperative context, desegregation in schools may have a negative impact, with students feeling threatened and becoming more prejudiced (Johnson & Johnson, 1981). Johnson, Johnson, Stevahn, and Hodne (1997) define "the three Cs of safe schools" (p. 8) as a cooperative context with conflict resolution and civic values, representing "a gestalt in which each component enhances and promotes the other two" (p. 13).

We know that a low threat environment which is characterized by positive affect enhances higher level thinking and creative problem-solving (Izard, 1991; Goleman, 1994; Sylwester, 1995). This environment also enhances our ability to form attachments and build prosocial relationships. Hawkin's voluminous research has shown that the children in high-risk environments who navigated the risks and became productive, healthy, non-violent "contributing members of the community" often noted the important role of attachment: "a parent, an aunt, a grandmother, a teacher, a youth worker, a minister, a business person— established a bond of affection and cared enough to reach out" (Hawkins, 1995, p.14).

Poor affect regulation, poor social skills and "deficits in social problem solving and social cue reading" (Norman et al., 1993, p. 1014) often predict peer rejection, weak attachments, and the alienation that leads to academic failures. Crawford and Bodine (1996) state that when a school develops a conflict resolution program, it strengthens students' resilience in three ways. First, "resolving conflicts in principled ways promotes and preserves relationships thereby facilitating the bonding that is essential" (Crawford & Bodine, 1996, p. 73); second, the conflict resolution education helps students control their behavior and make smarter choices; and third, setting up a conflict resolution program empowers students by encouraging them to solve their own problems rather than having them controlled by teachers and staff. Without such a conflict resolution program, negative conflicts predict "detachment from school and lower grades" (Johnson & Johnson, 1996, p. 482).

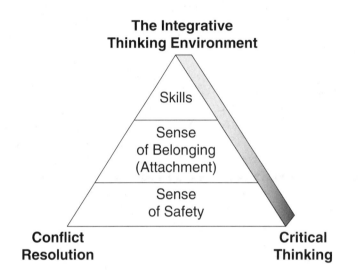

Positive changes are seen in students' strengthened school and community attachment within weeks of implementing a conflict resolution program. Skills are further strengthened when the school environment provides opportunities for social co-cognition in the integrative thinking classroom. This increased caring and cooperation in classroom climate increases critical thinking and metacognition (Davidson & Worsham, 1992). On free recall and cued recall tests researchers have found that "happiness significantly increased learning and memory" (Izard, 1991, p. 168). In summary, researchers Roeser, Midgley, and Urdan (1996) suggest that school environments characterized by caring and respect for individual differences "are related to a more adaptive pattern of cognition, affect, and behavior" (p. 417).

Roeser, Midley, and Urdan (1996) studied the mediating role of attachment or belonging on academic achievement. Students' perceptions of the school environment and students' relationship with teachers shape their school-related beliefs, sense of school belonging, and academic achievement. An environment where students feel self-conscious or threatened may cause alienation and "impaired" ability to concentrate, a fear of taking academic risks, and other performance threatening behaviors (p. 416). Although "48 percent of the variance in academic self-efficacy was explained with prior GPA, personal task goals, and feelings of belonging emerged as the strongest predictors" (Roeser et al.,

1996, p. 416). "The quality of teacher-student relationships" (p. 22) was the strongest predictor of feelings of school belonging.

Students in low-threat, high-challenge environments that create "relaxed alertness" (Caine & Caine, 1997, p. 153) may achieve academic flow—increased performance and critical thinking. Safety, coherence, respect, orderliness, and a sense of community are all aspects of the high-challenge, low-threat environment. Caine and Caine (1997) have recommended that conflict resolution programs be established in all schools to maintain a "healthy discussion" (p. 250) of different perspectives and a healthy environment. Perhaps the most significant development beyond establishing safety is the "recognition of the nature of the students' emotional and social brain" (p. 104). Vygotsky introduced many educators to the concept of a social construction of knowledge (Caine & Caine, 1997). As Caine and Caine (1997) review the research on the brain's psychophysiology and cognition, they suggest that students' social brain has been "sadly neglected" (p. 90). Low-threat environments are essential for optimal learning and, fortunately, these conditions are attainable with conflict resolution programs.

FROM ALIENATION TO ACTIVISM: ATTACHMENT IN THE INTEGRATIVE THINKING CLASSROOM

It is alienation and detachment from the school community, not an IQ deficit, that predicts student problems in most cases (Hawkins & Catalano, 1993). As researchers reviewed programs that included constructive conflict resolution, non-violent problem solving skills and community building, they concluded that "students work harder, achieve more, and attribute more importance to school work in classes in which they feel liked, accepted, and respected by the teacher and fellow student" (Lewis, Schaps, & Watson, 1996, p. 141). However, in schools where students feel rejected or unsuccessful, as the extensive work of Hawkins and Catalano (1993) has shown, "It appears that the experience of failure . . . increases the risk of problem behaviors." (p. 4). David Hawkin's years of research have convinced him that having a positive way to belong and to help in the community is essential to adolescent development and mental health (Hawkins, 1995).

Helping each other, rather than hurting each other, may not only be healthy and natural but may be good medicine in hard times. Selye's work convinced him that the community volunteer or altruist may "have hoarded good feelings for bad times, in much the same way [that] squirrels hoard food" (Padus, 1992, p. 55). Linda Nilson "goes so far as to say altruism may be part of our survival instinct" (Padus, 1992, p. 56). Other medical researchers tell us that "caring is biological" and "the more connected you are . . . the healthier you are" (Padus, 1992, p. 56).

What happens to the many children who don't experience attachment and success? The most obvious result is that we have children who will be less likely to show consistent prosocial behavior and resilience.

Additional signs of alienation and lack of attachment are gang and hate group membership. Years of research have upheld Allport's classic studies that found that the typical child in a hate group is alienated and fearful of others and of his social environment. This lack of attachment is characterized by the prejudiced youth's need for structure even if it is a false, narrow, and inadequate structure, as provided by a hate group membership. Gang or hate group membership offers "a sense of connection, belonging, and self-definition" (American Psychological Association, 1993, p. 28). One of the strongest "protective factors against aggressive, violent destructive behavior and gang membership is the sense of belonging" to a family or school community (APA, 1993, p. 19).

THE BIOLOGY OF SUCCESS IN THE INTEGRATIVE THINKING CLASSROOM

From another vantage point, recent neurological research corroborates what teachers have known for years: Students can't learn in an environment where they feel alienated or threatened socially, psychologically, or physically. What happens to us under conditions of fear and anxiety starts in the primitive part of the brain. The amygdala is a brain structure in the limbic system—our "emotional brain" (Goleman, 1994, p. 4). Fear, rage, and fight or flight reactions arise in the amygdala. The speed with which the amygdala hijacks the brain from the cerebral cortex can provide an adaptive safety mechanism. It is essential that our attention be hijacked in this way, allowing us an instant flight reaction to the sight of a snake in the grass (Bloom, 1997). The amygdala makes all of that possible. We focus on the singular issue of survival when our brains are hijacked. Creative and critical thinking are postponed.

Many teachers report that when students fear ridicule or conflict they can't concentrate on their work. The amygdala may cause downshifting, a "psychophysiological response to threat" which "results in less sophisticated use of the brain" (p. 41). Although this fight or flight reaction is adaptive in some environments, it does not enhance learning. The "downshifted learners bypass much of their capacity for higher-order functioning and creative thought" (Caine & Caine, 1997, p. 18). To prevent downshifting, students need a safe, low-threat, high-challenge, critical thinking environment: "Processing content consistently and with appropriate positive social interaction may prevent downshifting" (Nummela & Rosengren, 1986, p. 51).

Studies suggest that a fear response in the amygdala has a very small time advantage in the brain, probably no more than a twenty-fifth of a second, during which the emotional brain can override the cerebral cortex response. The amygdala plays an important role in the storage of memory as well. The "structural relationship between the amygdala and cortex offer a crucial insight . . . the connection from the cortex to amygdala are only inhibitory. While the amygdala can hijack the brain, the cortex can only put the brakes on" (Goleman, 1994, p. 4).

While the cerebral cortex may help us override a reaction, we can not decide when to have such a reaction. The cerebral cortex *can* help us decide *what* to do with it, however. "Emotions or feelings are conscious products of unconscious processes" (LeDoux, 1994, p. 57). Although emotional and declarative memories seem to be joined "seamlessly in our conscious experience" (p. 57), they are in fact products of separate functions. The amygdala and the unconscious emotions exert "a powerful influence on declarative memory and other thought processes" (p. 57). Because we can not choose to turn off the amygdala, we must instead choose to concern ourselves with the classroom climate, anger management, and self-control. Because "a child's ability to learn academic material is profoundly affected by emotional states" (Elias et al., 1997, p. 49), and emotional states are affected by classroom climate, a sense of safety is our first goal in the conflict-positive classroom.

Joseph LeDoux (1996) suggests "that emotion and cognition are best thought of as separate but interacting mental functions mediated by separate but interacting brain systems" (1996, p. 69). Although the emotional brain responds automatically, our "cognition gives us choices" (p. 69) once we begin to understand our emotional reactions. We need to learn to understand how to handle our emotional responses in a non-threatening environment—the first goal of a successful conflict resolution program.

Chronic stress causes "high cortisol levels which can lead to the destruction of neurons in the hippocampus associated with learning and memory" (Sylwester, 1995, p. 38). Temporary, short-term elevation of "cortisol in the hippocampus can lead to an inability to distinguish between important and unimportant elements of a memorable event" (Sylwester, 1995, p. 38), making the roles of teaching or learning untenable. On the other hand, "exercise and positive social contacts" (Sylwester, 1995, p. 38) elevate the brain chemicals that "can increase the possibility that students will learn how to solve problems successfully in potentially stressful situations" (Sylwester, 1995, p. 39). Although "we don't learn emotions" (Sylwester, 1995, p. 75) we can learn to recognize and work constructively with them.

A state of mild stress or excitement may "facilitate recall" (Restak, 1984, p. 175); however, students in a physically or psychologically threatening environment will become "too anxious to take in new information and have difficulty recalling previously acquired information" (Restak, 1984, p. 175). Their "performance deteriorates . . . increasing disorganization" (p. 175). Anxiety may cause the pupils of the eyes to dilate, making simple "reading more difficult" (Restak, 1984, p. 175). Researchers (Beyth-Maron, Rischhoff, Jacobs, and Furby, 1989) often find that "greater anxiety leads to shorter and less effective decision processes" (p. 10). According to Stosny (1995), "cognitive rigidity experienced during anger arousal causes a polarizing cognitive effect, making any critical thinking or creative consideration of multiple perspectives highly unlikely, if not impossible" (p. 59).

Inhibition and inability to express negative emotions or resolve negative conflicts is associated with "potentially deleterious changes in the ways we think. In holding back significant thoughts and feelings . . . we typically do not think about an event in a broad and integrative way" (Pennebacker, 1997, p. 9). If a student does not talk about a negative event, he usually will not translate the event into language" (Pennebacker, 1997, p. 9) which will prevent him from "understanding and assimilating the event" (p. 9). Izard (1991) and her colleagues have found that positive emotions facilitate "cognitive processes such as thinking, remembering, categorization, and creative problem-solving" (p. 1678). In fact, subjects who interact with a happy, positive evaluator (versus a negative, critical evaluator) to establish mood and climate, show higher level thinking on intelligence tests that follow (Izard, 1991).

A relaxed, positive environment with some positive social interaction will "stimulate more efficient functioning for the entire cortex and increase learning and reasoning potential" (Nummela & Rosengren, 1986, p. 50). The research findings clearly favor non-threatening, caring learning environments for our children in the interests of achievement and psychological well-being. Conflict resolution programs reduce alienation and academic failure and increase attachment, transforming the learning environment (Johnson & Johnson, 1996, p. 482). Much like language acquisition, there is evidence that the "language of mediation" is easily learned and conflict resolution steps internalized when taught to younger children (Meredith, 1987; Miller, 1987).

Conflicts that students resolve between themselves using peer mediation or conflict resolution techniques are more enduring and the resolutions are more meaningful for all parties (Miller, 1987). Students who study mediation can also "engage a listener . . . and make their purpose clear" in other social and peer interactions (Miller, 1987, p. 12). The skills may transfer and positively affect other areas of the student's life such as "dramatic positive increases in self-image, social morality, and vocational-educational attitudes" (Miller, 1987, p. 12; Van Slyck & Stern, 1991). Evaluations reveal increases in student self-esteem, improved school climate, improved behavior and communication skills among students, and improved teacher morale in schools with conflict resolution and/or peer mediation programs (Miller, 1987). Teachers also report having more time (fewer disputes and interruptions) after the initial time investment to begin the program.

Ironically, not only are "trouble makers transformed," but they are often among the best mediators, seemingly "relieved finally to have discovered a method for dealing with their own problems" (Miller, 1987, p. 14).

THE COOPERATION-CONFLICT RESOLUTION CYCLE

Polling teachers using the critical incident technique, researchers found increased use of cooperative learning strategies as the most frequently cited change in classes which had conflict resolution programs (Heydenberk & Heydenberk, 1997b). The increased social communication skills developed in the conflict-positive classroom enabled students to work together more productively in cooperative groups. A meta-analysis of 122 cooperative learning studies conducted by Johnson, Maruyama, Johnson, Nelson, and Skon (1981) found 286 effects. These effects indicate that "cooperation promotes higher achievement than does competition by 65 to 80%" (Johnson et al., 1981, p. 51). Cooperation also "promotes higher achievement than do individualistic effects" (Johnson et al., 1981, p. 51). Cooperation is superior to individualistic efforts in promoting productivity. Increasing cooperative learning promotes attachment, achievement, and productivity.

Gabbert, Johnson, and Johnson's (1986) study of cooperative learning versus individualistic learning effects on achievement in a randomized, stratified sample of elementary students found that achievement gains "transferred to individual testing situations for three higher-level reasoning tasks" (p. 265). Interestingly, there were no group differences on lower level tasks. Johnson and Johnson (1992) point out that hundreds of studies have shown the effectiveness of cooperative learning structures; however, "simply placing students in groups and telling them to work together does not in and of itself promote higher achievement and higher level reasoning" (p. 121). Groups must possess the essential elements of positive interdependence, which is the hallmark of the integrative thinking classroom.

Johnson, Skon, and Johnson (1980) studied forty-five students randomly assigned to cooperative, competitive, and individualistic conditions. As in their twenty previous studies, the students in the cooperative condition used higher quality reasoning strategies when tested individually on a battery of critical thinking tests. Furthermore, the higher ability students consistently outperformed the higher ability students in the competitive or individualistic conditions. The cooperative condition students out-perform a stratified random sample of their peers on problem-solving tasks and they consistently used "superior [thinking] strategies for deriving their answers" (Johnson, Skon, & Johnson, 1980, p. 91). Some concerned critics of cooperative learning environments have explained gains by suggesting that low-ability students may benefit from the brighter students' tutoring in the cooperative context. These studies show cognitive benefits to students of all abilities.

Many studies find improved interpersonal skills as a result of conflict resolution training (Johnson & Johnson, 1996). This increase in interpersonal skills has inspired some teachers to increase their use of cooperative learning strategies after conflict resolution training (Heydenberk & Heydenberk, 1997b). This increase, in turn, provides opportunities for students to hone their conflict resolution skills, communication skills and critical thinking.

Stevahn, Johnson, Johnson, and Real (1996) studied the effects of a cooperative (versus individualistic) context on the success of conflict resolution training. The students in the cooperative context scored higher on conflict resolution and academic achievement measures. Students' conflict resolution skills were enhanced in the cooperative environment as was their content comprehension. Conflict resolution training and cooperative learning strategies appear to enhance each other, creating an upward spiral of increased achievement and improved behavior in the classroom.

Tolerance and appreciation of diversity are also enhanced in the conflict-positive classroom. Fishbein (1996) contends that prejudice and discrimination have not been sufficiently reduced through mainstreaming or desegregation. He tells us that cooperative learning in classroom settings may be our best hope. Fishbein agrees with Johnson and Johnson's assessment that effective cooperation must include positive goal interdependence and complementary roles.

Fishbein (1996) examines dozens of studies that focused on prejudice education in cooperative academic settings. Three of the studies measured various multiple outgroup prejudices. Fourteen studies focused on racial and ethnic prejudice, three studies focused on gender bias, and the last six looked at prejudice towards disabled children.

Fourteen of the studies included in Fishbein's (1996) review "had children working in cooperative context as a single experimental condition . . . The control condition in eighteen of the studies involved children working individually" (Fishbein, 1996, p. 235). Six of the remaining studies included two experimental conditions—one cooperative and one competitive. The three studies of gender bias indicated that cooperative interaction "does reduce discrimination toward opposite sex classmates and prejudice toward unknown members of the opposite sex" (p. 235).

There were fourteen studies on racial and ethnic discrimination. The prejudice study outcomes were not as clear "although there are some limited data [indicating] attitudes toward outgroup classmates improve following cooperative interaction" (Fishbein, 1996, p. 240). All of these studies considered together provide strong evidence that "cross-racial discrimination decreases as a result of cooperative interaction" (Fishbein, 1996, p. 240) and the changes may be long-lasting. Furthermore, the effects may go past increased tolerance of race and ability differences toward appreciation of differences and actual friendships (p. 241). The results hold for children of all ages. The increased cooperation in the integrative thinking classroom may have effects that are more profound than simply lowering incidents of physical aggression and conflict in the classroom.

Johnson and Johnson (1979) have studied the effects of cooperation on conflict. They found that the context of the conflict was the most important factor in determining whether the resulting resolution would be constructive or destructive. In order for the outcome to be "constructive, information must be accurately communicated—with a cooperative context" (Johnson & Johnson, 1979, p. 58). In a competitive context, "communication tends to be nonexistent or misleading" (p. 58). The second requirement was that the resolutions occur in a "supportive climate in which people feel safe enough to challenge each other's ideas" (Johnson & Johnson, 1979, p. 58). Constructive problem-solving outcomes were those that dealt with understanding the feeling involved in the conflict or controversy as well as the ideas. The quality of the resolution or solution was also affected by how the problem was defined (e.g., a joint concern) and how well students could identify similarities and differences between opinions or positions. Whether or not the outcome of a conflict will be violence or a peaceful resolution depends on the skills of the disputants, not the details of the dispute.

The effects of a cooperative climate as reviewed by Kohn (1986) are increased individual and group productivity, increased individual learning and comprehension, increased social skills and dispositions regarding the learning tasks. However, "despite this evidence . . . we continue trying to succeed at the price of other peoples' failure" (Kohn, 1986, p. 183).

As Kohn (1986) points out, the most competitive business environments are characterized by cooperation among workers within the company in order to achieve success. Although we incline to "attend instead to the far more visible instances of struggle" (Kohn, 1986, p. 18), the truth is that the "vast majority of human interaction in our society as well as in other societies is not competitive, but cooperative interaction" (p. 18). Kohn (1986) agrees with Ashley Montagu and David and Rodger Johnson when he states that "without the cooperation of its members society cannot survive" and, furthermore, "the society of man has survived because the cooperativeness of its members made survival possible" (Kohn, 1986, p. 18). Cooperation is, according to conflict theorist Morton Deutsch, "inherent in the very idea of society" (p. 19).

Children are naturally anxious to play together, to communicate, and to exhibit the "so-called prosocial behaviors—cooperation, helping, sharing, comforting" which "occur in almost every child" (Kohn, 1986, p. 19). It is the child who is the exception, the bully, the shy child, or the troubled child, who, understandably, gets our attention and the vast majority of our research efforts. We must remember that the majority of our children seek ways to socialize and create friendships. Although we may learn how to exhibit cultural conventions, (manners and prosocial behaviors), the "inclination to help . . . exists literally from the beginning of life" (p. 119). Even Charles Darwin reminded us that the struggle for existence was largely successful because of our cooperative skills (p. 21).

The increased cooperation and co-cognition in the integrative thinking environment provides students with the sense of safety and the tools they require to engage in the highest levels of critical thinking. Ironically, despite our faith in a very competitive academic environment, it is the more cooperative environment that increases students' creativity, sense of responsibility, and individualism. The cooperative integrative thinking environment fosters cognitive flexibility and growth. In fact, "the inclination to take risks is stifled by competition" (Kohn, 1986, p. 130) in the classroom. As Kohn (1986) tells us, levels of competition create an environment of "sterile . . . safety" (p. 131) where students tend to avoid more challenging tasks and rarely indulge in true reflection in a highly competitive distributive (win–lose) environment where "competition affects the personality . . . and turns us into cautious, obedient people" (Kohn, 1986, p. 131), students are afraid to challenge themselves or each other.

An exclusively competitive environment fundamentally changes the way students think. A non-cooperative, highly competitive environment causes students to focus on an external locus of control academically, and dramatically inhibits performance as students lose sight of the intrinsic values and the interest of the subject matter. Students focus exclusively on the punishment or reward involved in a highly competitive classroom (Kohn, 1986).

Extremely competitive academic environments have been shown to cause shallow, flawed, and dichotomous thinking (Kohn, 1986). The simplistic, shallow thinking characteristic of a competitive environment leads to the short form of thinking . . ."either/or to good/bad to we/they to we against them" (Kohn, 1986, p. 128), instead of the reflective search for balance and understanding. This faulty, simplistic reasoning invites battle and blame (Kohn, 1986). Those who have learned to see the world in an either/or, dichotomous fashion are "attracted to competition, but, by the same token, competition will help to shape such an orientation" (Kohn, 1986, p. 24). They may become uncomfortable with more complex reasoning tasks. This is the downward spiral of the non-cooperative classroom.

The cooperative integrative environment fosters a sense of academic safety that allows for more complex thinking and intellectual challenge. Conflict may become the strongest academic tool within such an environment. Despite concerns, a cooperative environment does not "sacrifice either an academic orientation or a strong sense of self" (Kohn, 1986, p. 155), and in fact fosters individualism and self-knowledge in students. In order to "rescue cooperation from yet another misconception" (p. 156), Kohn points out that the cooperative classroom "does not imply some idyllic state of harmony among participants" (p. 156). Students are, in fact, more likely to express, consider, and discuss differences in the safety of a cooperative context. Johnson and Johnson's work (1992) shows that students may discuss their differences of opinion more often in the safety of the cooperative context. Rigid agreement and lack of conflict is unnatural and indicates an environment of students in fear, "bereft of their rational faculties—as the total agreement among cult members" (Kohn, 1986, p. 156).

Constructively resolved conflict often leads to an expanded understanding for the parties involved. Research on cooperative conflict resolution shows that students prefer it to the forced "concurrence-seeking model" (Kohn, 1986, p. 157). Destructive conflict and debate were strongly disliked by the same students. Students of all ability levels learn from cooperative conflict and show increased comprehension on achievement tests when working in the cooperative conflict environment. Students show higher attachment levels and "greater accuracy of perspective taking in cooperative conflict than in concurrence seeking, debate or independent learning situations" (Kohn, 1986, p. 157). The dramatic increases in cooperative interaction in the integrative thinking environment affects students in several ways. Students interact more effectively and think more clearly even when working alone in a calm, cooperative climate.

For Piaget, "cooperation is really a factor in the creation of personality . . . the self that takes up its stand on the norms of reciprocity and objective discussion and knows how to submit to these in order to make itself respected" (Piaget, 1997, p. 95). Furthermore, for Piaget "It is the cooperation that builds genuine respect . . . not to be confused with the mutual consent of two individual selves capable of joining forces for evil" (Piaget, 1997, p. 96). The cooperation in the integrative classroom fosters superior thinking skills for social and academic success.

The opportunities we provide for our students to build a sense of community in our integrative thinking classrooms and schools will enrich their education and protect them at the same time. Teachers have always been there for their students, but the greater gift is to show them how to be there for each other and for themselves. Having worked on our problem-solving skills in Part One, Part Two presents the essential components of conflict resolution programs to help us build a sense of community within our schools, ensuring all of our students and teachers the safety and success they deserve.

CHAPTER 4

United without an Enemy: The Conflict Resolution Program

If I can stop one heart from breaking, I should not live in vain.
—Emily Dickinson

Chapter 4 presents a complete conflict resolution skills program. Students examine their conflict resolution styles before learning the keys to effective communication and the conflict resolution steps. Increased social skills and emotional understanding powerfully predict increases in academic performance and school attachment, as well as success and satisfaction in life.

EXPLORING ATTITUDES ABOUT CONFLICT

At first, other teachers asked me how I always got all of the good kids,
and now they ask me what I'm doing in my classroom.
—Classroom teacher

Exploring Attitudes about Conflict introduces students to conflict as a concept that is distinct from fighting and aggression. Students define conflict and explore attitudes about conflict. The effect that attitudes and assumptions have on conflict situations is explored, as well.

CR-CT Skills Developed

Main idea

Classification

Communication

Active listening

Analysis

Divergent thinking

Procedure

- The teacher writes the word conflict in the middle of the board and circles it. Students are asked to brainstorm word associations and examples of conflict.

- After the brainstorm has been completed, students are then asked to count the number of negative and positive words used to define conflict.

   The teacher asks how a conflict is different from a fight or violence. Are they the same?

   Can a conflict be an opposition of ideas or interests without a fight?

   Examples might be:

   My parents belong to different political parties but they don't fight about political differences.

   My best friend and I have different favorite football teams but it doesn't cause us to fight.

   My sister and I share a small bedroom but we don't fight about space.

- The teacher asks the following:

   Can a conflict be inside of a person?

   Can a person have a conflict about what to eat for lunch?

   Can there be conflict about what movie to watch?

   Can there be conflict about which friend to call?

   Can a conflict be a friendly discussion about which present to buy for a mutual friend?

   Can two friends have different, conflicting ideas about something and still remain friends?

   Students respond, clarifying their responses.

- Students are asked to define conflict. "If all conflicts don't end in a fight, what will our definition be? What characterizes all conflict?

- Students contrive a new definition of conflict, one which includes constructive outcomes.

   Given the model shown below, students are asked to brainstorm what makes conflict worse, such as yelling, pushing, tone of voice, or not listening.

- Using the same model, students are asked to describe the behaviors that would improve a conflict situation. Use previous examples or student examples to facilitate discussion.

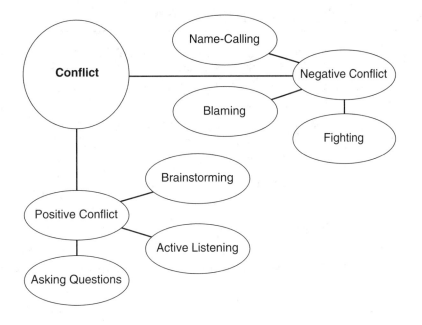

- Students are asked to consider what the following questions (and attitudes) have to do with resolving conflict: "If you don't believe that there is a store or cinema on your block, are you likely to make plans to get there?" "If you don't believe conflict can be constructively resolved are you likely to try using conflict resolution?" "How do our attitudes affect our potential for problem solving?"

- Students are asked, "Does your knowledge about what conflict is, affect how you might deal with conflict?" "Can your attitudes about resolving conflict affect the outcome of a disagreement?"

- Students are asked to recall a conflict situation in which they wish they had responded differently. They could be asked to identify the conflict, indicate who was involved, how the conflict situation progressed, how the conflict situation was resolved and how they could have acted differently in the conflict situation.

Extending Activities: Journal Response

How can my beliefs about conflict affect how they are resolved?

Portfolio Pick

CONFLICT RESOLUTION TWISTER

As in previous twister activities, students brainstorm the most effective ways to *prevent* a positive outcome. Students begin to create a conflict resolution twister with scenarios provided and then transfer the activity to the classroom conflict.

CR-CT Skills Developed

Divergent thinking

Communication

Procedure

- Students review and brainstorm the conflict resolution attitudes and behaviors from the previous activity, *Exploring Attitudes about Conflict.*

- The teacher introduces the Twister Brainstorm:
  1. "What behaviors can we use to increase conflict?" and
  2. "What attitudes and behaviors did we choose that increased anger in a conflict situation?" Some responses might be: name calling, eye contact, making faces, not listening, attacking the person, not the problem, mimicking, threatening, and refusing to communicate. Students should be allowed to share the situations in which the example or behavior was drawn.

- When the list is complete, students reverse or *twist* their answers to begin development of a list of conflict-positive behaviors and attitudes. The model provided below may be used as students generate behaviors.

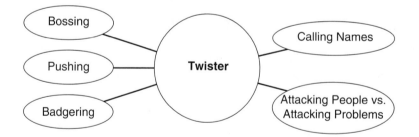

Extending Activities: Response Journals

How many conflict twister behaviors do I use? Do they make my conflicts better or worse?

Portfolio Pick

CONFLICT RESOLUTION STYLES

Now he's lost his mother [to violence]. He knows how important conflict resolution is. He teaches the other students to be conflict managers. He's a good mediator. He still has so much hope. When I get overwhelmed I look at him and think, Wait a minute, who am I to give up hope?
—Elementary school principal

How students define and approach conflict is a stronger determinant of the conflict's outcome than the nature of the conflict itself. In this activity we help students develop an awareness of how they habitually approach or avoid resolving conflicts.

CR-CT Skills Developed

Metacognition

Analysis

Procedure

- The teacher draws a large circle on the board and divides it into quarters. The quarters are labeled as shown below.

- The teacher questions whether anyone has ever sought help from a parent or teacher in solving a conflict instead of resolving it themselves. A couple of student examples are merited here. This is called an appeal to authority.
- It is important to convey that it is sometimes important to appeal to authority in resolving issues, especially when danger is threatened.

Most of the time it isn't necessary to appeal to authority. Students identify cases requiring an appeal to authority and those that do not require such intervention after reviewing the examples below:
A classmate threatens to bring a weapon to school. (Appeal to authority is appropriate and necessary)
A friend borrows a CD and forgets to bring it to school; you wanted it that night. (Personal conflict resolution communication is appropriate)

- Students generate examples of appropriate times to appeal to authority and times to resolve issues themselves.

- The teacher asks whether anyone has ever walked away, lied, pretended to agree, or pretended to not hear something in order to avoid a conflict.

- Students respond and divulge answers.

Again, it is appropriate to resolve the conflict if it meets the Safe, Smart, and Successful criteria cited in earlier activities. If resolving it personally poses any danger, then another action must be taken.

- Students assess the appropriate response to conflict in the following scenarios:
    1. One of your friends cancels plans with you only to do something else with a mutual friend. Do you avoid conflict by quietly accepting it or face the conflict with your friend? How would you feel about this kind of action?
    2. You're walking down the street and a stranger begins screaming names at passersby around you. Do you continue walking or verbally engage the person?

Has anyone ever hurt, screamed, ordered someone to get what they wanted just because they were too impatient or didn't want to bother explaining or working the problem out?

- Students respond and generate examples.

- This action is classified as a win–lose conflict resolution. Students generate examples of appropriate avoidance and conflict resolution styles.

- Next, students answer the following two questions individually:
When I get angry I . . .
When I disagree with someone it usually ends up . . .

- When they're finished the teacher asks for some students to share responses at the board. The responses fall into one of four categories. Students help the teacher categorize responses as follows:
Avoid conflict
Appeal to authority
Win-lose approach
Win-win approach

Extending Activities: Response Journals

Does my conflict resolution style change depending on the person with whom I disagree?

Would I be better off trying a new conflict resolution style with someone I fight with often?

THE THREE R'S OF CONFLICT RESOLUTION

After the initial step in conflict resolution which asks students to stop before an impulsive outburst, the Three R's of conflict resolution are the tools needed to reframe the problem and make it amenable to resolution.

CR-CT Skills Developed

Analysis

Active listening

Communication

Paraphrasing

Metacognition

Procedure

- The teacher introduces the Three R's of conflict resolution:
  1. **R**eset (tone)
  2. **R**estate (paraphrase and clarify)
  3. **R**eframe (define the issue as a problem to be solved, not a win–lose power issue)

- The teacher introduces the scenario below:

    Tanya screams at Ryan, "You never do anything you say you're going to do, so don't even come over here and sit with us!"

    Ryan smiles and says, "Wait a minute. I'm really sorry you're mad that I missed the meeting yesterday. I hear you waited for me. Hey, what should I do if I find out I can't make a meeting and you guys are already at school? Who could I call?"

- The teacher then asks students to consider that if Ryan didn't reset the tone, it might sound something like this: "Fine. Finish it yourself!" which would copy Tanya's tone.

    If Ryan doesn't reset the tone or restate the issue, how could it sound? How would the problem be resolved differently in each condition?

- Students work in groups to Three-R the following scenarios:
  1. Kendra waited for Roberta in front of the theater and missed the first minutes of the movie. Roberta never showed up or called. Kendra screams at Roberta before class.
  2. Samantha heard that Julia was spreading rumors about her boyfriend and she angrily confronts Julia at lunch.

  Students are asked to write the Three R's for the two cases above. They should reflect the following:
  Reset—use a calm tone
  Restate—paraphrase using, "I can see", "I understand"
  Reframe—redefine the problem to be solved rather than the blame to be assigned

- Groups may share their examples as time permits.

Portfolio Pick

City at Peace mediators teach Santa Barbara's young people conflict resolution skills and improvisational theater techniques to help them explore conflicts in their lives. NANCY DAVIS, DIRECTOR, CITY AT PEACE, SANTA BARBARA, CA. PHOTO: BARBARA PARMET.

CONFLICT STYLE THEATER

Conflict Style Theater is an effective and memorable tool for helping students identify and create conflict style choices.

CR-CT Skills Developed

Main idea

Synthesis

Categorizing

Procedure

- Students are placed in groups of three to five. Each group is given two cards: a scenario description card and a style card.
- Each group designs an ending to their assigned scenario that characterizes the style. They act out the scenario to the class.
- The class is asked to guess which conflict style the group was assigned. When each group is done they shuffle the cards and hand them out again. It is okay if a group gets the same scenario card with a different style card or the same style card with a different scenario card.

Distributive (Win–Lose) Style or Aggressive Style	**Appeal to Authority**
Integrative (Win–Win) Style	**Avoidance (Passive) Style**

- Conflict Style Theater Scenarios:

1. Kathy and Martina are good friends who are discussing what to do on Friday night. Kathy wants to get a bite to eat and then go to a friend's

party. Martina wants to see a movie that just opened on the other side of town and doesn't particularly like the girl having the party.

2. Tiara and Heather are working on a paper at Tiara's house. Tiara's mother has new white carpeting in the house. Heather knocks over the drink Tiara left on the back of the couch and it spills on the couch and the new rug.

3. Tony borrows Jared's favorite CD on Thursday. He promises Jared he'll bring it to school Friday. Jared doesn't get it on Friday. Now it is Monday and Tony still didn't bring it to school.

4. Kendra promises Vicki she'll stop by after school on Monday so they can work on their papers and go to Vicki's sister's soccer game. Vicki waits and waits and doesn't get the paper done and they miss seeing the game. Kendra never shows up but Vicki finds out that Kendra was at the game with some other friends.

5. Carmine's aunt is moving next weekend. His friend David is going to help her load boxes and awkward items into the truck. The boys are getting paid well and Carmine has already decided how to spend the money. When moving time comes, David never shows up. Carmine can't move the tables and boxes alone.

Extending Activities: Response Journals

Which conflict style made your scenario more difficult to resolve? Which conflict card would make it easier to resolve?

COMMUNICATION KEYS

Students are introduced to the power of transforming their communication from aggressive, offensive, or threatening to the kind of communication that opens the door to problem solving.

CR-CT Skills Developed

Analysis

Divergent thinking

Revising

Active listening

Communication

Procedure

- Students review the types of communication that may shut the door to further communication and problem solving and try to rewrite the communication in a more positive way that invites further dialogue. Students should review and use the 3 R's of Conflict Resolution as well as review the list of what not to do (The Conflict Resolution Twister Activity) in order to get ready for this activity.

- Students then work in groups to choose a typical home or school conflict (no names of real people, please) and then write or role play the scenario with their conflict resolution communication skills.
- After each group reads or role plays their scenario, classmates may discuss which keys to communication were used to keep communication open.
- Students may fill in the keys on the next page.
- Students analyze classmates' keys.

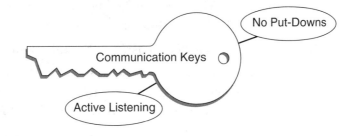

BOOMERANG

Students trace the effects of conflict-positive and conflict-negative communications using the scenarios we've provided and designing their own as time permits.

CR-CT Skills Developed

Metacognition

Analysis

Communication

Active listening

Procedure

- The teacher asks students to consider the following: When walking down the street you say hello to someone you know. They glare and ignore you. What do you do? How do your actions come back at you?
- If you want to make someone smile when you are walking down the hall, how do you do it?

- The teacher introduces the boomerang metaphor. A boomerang is a bent throwing instrument that can be thrown in such a way that it goes out and comes back to you. An action or language that is used may also come back to haunt the speaker.

- Students read or listen to the following:

  Sandy walks into a restaurant and sees her friend, Yashika. "Hey, Yashika, I heard you got a role in the play. You'll be great! Congratulations." Megan walks in and says, "Yashika, are you really in that silly play? Why? Some of us have a life, I guess."

  Who do you think Yashika will invite to the opening night party, Sandy or Megan? Why? How do Sandy and Megan create their own, but different, boomerangs?

- The class is asked to listen to the following:

  Tony walks into class and says, "Kevin, new shoes? Did your mommy give you your allowance?" Joey walks into class and says, "Kevin, nice shoes. Great for basketball!"

  Who does Kevin invite over for a game that afternoon? How did Joey and Kevin each create different boomerangs?

- Using the attached cards, student pairs role play the following;

You get your teacher to smile and say hello in the hall.	You anger a stranger on the street.
You get your classmate to avoid you.	You get a stressed friend to calm down.
You get your sibling upset with you.	You get a sad friend to cheer up.
You get a smile from a stranger on the street.	You make your parents laugh.

- Students brainstorm the behaviors and communication skills they would use to achieve the following:
  Getting someone to smile
  Getting an angry response
  Letting someone know you're angry
  Getting someone to calm down

Extending Activities: Response Journals

Is there anyone I disagree with that I can approach differently?

MEETING ON THE MOBIUS STRIP

After a brief introduction to the Mobius Strip, students make a model of the Mobius strip and discuss it as a metaphor for integrative thinking.

CR-CT Skills Developed

Active listening

Metaphorical thinking

Communication

Procedure

- The teacher explains that in the 1800s a man named August Ferdinand Mobius studied topology and mathematics. One of his favorite issues to study and write about was the Mobius strip—a strip that is in one perspective two-sided, and in another sense, one-sided.
- Students cut strips of paper about 18 inches in length for the Mobius strip. When the Mobius strip is laid flat on the desk the students turn one end of the strip face down to achieve a half turn.

Mobius Strip

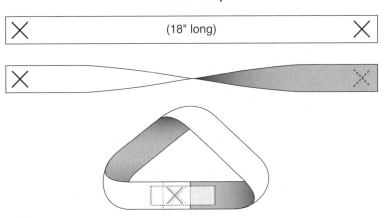

After writing Xs on the ends as shown, students then twist one end over so that only one X is showing. Then students bring the two ends together so that both Xs are touching each other on the inside of the circle. The joined edges are taped.

- Students then take pens or pencils and draw a line down the middle of the strip without lifting the pen, turning it slowly until they come to the place where they started.
- Students are then asked to find the other side of the strip—the unmarked side. There is no "other side" to a Mobius strip.
- Students may then cut the Mobius strip down the middle to make a larger circle.
- Students discuss how the Mobius strip is a metaphor for conflict resolution and mediation. How do we get two sides to become one?
- Students are then introduced to the concept of integrative thinking: Integrative thinking is a type of problem solving in which the solution that is sought ensures that all parties achieve their goals and agree on the solution. Integrative thinking often requires that a larger perspective be taken—a new definition of the problem. Distributive thinking is when the solution sought will result in a win–lose solution in which only one party can win. This slows the decision-making process and creates negative feelings on the part of the loser after the decision is made.

GROUND RULES, GUIDELINES, AND GOALS

In order to achieve a win–win or integrative conflict resolution outcome, it is helpful for students to agree on the ground rules and guidelines that support integrative win–win thinking. By reviewing and posting the ground rules, guidelines, and goals the students may begin communicating more productively, despite destructive conflict resolution styles and habits.

CR-CT Skills Developed

Analysis

Communication

Active listening

Procedure

- Students are asked to create a brief conflict situation which meets the Safe, Smart, and Successful criteria established in an earlier activity. Students should create one which could be constructively resolved by students only.

- Students are asked what could be done to create a win–win solution to the conflict. Students recall and post a definition of win–win.

- Students discuss what ground rules and guidelines could be used to help two angry disputants. Students brainstorm independently for a few minutes, after which they share their solutions with the class. Their responses are written on the board by the teacher or by a volunteer recorder.

- The Ground Rules should include:
  No name calling
  No interrupting
  No changing the subject
  No attacking the person
  No involving others

- Students are then asked to state these behaviors in the positive: "What are the *shoulds,* not just the *shouldn'ts,* as introduced in previous chapters?" Their responses might look like:
  Take turns talking
  Listen carefully to the other person
  Ask the other person to clarify something if you don't understand
  Stay on the subject

These Ground Rules can be refined and expanded and then placed on a bulletin board or chart for ongoing student reference. The Ground Rules are to be reviewed before attempting to resolve any conflict.

Extending Activities: Response Journals

How could these ground rules be used in everyday communication? If we used these ground rules in all of our conversations would it influence the conflicts we have?

Portfolio Pick

ACTIVE LISTENING

After reviewing Sound Scavengers, another active listening activity from Chapter 1, students review the importance of listening as the first step in successful conflict resolution and communication. Sometimes just practicing active listening is enough to diffuse a conflict. Active listening gives us information and increases empathy before we begin problem solving.

CR-CT Skills Developed

Active listening

Analysis

Metacognition

Procedure

- After reviewing one or more of the listening activities in Chapter 1, the teacher asks whether anyone has ever had a disagreement with someone and found out that they did not really understand the other person's point of view, or found out that the other person didn't understand their point of view. Destructive and often angry communication results.
- The teacher introduces the first step of conflict resolution. Once students have cooled off enough to review the win–win conflict resolution guidelines and agree to them, they are asked to sit down and begin conflict resolution by active listening.

  Active listening includes eye contact, attentive posture, non-hostile expressions, silence, and asking appropriate questions.

- Students form groups of three to role play effective and ineffective listening strategies using the scenario and listening style cards attached.
- After each student group models their listening strategy the class guesses which card they had and explains their choices.
- Students may design their own scenarios and act them out if time permits.
- Discuss how the resolutions would be affected by each form of listening behavior.
- Speakers are then asked to review how they felt under each different condition.

Scenario Cards

One friend is trying to tell another about a trip

One friend is trying to tell another about a family party

One friend is trying to tell another about a fight he had with another friend

Listening Style Cards

Active listening
  eye contact
  no interruptions
  asking questions

Poor Listening
  interrupting with comments
  no questions—uninterested
  changing the subject

Active Listening
  eye contact
  no interrupting
  asking questions

One friend is trying to tell another about a problem with a homework assignment	Poor Listening
	  interrupting with comments
	  no questions—uninterested
	  changing the subject

- Students may be encouraged to create their own cards.

FEELINGS WORD WHEEL

The Feelings Word Wheel is an engaging activity that asks students to reflect on their affective vocabulary and develop a "retrieval system" so that they do not have to wade through a long alphabetical list when their emotions are running high.

CR-CT Skills Developed

Comprehension

Analysis

Procedure

- All students have the Affective Vocabulary List shown below.
- The teacher draws a circle on the board. How many ways can we group these words, starting with positive and negative emotions?

Affective Vocabulary List

Positive	Negative
happy	sad
proud	angry
calm	disappointed
hopeful	confused
excited	hurt
loving	afraid

- Within the positive and negative sides we can group subsets, or similar terms, to help in locating them in the future.
- The teacher draws a circle on the board. Students group and illustrate word wheels for conflict resolution folders and for the conflict resolution table.

ACE PARAPHRASING

Students may use this effective, memorable tool to help them focus on the various parts of effective paraphrasing.

CR-CT Skills Developed

Active listening

Communication

Metacognition

Procedure

- The teacher introduces ACE Paraphrasing:
  Affirm—acknowledge facts, validate
  Clarify—ask questions (not to judge)
  Express—to show understanding; to check understanding

- The teacher and students role-play the following. Students read:

  I've been sick for two weeks and I walked into the class and the substitute gave us a test. I told him I couldn't take the test. The substitute sent me to the principal's office before I could explain.

- Teacher paraphrases, using the ACE method:
  A—Affirm:

  I think you seem a bit frustrated and upset because you got punished for being sick, and therefore not prepared to take the test. Am I correct?

C—Clarify:

Apparently you didn't get a chance to explain the situation, right? Am I right about what happened and how you feel?

E—Express:

Okay, you're upset because you were sick and you had no time to make up missed work and the substitute didn't understand, so he punished you. Am I right about what you are saying and how you feel?

- Students can use the following scenarios for ACE Paraphrasing:
  1. "I just found out that we are going to Italy to visit my Grandmother this summer. I thought I was going to be on the summer team, but I guess I can't do it."
  2. "Rachel told me she was having a party this weekend and then I never heard from her. Lots of people have told me that it was a great party. I don't know if I should say anything to her or not. She always comes to my house when I have a party."
  3. "Jamal was supposed to come over last night to work on the report. I finished my part of the report. I think it's pretty good, too."

- Students may write their own scenarios to use for ACE Paraphrasing practice.

THE ALTERNATIVE "I" MESSAGES

I used to pretend that I was sick so I could stay home from school.
Now when I'm sick, I pretend that I'm okay so I can go to school.
—High school student

Reviewing the "I" message in Chapter 1, the Assertive "I" is a three-part message that helps students effectively assert their feelings about a problem and explain why they feel that way without assigning blame and inviting defensiveness or aggressive reactions.

CR-CT Skills Developed

Analysis

Active listening

Communication

Procedure

- The teacher introduces the Assertive "I" Message by using the following example on the board:

I feel disappointed *when* you lose your journal *because* I know how hard you worked on it and how important it was to you.

The three essential parts of the Assertive "I" Message are identified:
1. I feel . . .
2. when . . .
3. because . . .
   Another example would be:

   I feel frustrated when you are late for class because I know you missed important information that you will need later.

   "I" messages introduce feelings and reasons useful in resolving an issue. "You" Messages are interpreted as attacking the other person.

- Students are asked to identify the *you* characteristics in the following:
  You always lose things. Now you have lost your journal.
  You are always late. I won't repeat the assignment.

  Which statements would evoke a more positive response?

- Students can practice Assertive "I" stems like the ones below:
  I feel *(state feeling)* about *(state event)*. Or
  When *(state action)*, I feel *(state feeling)*
  Because *(state reason)*

Alternative "I" Messages

The Alternative "I" is much like the Assertive "I" but with somewhat more casual vocabulary and flexible structure.

It bothers me when people call me Mike. It's not my name. Call me Michael.

I get frustrated when I have to wait and I miss the bus. Can't we leave earlier?

I get upset when we're late.

Call me Nick because I like my nickname.

I get frustrated when we're late because we miss the bus.

- Students analyze how these "I" messages are different.
  Students may be more comfortable with *I get* rather than *I feel* in a casual situation.
- Students discuss how removing the *you* affects the sentence in the Alternative I.

THE BLAME FRAME

Truth is generally the best vindication against slander.
—Abraham Lincoln

It is always tempting to jump to judgment and blame in order to find the solution, but it is seldom effective. In the Blame Frame, students will practice reserving judgment to keep the lines of communication open.

CR-CT Skills Developed

Active listening

Communication

Analysis

Procedure

- The teacher reviews the Assertive "I" Message by reminding students of the three parts:
  I feel . . .
  when . . .
  because . . .

- It is sometimes more natural to use:
  I get . . .
  when . . .
  because . . .

- Students use the following scenarios to write a three-part Assertive "I" message (either *I feel* or *when*) and a Blame Frame (a personal blame or a *You* message).

- The teacher draws student attention to the following:

  A friend of yours tells everyone a secret that you trusted him with. "You lied and betrayed me by telling everyone."

  What message is sent in the above Blame Frame?
  How is conflict resolution affected by such Blame Frames?
  Change the above to make it into a positive or Assertive "I" message.
  "I felt betrayed because I trusted you; I thought we were friends."

- Students work on the following scenarios to design Assertive "I" messages and Blame Frames.
  Other scenarios that may be included are as follows:

  1. A student demands that everyone do a project that some don't want to do.
  2. One student does work that is unacceptable.

The Blame Frame

Scenario	The Blame (You) Frame	The Solution (I) Frame
A student is on the computer and another demands that he/she get off so they can use it.	"You can't tell me what to do. Besides, you should've finished a while ago."	"I can see you need this but I have to finish what I'm doing. I'll let you know when I'm done."
A student hears that another student is spreading lies about him/her.		"I'm getting confused. Can you explain to me what you told everyone about me?"
One student in a group criticizes everything that the others come up with.	"All you do is criticize. You don't do anything else. We don't want you in our group."	
One student in a group doesn't participate or share his/her ideas.		

3. A student gets mad because another in the group offers criticism of an idea.
4. One student threatens to get even with another student if he doesn't get his way.
5. One student thinks another student has intentionally shoved him in the hall.
6. One student thinks another student was laughing at him in the hall.
7. One student makes fun of another student's aunt because she has an accent.
8. One student in a group invites all but one group member out to work on a project.
9. One student in a group demands that the others snub a new student.
10. One student in class trips a younger student in the hall and tells the others to lie about it.

- When completed, students read and defend their responses by telling how each would influence communication and resolution outcomes.

Portfolio Pick

APPRECIATION AND AFFIRMATION "I" MESSAGES

We shall show mercy, but we shall not ask for it.
—Winston Churchill

Introduction

"I" messages are very effective for maintaining or initiating a friendship as well as saving one. In this activity students have an opportunity to write each other an appreciation "I" message. This is a good classroom community building activity.

CR-CT Skills Developed

>Communication
>
>Writing
>
>Empathy

Procedure

- The teacher models: "I feel happy when you get involved in your conflict resolution lessons because these are important life skills. When you appreciate each other and work well together I feel hopeful about your future because friendships are the true riches in life."
- The teacher asks what is different about the above "I" message.
- The teacher explains that today each student is going to write a classmate an Affirmation "I" message. The directions are:
- Everyone writes their name on top of the paper and numbers every other line for the number of students.
- The paper is circulated to every desk. Students may or may not sign their names after they write what they appreciate most about their classmate on one of the numbered lines below the classmate's name.
- The paper may be kept in students' portfolios.

Extending Activities: Response Journals

How can the Affirmation "I's" help you when you're in a conflict with a classmate?

Portfolio Pick

BRAINSTORMING BREAKTHROUGH

After reviewing the rules of creative brainstorming, students begin to brainstorm solutions to real social conflicts, which is often the most compelling way to teach any skill as well as being the most emotionally charged.

CR-CT Skills Developed

Divergent thinking

Active listening

Communication

Procedure

- Students review the rules of brainstorming (generate as many ideas as possible, don't evaluate, and don't set limitations).

- Students then work in small groups for five minutes to generate solutions to the following scenarios:
  1. The school choir has been invited to compete at the state level, but the school board will not approve the funds for the trip. How can we raise enough money to attend the competition?
  2. Gymnastics might be discontinued as a school sport because some people think it is too dangerous. How would you convince them otherwise?
  3. Jarret and Don are best friends. Don has previously agreed to go to a friend's house on the day of Jarret's birthday party.

- Student groups review their brainstorm solution lists with the class.

"PEACING" IT TOGETHER

Your luck is how you treat people.
—Bridget O'Donnell

Finally, in the last part of the conflict resolution process we must choose solutions, combine solutions, and synthesize a resilient resolution.

CR-CT Skills Developed

Active listening

Communication

Evaluation

Synthesis

Procedure

- When students have exhaustively explored the brainstorm session they begin by intuitively choosing good solutions. When simple choices are made students review the solutions *not* chosen to see if any could be combined to form a suitable solution.

    The criteria for a resilient solution should start with our Safe, Smart, and Successful foundation guidelines. Obviously, no solution that endangers anyone or makes things worse should be chosen.

- Students then brainstorm or add other win–win guidelines—for example, the best solution:
  Helps prevent future problems
  Is fair to all
  Meets the needs of the disputants
  Is worth the time or expense

- Students construct a list and compare solutions to the criteria they've designed and formulate a plan to evaluate using the various proposed solutions.

Portfolio Pick

CONFLICT JOURNALISM

To help students understand the nature and frequency of conflict, they may conduct conflict interviews of each other as well as willing friends or family members.

CR-CT Skills Developed

Communication

Active listening

Paraphrasing

Critical questioning

Procedure

- Using the reporter's form provided below, students interview any friends or family about the types of conflicts they experience and how they would like to resolve them.

Conflict Interview Form

Ask an adult to tell you about a conflict he or she had with another person. Write down the adult's answers to these questions, paying special attention to how the conflict was resolved.

1. How did the conflict start? _____
2. What was the conflict about? _____
3. What did you think the problem was? _____
4. What did the other person think the problem was? _____
5. How was the conflict resolved? _____
6. Were you happy with the resolution or outcome? _____

• Students should compare their findings.

Portfolio Pick

CONFLICT RESOLUTION TABLE

> *To have ideas is to gather flowers: To think is to weave them into garlands.*
> —Anne S. Swetchine

In order for students to use their skills, Conflict Resolution tables or corners must be available in the classroom. The mediation table may be a desk or even just chairs in a back corner of a room or an entire room or office. The essential thing is that the students have a place to go to resolve misunderstandings and conflicts and that the designated place is equipped with the conflict resolution steps, affective vocabulary list, and paper and pencils.

CR-CT Skills Developed

Critical thinking

Integrative thinking

Procedure

• Students are introduced to the concept of a mediation table and mediation tools. Students decide on which tools go in the mediation areas. The list should include:
A sign-in sheet
A word wheel
A conflict resolution plan sheet (following)
A chart of the conflict resolution steps (following)
Students may help assemble and decorate the area.

Conflict Resolution Plan Record Sheet

Name: _____

Problem: _____

_____

Each disputant's understanding of the problem: _____

_____

Steps taken: _____

_____

Evaluation: _____

_____

Alternative if plan fails: _____

_____

Conflict Resolution Steps

Step 1: Review ground rules

Step 2: Each person tells their story (no interruptions)

Step 3: Each person asks clarification questions and uses ACE Paraphrasing to check their understanding of the problem.

Step 4: Brainstorming—creating a solution

Step 5: Choosing resolutions that both parties can agree to

CONFLICT RESOLUTION TOOLBOX TOUR

The teacher asks students to review the conflict resolution steps introduced in Part 1 of Chapter 4. Students then reflect on any changes in the ways they react to conflict.

CR-CT Skills Developed

Metacognition

Integrative thinking

Summarizing

Procedure

- Students create a list of conflict resolution steps and strategies for the CR-CT portfolio.
- After listing the essential tools, students briefly describe each tool or give an example of each step.

Portfolio Pick

Conflict Resolution Toolbox Tour

Conflict resolution styles:

    Avoid appeal to authority

    Win–lose

    Win–win

The Three R's

    Reset

    Restate

    Reframe

Ground Rules

    No name calling

    No interrupting

    Attack problems, not people

    Take turns

    Use active listening skills

Portfolio Pick

CHAPTER 5

Lions and Tigers and Bears: No Problem

Lions and Tigers and Bears: No Problem provides activities to help us develop, enhance, and maintain cooperative learning and cooperative communication in the integrative-thinking classroom. We all know that learning is enhanced in a socially rich environment, but not every student arrives in our classroom ready and willing to engage in productive social co-cognition. Building on the skills we've developed through conflict resolution training, we now develop conflict positive cooperation and communication skills. Included are activities that help students create a sense of community among classmates and appreciation of the diverse talents in their classroom and in their communities.

CONFLICT-POSITIVE COMMUNICATION (CPC)

Conflict begins at the moment of birth.
—Jean Baker Miller

Conflict-Positive Communication (CPC) is introduced to students to directly facilitate transfer of their conflict resolution skills to the cooperative learning setting. We begin by reviewing the concept of conflict-positive communication from previous sections.

CR-CT Skills Developed

Integrative thinking

Divergent thinking

Analysis

Active listening

Communication

Procedure

- The teacher introduces the concept of Conflict-Positive Communication: Conflict-Positive Communication is constructive (builds relationships rather than breaks them) and productive (leads to expanded understanding if and when different perspectives arise).
- Students generate or review examples (from Blame Frame, Assertive "I"s and other activities) of conflict-positive versus conflict-negative communication styles.
- A Conflict-Positive Communication concept map is developed and then discussed after the teacher models it on the board using as many conflict resolution tools as possible: active listening, no put downs, no interruptions, clarifying, and paraphrasing.

    For instance, "Let's each brainstorm all that we can that is related to conflict positive-communication."

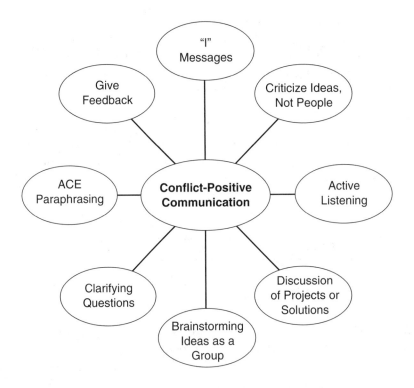

- Students identify the many ways our conflict resolution skills can increase communication and cooperation, even when we're not in a conflict.
- The teacher asks, "What is cooperative learning?" Students' responses might include sharing and working together.
- The teacher introduces cooperative learning as distinct from just sitting in a group working next to each other. Is mere proximity cooperative learning? What makes cooperative learning different? How do we cooperate?
- The teacher presents the following traits of cooperative learning:

1. Positive interdependence: Group members depend on each other and themselves to work toward the group goals. Each group member has a role that contributes to the success of the group's work. Each group member is concurrently responsible for contributing to the social and academic success of the team or group.
2. Face-to-face interaction is also considered an essential aspect of cooperative learning. Conflict-positive communication is the hallmark of productive face-to-face interaction in cooperative group work.
3. Individual accountability: At any given time each group member should be able to describe the group's work and the content that is being studied. Active listening and paraphrasing are important skills for assessing each group member's understanding.

- Students review the CPC brainstorm to identify how each of these CPC skills will be useful for cooperative group work sessions. Our CPC skills are the same skills we need for successful group interaction.
- A large class CPC skills chart should remain posted in the classroom. Individual charts may be placed in journals or portfolios.

Portfolio Pick

CONFLICT-POSITIVE COOPERATION PLAN: SKILL STORM

Alone we can do so little; together we can do so much.
—Helen Keller

Students help to create a conflict-positive cooperation chart using the Conflict-Positive Cooperation maps. These charts will serve as a template from which to develop plans and evaluations of our cooperative group work.

CR-CT Skills Developed

Active listening

Communication

Metacognition

Integrative thinking

Procedure

- In order to develop cooperative interaction in a way that benefits all learners we need to incorporate our conflict and cooperative skills. We will develop a chart to keep in the room which will reinforce our CPC skills and keep us on the right track when we're working.

- Using the CPC maps (from the brainstorm activity in the previous CPC activity) the class lists the CPC skills on the board; students contribute to the list.

- The class groups related items in order, such as:
  Active listening
  Not interrupting
  Clarifying questions
  ACE paraphrasing
  Brainstorming
  Using "I" messages
  Giving feedback
  Offering ideas and solutions
  Criticizing ideas, not people
  Collaborating to look at ideas (integrative problem solving)

- In groups, students design a CPC Chart with all of the CPC skills listed. The final version of the CPC Chart is posted in the room for reference when needed, replacing or supplementing the CPC brainstorm map.

  The class may discuss the following: As we work we need different tools to complete a project or solve a problem. For instance, for everyone to be informed of every piece of the project we can use summarizing and paraphrasing and clarifying messages, too.

  During the project we need to question our progress. We can give feedback, remembering to criticize ideas, not people.

  If the project requires that we find or choose a solution, what CPC skills would we use?

  We can use our CPC skills to brainstorm, problem solve, and mediate choices and solutions.

- Finally, since everyone in the group has to be individually accountable for the information your group works on, which skills can we use to make sure that each of our group members could explain our project if chosen by the teacher to represent the group? Summarizing, paraphrasing, and clarifying would be appropriate choices. Each student should have an individual copy of the CPC Chart.

Portfolio Pick

COOPERATION CRUNCH TWISTER

> *Our race became a dominant form of life because
> we tended to help—not kill—one another.*
> —Robert Sylwester

In keeping with the tradition of all of our other twisters and brainstorms, the Cooperation Crunch Twister asks students to brainstorm great ways to *prevent* cooperation among students. We then reverse the items to see if we can add anything to our Conflict-Positive Cooperation plan.

CR-CT Skills Developed

Divergent thinking

Cooperation

Communication

Integrative thinking

Procedure

- Students are assigned to small groups. The teacher introduces the Cooperation Crunch Twister. The group is asked to brainstorm behaviors which reflect *uncooperative* behavior.
- The groups provide behaviors which harm group interaction; the teacher records them on the diagram provided below:

- After the chart is developed, one student from each group records the cooperation crunches for his or her group.
- After the discussion is closed and the twister is complete, students work in groups to reverse the listed items and compare these to the items already listed on the CPC Plan skill storm.
- New entries can be added to the CPC if teachers and students agree (for example, taking turns, controlling anger, no put-downs, and staying on task).

Portfolio Pick

FRAMING FEEDBACK

Many argue: not many converse.
—Louisa May Alcott

Students use the Blame Frame scenarios to practice using simple or complex messages and ACE Paraphrasing within the context of the cooperative group. Practicing these conflict-positive communication skills encourages students to phrase concerns, questions, and criticisms in a productive manner so that students focus on the task at hand without becoming passive or defensive.

CR-CT Skills Developed

Communication

Cooperation

Integrative thinking

Procedure

- The teacher initiates a review of ACE Paraphrasing and "I" messages in the CPC context. Two examples are provided:

Blame Frame—"You" Statements

"You didn't get enough books on Ancient Greece for us to begin the project."

"I" Statements

"I'm not sure we have enough books to begin our project. Do you think we need more?"

- Students identify which scenarios are more productive, and why.

    1. Sarah and Rosa are working on a social studies project. Sarah has been out of school for a week on a trip. She comes back and criticizes all of Rosa's work. Rosa responds.

*The bottom line for us is to prepare them for . . . successful lives . . .
and we'll do whatever is in our power to make that happen.*
HENRY ODI, COFOUNDER, S.T.A.R. ACADEMY. PHOTO: ELIZABETH COLLEY.

2. John borrows Malcom's bike and it is stolen. Malcom responds.
   - Use a blame frame "you" statement and an "I" statement for each.
   - Students may create similar scenarios; they are discussed in class.
   - Students may choose typical or common conflicts in order to practice "I" and "you" statements.

EACH ONE TEACH ONE

> *We remember 14% of what we hear, 22% of what we
> both see and hear, and 91% of what we teach.*
> —Michael Jones

Because individual accountability is an essential element in the cooperative classroom, Each One Teach One reminds students to be accountable for the lesson they are working on as a group. Each One Teach One is a quick strategy for reminding students of the individual accountability goals.

CR-CT Skills Developed

Summarizing

Paraphrasing

Communication

Procedure

- At any time when the teacher calls out "Each one teach one," all students are required to write a quick summary of what they've accomplished as a group. The teacher may select one or more to be paraphrased and discussed with the class.

HELP WANTED

Because the best-laid plans sometimes need revising and review as a project goes on, any member of a group can post a "Help Wanted" to bring everyone's attention to a stumbling block, point of confusion, or contention. In addition to fostering cooperative learning, Help Wanted is a fine metacognitive activity.

CR-CT Skills Developed

Metacognition

Listening

Procedure

- Students review previous cooperative team projects and any problem areas.
- Classmates offer solutions or recommendations from their experience.
- Each group designs a Help Wanted sheet to keep track of any problems or questions during a group project (for example, I can't find any books on Ghandi's childhood; I'm not sure whether I should do the display this way or another way).
- As students work they can fill out the Help Wanted sheet to trouble-shoot potential problems as a group during the team check-ins or check-outs.

COOPERATIVE METAQUEST: QUESTIONING OUR QUESTIONS

For the first four years no new enterprise produces profits.
Even Mozart didn't start writing music until he was four.
—Peter Drucker

Cooperative Metaquest is a cooperative team version of the Metaquest activity, which asks students to question themselves one last time before embarking on any problem solving.

CR-CT Skills Developed

Metacognition

Cooperation

Critical questioning

Analysis

Procedure

- The students are asked to individually review their Metaquest Charts from Chapter 2 and revise them for their group project.
- When each group has revised their chart, the classroom chart (combining the questions that each team has chosen) is assembled.

TEAM CHECK-OUT LIST

Democracy is based upon the conviction that there are
extraordinary possibilities in ordinary people.
—Harry Emerson Fosdick

A variation on the classroom Check-In and Check-Out, the teacher allows all cooperative group members to review progress, express concerns, ask questions, and summarize or paraphrase their assessment and understanding of the project or lesson.

CR-CT Skills Developed

Communication

Metacognition

Cooperation

Analysis

Procedure

- Depending on the type of content task they're working on at the time, students may help develop a master list of issues to consider when a team work session is completed or a unit is finished.
- During times designated by the teacher, students respond to the list. In addition to other items, a Check-Out List might include the following:

Check-Out List

Do we have the resources we need?

Are we/am I making progress as planned?

Is our project:

    organized?

    clear?

    interesting?

    creative?

    making reasonable conclusions?

Do we need to revise our plan?

Did everyone:

    contribute?

    participate?

    use CPC communication skills?

Did we/I solve all "help wanted" issues?

Does everyone understand the project well enough to present the Each One Teach One?

Were all conflicts resolved positively?

Goals, notes, and suggestions for next session?

COOPERATIVE CRITICAL INCIDENT REPORTS

When first working with cooperative groups, and occasionally after the groups are well established, the Cooperative Critical Incident Reports allow us to assess and share where we've been and where we're going. The reports ask students to reflect on their academic and conflict-positive communication progress.

CR-CT Skills Developed

Analysis

Communication

Cooperation

Procedure

- The teacher introduces the Critical Incident Report as a very fast, effective way to check-up on progress.
- Students are given the form below to complete individually. They are invited to share their responses with others if they feel confident about doing so.

Cooperative Critical Incident Report

Instructions: Write your responses to the items below. There are no right or wrong answers. Your responses will not be graded. You may share your responses with others only if you wish to do so.

1. The most important thing we learned, studied, discovered, or accomplished today was: _____

   _____

   _____

2. The skill we used most effectively was: _____

   _____

   _____

3. The skill we need more work on is: _____

   _____

   _____

4. The achievement goal we need to meet is: _____

   _____

   _____

5. The issue that I am confused/concerned about is: _____

   _____

   _____

This sheet may be kept in students' portfolios.

INTRODUCTION INTERVIEWS

> *If I don't have friends then I ain't got nothing.*
> —Billie Holiday

A classic community or team-building activity, Introduction Interviews allow people to be introduced to the class and to meet and learn something about each other. Ideally suited for the beginning of the school year, it may be done periodically throughout the year: students change rapidly and students view each other differently as they get to know each other more thoroughly. This proves to be an excellent listening activity, as well.

CR-CT Skills Developed

Active listening

Communication

Paraphrasing

Procedure

- The teacher asks the class to count off by fours, i.e., 1, 2, 3 and 4; 1, 2, 3, and 4, to establish groups.
- Students who are "1's" and "3's" sit next to each other; students who are "2's" and "4's" sit next to each other. This is done to break up close friends for the exercise.
- Students gather information about the person they have been assigned to and prepare to introduce their partner to the class. Students are asked to interview each other. The first interviewer has four minutes. When the time is called the pair switch roles. The interviewer may only give information their partner wishes to share with the class.
- When individual interviews are completed, the students introduce each other to the class.

Introduction Interviews can be repeated throughout the year using different sets of people with different stimulus questions, such as: favorite holiday, favorite movie, favorite food, where you would like to visit, who you would like to meet, the most interesting thing about you that others aren't aware of, and how you have changed this year.

CIRCLE THE ELEPHANT

Everyone has a piece of the truth.
—Gandhi

After reviewing the classic tale about the Blind Men and the Elephant, students are introduced to Circle the Elephant. This exercise asks students to describe an aspect of their group project on which they gained a new perspective or acquired new information.

CR-CT Skills Developed

Analysis of perspective

Active listening

Paraphrasing

Communication

Procedure

Cooperative learning is presented to the class as a way to increase our understanding and gain a larger perspective. The metaphor of circling the elephant or getting more information is presented through the tale of the Blind Men and the Elephant, presented below.

The Tale

Long ago in a far away land there were six blind men who became good friends. They learned to explore and understand their environment in different ways—by carefully touching, listening, smelling, and tasting. One day they heard the news that there was a new elephant at the prince's castle nearby. The blind men were curious about this huge animal.

The blind men all packed their bags and began the long trek to the castle. The guards greeted the blind men inside the castle gates and escorted them to the new elephant. At last, the men had a chance to find out, first hand, what a real elephant was like.

The first of the six friends walked over and carefully stroked the elephant's side. "This animal is rough and strong and wide—like a mud wall," he announced.

The second blind man touched the elephant's tusk. "This animal is as smooth and cold as ice and as sharp as a spear," he stated.

The third blind man, holding the elephant's ear, exclaimed, "This elephant is soft, thin, and flexible—like a huge leaf or a fan."

"No, no, no," exclaimed his friend, the fourth blind man, who was holding the elephant's trunk. "This animal is long and round like a huge snake."

"A snake?" the fifth blind man asked. "Did you say a snake? Most trees don't have this wide a base. This animal is like a tree with a huge round tree trunk rising up from the ground," he explained, running his hand around the elephant's leg.

The sixth blind man said, "This is neither as thick as a tree trunk nor as thin as a snake. This is more like a small rope," as he touched the elephant's tail. "And it doesn't go near the ground. What are you all talking about?"

The blind men began to argue about the nature of the elephant.

"The elephant is like a tree!" one exclaimed.

"No, it's like a rope," professed another.

"It's more like a cold, sharp sword," said another blind man.

"No, no, no, it's like a snake!" a blind man shouted.

Upon hearing the shouting, the prince and the guards came running.

"What is it?" asked the prince.

The blind men each explained their perception of the elephant and the problem.

"Who is right?" asked one blind man.

"You are all right and you are all wrong." the prince answered. "The elephant's tail is like a rope; his trunk is like a snake; his side is like a mud wall; his leg is like a tree; his tusk is like a cold sharp spear; and his ear is like a huge leaf. You may each circle the elephant and see your friends' perspectives," the prince suggested.

"Ah, ha!" said one blind man.

"Very interesting!" exclaimed another blind man, and the guards helped the men to mount the elephant for the long ride home.

- Students are asked to Circle the Elephant by interviewing each other about their understanding of the current assignment, either within the group or between groups, and return to their desks to note one new, interesting fact that they learned from their classmates.
- If students within the groups are studying different parts of a problem the circle interview may take place within the group. If not, the group members each send one reporter to interview members of another group and then return to their original team.
- When students have completed the Circle the Elephant interviews, the most interesting new fact or perspective is shared with the class.

COOPERATIVE CONSENSUS

One way to solve problems and/or make decisions is by building consensus. There are many decisions that are already made for students by teachers and staff. However, on occasions when the teacher believes it is appropriate to include student voices in problem solving or decision making, consensus may be the goal.

CR-CT Skills Developed

Integrative thinking

Communication

Active listening

Paraphrasing

Analysis

Procedure

- The teacher solicits and discusses a couple of definitions of *consensus* provided by students. Erroneous perceptions about consensus which the teacher should address are: (1) Consensus is *not* a majority vote, as in elections; (2) consensus is *not* a unanimous vote, indicating total agreement.

  Historically used by Native Americans and Quakers, the purpose of consensus is to get everyone to work together to decide on a course of action.

  A recent newspaper article or a school issue is chosen by the students or teacher to begin the discussion.

- Students discuss the issue in small groups.
- A group reporter summarizes the group's definition and understanding of the problem.
- Groups then work together spending five to ten minutes brainstorming to generate possible solutions or resolutions related to the issue.
- Each group chooses three to four solutions to share with the whole class.
- As groups share solutions the teacher writes responses on the board.
- Using our foundation criteria designed in a previous activity (the Safe, Smart, and Successful guidelines), we decide which solutions are best. Is the solution realistic? Is the solution fair to all? Is the solution safe? Can we combine solutions to reach a more balanced, stable solution?
- The class votes on proposed solutions, using the voting system given below.

Voting System

A raised fist means: I completely disagree.
One raised index finger means: I step aside. I don't love the idea but I'll go along; I will not help but I will step aside.
Two raised fingers means: lukewarm support.
Three fingers raised means: shows a vote of support, if not first choice.
Four fingers mean: strong support of the decision.

- Although all class members are not likely to agree completely on a single best choice, consensus is reached when there are no raised fists when the vote is taken.

• Students continue to communicate and clarify, provide options, and to vote until no raised fists appear during voting.

THE CPC CLASS MEETING

Absence of participation tends to produce lack of interest and concern on the part of those shut out. The result is a . . . lack of responsibility.
—John Dewey

As students become better at conflict-positive communication, their reward is increased self-responsibility and decision making. Class meetings are an effective tool for community or team building, problem solving and raising academic and social skills. The concept of consensus is reviewed.

CR-CT Skills Developed

Metacognition

Active listening

Communication

Procedure

• The class is arranged in a circle or semicircle to allow face-to-face communication to occur.

  The teacher engages students in a discussion, reviewing the conflict positive communication skills learned in previous lessons. They might include: eye contact; active listening; no put-downs; attack problems, not people; and clarification questions, among others. These are the essential communication skills for successful meetings, as well.

• The concept of consensus problem solving is reviewed.

  We will use these three criteria to make our meetings successful and productive:
  1. Content: Do we have the real issue? Does the issue deserve to be discussed by our class? Is the issue worthwhile?
  2. CPC Climate: Was our meeting characterized by conflict-positive communication and respect?
  3. CPC Process: Did we use our integrative problem solving skills? Did we consider all aspects of the problem?

• Students use the chart on the next page to review their meetings, keeping notes on all three areas (listed above) and what went well or what needs attention.

CPC Class Meeting

1. CPC Content: _____

_____

_____

2. CPC Climate: _____

_____

_____

3. CPC Process: _____

_____

_____

TOWN TEAMS

> *Where the people rule, discussion is necessary.*
> —William Howard Taft

In Town Teams, students are encouraged to identify a town team outside of school such as: a medical practice team, an EMR team, rescue squad, fire department, restaurant staff, office teams, school board, or a local softball team.

Students are assigned to interview members of an identified team to determine how the role each plays contributes to the group's mission. Students may interview in pairs or small groups if few teams are available. In advance of the interviews, students should design their questions and learn about successful interviewing techniques such as: make the person comfortable; make eye contact; listen actively; don't rush; phrase questions clearly; don't interview yourself; and other traits of conflict-positive communication.

CR-CT Skills Developed

Active listening

Paraphrasing

Summarizing

Procedure

- Students engage in a class brainstorm to identify potential teams in the area. The teacher may prompt the effort by citing a few possibilities.

- Students are asked to choose a town team and map out possible roles of the members within the team.

- Teams or members of teams are contacted for potential interviews. If possible, some team members might come to the classroom to explain their job and how it fits within a team, for example, a heavy equipment operator works as a part of construction team. Students often enjoy volunteering their parents.

- Students design interview questions to begin their projects and review how to use their CPC skills to ensure a successful interview. Sample questions are:
  What is your role?
  How do you work as a team?
  Could you do this job alone?
  How is being part of a team productive, rewarding, or frustrating?
  What makes a team successful?
  What have you learned from your team?

- When interviews are complete, students may present them in written or oral form to the class.

Portfolio Pick

INTRODUCTION TO CHECK-INS

I've worked with them and played with them. I've laughed with them,
and at times, I've even cried with them.
—Classroom teacher

The Check-In is one of the most powerful classroom strategies for increasing school attachment; enhancing peer relationships; increasing affective vocabulary; and enabling students to acknowledge destructive or distracting issues. Initially, Check-Ins may take up to fifteen minutes per session. When the procedure becomes routine, four to five minutes will suffice. Many teachers use Check-Ins on a daily basis; some find two to three per week to be adequate. Because it may take a week or two for students in a new classroom to feel comfortable with true Check-Ins, this activity may be a more appropriate version to begin the school year. Our research has shown that the Check-In is second only to conflict resolution education in terms of increasing levels of school attachment for students.

CR-CT Skills Developed

Active listening

Communication

Development of affective vocabulary

Procedure

- Teachers ask every student to think for a minute about the two things that they've done that they are most proud of. They are then asked to share a sentence or two about each choice. After a minute or so, the students take turns sharing.

- Other themes to introduce Check-Ins might be:
  Two things I hope to learn this year
  Two things most interesting about my family
  Two favorite hobbies or pastimes
  The two most important qualities in a friend
  My two favorite books
  My favorite actors
  My favorite athletes or sports

Procedure

- The teacher distributes the handout, "A List of Feelings" (attached).
- Each student is asked to pick the feeling that most closely describes the way they feel.
- Students are asked to briefly explain why they picked that word. They should use "I" statements such as, I feel . . .
- The students are reminded that explanations cannot reveal anything personal or embarrassing about anyone and they should be brief.
- Alternative arrangements will be made for issues which require additional time or which are inappropriate for a classroom setting (e.g., using conflict resolution or arranging a discussion at lunch).
- The teacher begins the Check-In by saying, "I feel excited today because we're starting a new activity in our classroom . . ."
- The Check-In moves quickly around the room.

List of Feelings

Words That Convey Positive Emotional Experiences

appeased	calm	cheerful	clever	excited
compassionate	enthusiastic	friendly	gracious	grateful
happy	hopeful	inspired	joyous	loving
loved	nice	proud	trusting	silly

Words That Convey Negative Emotional Responses

abandoned	afraid	alone	angry	anxious
ashamed	bored	beaten	cold	cruel
confused	depressed	fearful	foolish	disappointed
distrustful	exhausted	disgusted	frustrated	hurt
horrified	insulted	jealous	regretful	sad
spiteful	tense	timid		

KIDS CAN, WE CAN

After reading the story about "We Can," students pick a problem in their school, community, or world that they would like to focus on during the year. This should be a team effort.

CR-CT Skills Developed

Active listening

Communication

Cooperation

Procedure

- After reading and discussing the "We Can" story, students begin to brainstorm problems in their school or community that they may wish to work on.
- After the brainstorming session, students develop criteria for making their final project decision. Criteria should include the foundation criteria introduced earlier (Safe, Smart, and Successful) as well as criteria regarding feasibility, cost, time available, and possible impact, and other pros and cons. Examples of projects may include fixing up the playground or front of the school; visiting a senior citizens' center; recycling; sending letters to children in a war-torn country; or sending books and toys to a local homeless shelter.
- After choosing a Kids Can project, students brainstorm ways to approach the problem. This stage may require research and interviews. Often the people interviewed for the Town Teams activity become an inspiration or a resource.
- When students, family members, and teachers have agreed on a plan, students may begin to write letters and garner support. The plan is developed further.

We Can:
The Guy Polhemus Story

As a young man Guy Polhemus made a bet with a friend. He had promised to spend several evenings as a volunteer in a local soup kitchen if he lost the bet. He lost. As it turned out, this was great luck for Guy, an army of homeless families, and our environment. Reluctantly, Guy began showing up at the soup kitchen to do as he had promised.

"At the time I did not really want to do it," Mr. Polhemus said. "But after a while it opened my mind and opened my heart. I saw that I was almost as close to the street as these people [coming into the soup kitchens] were.

"A lot of these people just had a bad run of luck, and they didn't have a father or a mother or a brother to bail them out.

"I really wanted to do more (for them)."

One Sunday at the soup kitchen several people asked Mr. Polhemus to watch their "empties."

He suggested that they go somewhere and turn in the cans they had collected, but they told him they couldn't.

"What do you mean?" replied Mr. Polhemus. "There's a bottle bill law here. Turn them in."

Apparently, it wasn't that easy. Many stores refused to take back the cans they had sold.

He went to a store with several of his homeless friends and the owner of the store asked: "What are you doing? Trying to save the world?"

Often the homeless collected cans and bottles just hoping to get enough money for a cup of coffee, something to eat, a newspaper, or a toy for a child, but as the incident illustrated, they had nowhere to take the empties. Everyone Guy talked to told him he couldn't recycle the cans in New York. But Guy Polhemus decided to keep trying.

A shop owner explained to him that he'd have a line around the block "two miles long" and no room in his store if he took back the recyclable cans. Another shop owner told Polhemus that if he would just come get the cans out of his store, he could have them all.

That shop owner had a thousand dollars a week in aluminum cans to donate.

With the cans piling up, Mr. Polhemus decided that he needed a redemption center. He could keep the cans and bottles off the streets and out of landfills—and perhaps a few people off the streets as time went on.

That's when he decided to call his project WE CAN.

Mr. Polhemus also felt the redemption center could be a "touch-point," where people could get outreach services, such as legal help, that were unavailable to them on the streets or in the soup kitchen.

When you don't have an identity, a home, or an address, it is very hard to get a job. The redemption center could provide an address.

"It's a beginning," said Polhemus.

There were many times when Mr. Polhemus thought that his efforts would come to nothing. The bottlers were not enthusiastic about recycling at first. However, WE CAN has, over the course of years, paid out almost $25 million to the poor and homeless. The organization employs dozens of previously unemployed homeless people at the redemption center and on the recycling trucks and has offered free services to many others.

In addition to the environmental and human benefits of Polhemus's efforts, the public has been informed regarding recycling and homeless issues, especially in the schools where WE CAN boxes stand ready to collect discarded cans and bottles.

Mr. Polhemus has received many awards, among them the Cranes Business Review, The Hope of New York, the Temple Award for Creative Altruism, the National Environmental Award, New York City Club's Earth Day Award, the Builders of Manhattan Award, and the Holland Society's Award for Distinguished Achievement.

CPC PROJECT PLANS

Students work together to draw up a Conflict-Positive Communication (CPC) Project Plan. The basic plan can be modified for each group project, but will serve as a template for organizing cooperative team work.

CR-CT Skills Developed

Analysis

Metacognition

Procedure

- The teacher introduces Project Planner, a design to be used whenever a new cooperative team project is initiated.
    The essential elements include:

    1. Description of the project
    2. Appropriate sequence
    3. Materials and resources required
    4. CPC skills useful for harmonious progress (for example, active listening, paraphrasing, or circling the elephant)
    5. Assignment of roles
    Resource persons
    Reporters
    Checkers
    Project coordinator
    CPC coach (encourages use of CPC skills)

Cooperative Project Planner

1. Project Description _____

_____

2. Individual Jobs _____

_____

3. Project Plan Sequence

    Step 1 _____

    Step 2 _____

    Step 3 _____

4. Materials and Resource List _____

5. CPC skills to be used for productive communication among team members _____

    _____

6. Team member roles

    Resource person _____

    Project coordinator _____

    CPC skill coach _____

    Other _____

Portfolio Pick

_____

THE VOCABULARY OF UNDERSTANDING

Never apologize for showing feeling.
When you do, you apologize for the truth.
—B. Disraeli

One of the most frustrating roadblocks to communication is a limited affective vocabulary. Many conflicts could be successfully resolved if they could be explained. Not only are some of the vocabulary words foreign to students, but it is even more difficult to choose the appropriate term when upset by a conflict.

CR-CT Skills Developed

Communication

Affective vocabulary

Procedure

- The teacher poses the following questions:

  "Has anyone ever been upset—but at a loss for words?"

  "Has anyone ever been frustrated and angry and unable to explain what they were feeling?"

- Students respond to the questions.

- The teacher then introduces the Word-a-Day Activity by giving the following directions:

  Each student is responsible for identifying and defining a new word each day. The definition should be placed in their conflict resolution journals by using it in a sentence or reflecting on an incident which involved the word.

- The class is asked to brainstorm words that fit in "I" messages. Examples are: angry, confused, disappointed, hurt, tired, thrilled, and hopeful. Students may refer to the List of Feeling handout (see pages 221–222).

- When the list is deemed adequate, the teacher arranges the class into five groups, one for each day of the week.

- The activity begins on Monday with the teacher writing the Group 1 word on the corner of the board. The same is done for Group 2 on Tuesday, and the activity continues throughout the week, ending on Friday with the word for Group 5. Each group is responsible for writing the definition for their word on the board and using it in a sentence for the class. The word sentence may be related to content-area studies (for example, "the general was disappointed . . .").

- On a weekly basis students may be given time to use the new words in their journals.

COMMON GROUND

> *Individualism and collectivism must have equal power.*
> —Michael G. Fullan

An effective team building activity, Common Ground shows students all the interesting things they have in common with classmates and, at the same time, shows them how different we are in many ways.

CR-CT Skills Developed

Analysis of multiple perspectives

Procedure

- Students move tables and chairs to the back of the room to create an open area. An auditorium or courtyard work well, too.

- Students make a line down the middle of the floor using chalk or tape. One side of the room is designated as the YES side; the other side is designated the NO side.

- The students are told that everyone who has ever been out of the country should stand on the "yes" side. Students comply.

- If time permits, students are asked where they have traveled; they discuss responses.

- The activity continues with the teacher asking that anyone who answers "yes" to any questions should go to that side of the center line:
  Anyone who has a pet
  Anyone who speaks more than one language
  Anyone who plays an instrument
  Anyone who has a hobby
  Anyone who likes music
  Anyone who doesn't eat meat
  Anyone who doesn't eat vegetables
  Anyone who does volunteer work
  Anyone who recycles
  Anyone who has a garden
  Anyone who has siblings
  Anyone who has an interesting friend

- The following questions are posed after the students respond to the above questions:

  "Have you ever met anyone with whom you didn't have *anything* in common?"
  "Have you ever met anyone with whom you had *everything* in common?"
  "What interesting information have you learned about a classmate?"

BEATING BIAS

> *Prejudice is the reason of fools.*
> —Voltaire

Bias and stereotyping are explored as thinking problems that affect both the biased thinker and those he thinks about, as well.

CR-CT Skills Developed

Metacognition

Analysis

Procedure

- The teacher offers a definition of "bias"—an inclination or tendency to perceive things in a slanted way. The biases we have may be a product of our experiences. For instance, the dislike and distrust of all dogs may be attributable to having been bitten by a dog; your fondness of strawberry ice cream may be due to early associations you had with the flavor.

- The teacher introduces a related word, "stereotype" or "stereotyping," that comes from one of the oldest forms of letter-press printing. Stereotype was a cast made of letters that was then filled with molten lead. The cast lead letters were used to imprint newspapers, magazines, and books. All paper that came in contact with the lead letters was imprinted in the same way.

- Students respond verbally or in writing to the following questions pertaining to stereotyping:

   How is the stereotype machine a metaphor for how people stereotype each other?
   Which lead letters do we carry around? How do we "print" on each other?
   How do we essentially print-over or ignore what a person has written about themselves or their individual characteristics when we stereotype?
   How can we learn to put our lead letters down?
   What are more useful tools for understanding people?
   How can we pick up more useful tools for understanding people?

- The teacher writes BEWARE OF BIAS AND STEREOTYPING on the board.

   The teacher asks, "What are the words that clue us in to biases and stereotyping?" For instance:
   "They all . . ."
   "Those people always . . ."
   "Those people like . . ."
   "They all dislike . . ."

- How do we stereotype with our choice of language?

   Other lead letters are "Oh, he's the exception," and any other statement that labels all of the evidence that doesn't agree with your lead letters as "just an exception" to minimize its truth as proof that you are wrong. Students may add to the list.

- The teacher next tells the class: "We can help change the sign to: BEATING BIAS by asking ourselves or others critical questions such as, "If we ignore opposing evidence by labeling it an exception, have we walked in their moccasins?" "Would we behave in a different way if we were in a different culture under different circumstances?" Again, students may offer suggestions.

Extending Activities: Response Journals

How do I lead-letter or label myself?

How do others label me?

How does it feel to be labeled?

LEAD LETTER DAYS

What's in a name? That which we call a rose
by any other name would smell as sweet.
—Shakespeare

Based on our metaphor from stereotyping, we will label each other with lead letters based on a classic activity that began with Jane Elliott, the now famous teacher in the "Eye of the Storm" documentary. This type of experience has been shown to increase empathy and academic achievement by increasing understanding and analysis of others' perceptions.

CR-CT Skills Developed

Analysis of multiple perspectives

Procedure

- Students write a letter to parents explaining stereotyping, the lead letter metaphor and our Lead Letter days: Lead letters are symbols for those who are stereotyped. Half the class will be wearing symbolic lead letter labels for half of the day; the other half of the class will wear the lead letters an equal amount of time. Parents should be invited to ask questions, or may choose to request that their child not participate if they are concerned by the nature of the activity.
- Each student chooses a label from a box filled with labels, half of which are labeled Lead Letter and half of which are labeled Red Letter.
- The Lead Letter students will sit in the back of the room and be required to do everything last. They should silently examine how they feel when they've been labeled with the lead letters of stereotyping.

- For the prescribed time allotment, Lead Letter students will sit in the back of the room. They will not be chosen to participate in class discussions. If one is chosen to answer a question or make a comment, the teacher will ask, "Can anyone find anything wrong with that Lead Letter comment?" and allow only Red Letter students to respond, or ask Red Letter students to paraphrase the Lead Letter student's comment. The Red Letter students' insights are complimented. The Lead Letter students' contributions are ignored.

- Lead Letter students are systematically ignored and judged more harshly throughout the session. Red Letter students are praised and encouraged throughout the session.

- The students reverse roles; the labeling process is repeated as every Lead Letter student switches labels with a Red Letter student.

- At the end of the session, all students will remove labels and process the experience. *It is essential that students do not leave the session without the processing step.*
  Questions might be:

  How did you feel as a Lead Letter student?
  How did you feel as a Red Letter student?
  What was hard about being a Lead Letter student?
  What made you angry?
  Did anyone feel they were accepting the Lead Letter label and giving up?
  How do we sometimes label ourselves and others?
  How did the questions asked of the class make you feel?

- All students should describe their experiences in an essay, seeking implications from the experience.

Portfolio Pick

GOING GLOBAL

Going Global asks students to research cultural traditions and how they may create cooperation and understanding or become the source of misunderstandings. These cultural differences may be interesting or devastating, depending on how we approach and attempt to understand them.

CR-CT Skills Developed

Active listening

Communication

Main idea

Procedure

Students are introduced to the concept of cultural differences in communication patterns: Conflict-positive communication may vary slightly from culture to culture. In all cultures finding a positive, peaceful, win–win way to communicate is important; however, it is not always that simple. In cultures all over the country and the world people may show respect and greet each other in different ways.

In many countries such as Italy and Spain, parts of the Middle East, and America, people greet each other with a kiss on the cheek or both cheeks. In Indonesia, however, it is considered extremely rude and even frightening to touch the head of a friend in any way. Children in France shake hands when they meet, like many American adults. Children in Japan and Malaysia may bow instead. Many Hindus place their palms together as they bow slightly and whisper, "Namaste."

In many parts of the world, shaking the head from side to side means no. However, in Bulgaria shaking the head side to side means yes and nodding up and down means no. In Greece nodding up and closing the eyes means no. Although good-bye and adios are derived words which mean "God be with you," they do not sound alike. They do, however, all say the same thing. In Japan it is considered bad luck to say good-bye; everyone says, please go and come back. In some cultures, women wear veils over their faces when out in public and have conversations with men only when they are married. Many women have to walk behind their spouses.

Some Japanese people believe that the eyes are "windows to the inner self" (Harris, 1998) and therefore may close their eyes if the "conversation topic is important or strained" (Harris, 1998). Although the intent is to concentrate and reflect on what is being said it is easy to see how an American could confuse this action with not paying attention. In addition, some cultures consider slurping and burping to be normal dining behavior whereas we might consider this quite rude. As well, people of some cultures do not like body contact but prefer a distant bow. A big friendly American hug or an arm around the shoulder would be considered an affront—a rude, aggressive imposition (Harris, 1998).

- Students work in groups of two to three and interview each other to provide a list of different customs they grew up with or experienced in their travels. They share with the class (for example, saying to each other "Bunny, bunny, rabbit, rabbit," an Irish greeting on the first day of the month). Kissing both cheeks of a close friend to say hello, giving a thumbs-up sign, or giving high-five hand slaps may be considered rude in many cultures. How might a wink be interpreted?
- Students share interesting aspects of their reports and interviews with the class.

Extending Activities: Response Journals

What universal greeting can be used when we meet people?

Does everyone smile?

Portfolio Pick

_____

CULTURE CLASH

When I was born I was so surprised I couldn't talk for a year and a half.
—Gracie Allen

In Culture Clash students learn to act as part of a different culture with different customs and attempt to negotiate and communicate with another group, representing yet another culture, about which they know very little. The resulting confusion and frustrations among these classmates and friends make this an important activity for increasing awareness about cultural communication differences.

CR-CT Skills Developed

Main idea

Communication

Procedure

- Students are asked to count off from one to four. All 1's, 2's, 3's, and 4's gather in the corners of the room with their culture, identified below.
- Each group has time to review their new culture, learn their new communication patterns and customs. Each new culture must have time to practice their new communication patterns and write rules in a notebook. Each culture makes ten trading cards (on index cards) with their culture's name and symbol on it as well as their colors (e.g., a flag or stripes) and then gives these cards to the teacher.
- After the cards are collected from each group, each culture is given ten assorted cards, two or three of each color.
- When the cultures are brought together, each culture must try to bargain to get their color culture cards back from the groups, respecting their cultural norms, traditions, customs, and communication rules. No one in any culture is allowed to break ranks by explaining culture clashes or customs to the other group members.
- When the teacher decides that the bargaining is over, the class returns to their seats to process their travels to another culture: How was it frustrating? How was it funny? What was most interesting?

Culture No. 1: The UNOS

Colors—black and white

Spoken language—none . . . only signs and gestures

Symbol and flag—"U"

Cultural characteristics:

UNOS speak to outsiders only when they are spoken to first.

UNOS close their eyes and shake their heads from side to side to greet new friends; up and down means no physical contact is permitted.

UNOS never point to anything. They consider that quite rude. They only point at dangerous criminals in their culture. When they wish to draw attention to something, they wave it in front of the others or gesture toward it with a full hand, never with a pointed finger.

UNOS consider any sound to be quite rude; therefore, they are forced to cut off communication when noise is involved.

Culture No. 2: The PEEK-A-BOOS

Colors—Yellow and orange

Spoken language—none, only signs and gestures

Symbol and flag—an eye

Cultural characteristics:

PEEK-A-BOOS say hello to everyone they meet by pointing at them and waving to them, although they avoid physical contact.

Head nodding up and down means yes.

Head nodding side to side means no.

PEEK-A-BOOS point at whatever they are attempting to communicate about and make lots of noise to show that they are friendly and paying attention (laughing, hissing, clicking, and direct eye contact).

PEEK-A-BOOS consider direct eye contact, friendly pointing, waving, and gesturing to be friendly behavior. Anything else is considered snobbery, and they therefore avoid further communication with offenders.

Culture No. 3: THE HUG-A-BOOS

Colors—red and pink

Spoken language—none, only signs and gestures

Symbol and flag—a heart

Cultural characteristics:

HUG-A-BOOS consider noises quite rude and instead smile and hug whoever they meet.

HUG-A-BOOS hold the forearm of whoever they are trying to communicate with. In any communication they try to keep direct eye contact.

HUG-A-BOOS always wear a heart on their sleeve and in their palms. While attempting communication, HUG-A-BOOS show their heart by holding their palm up to the other's face, about one foot away.

Culture No. 4: THE LOGOS

Colors—brown and green

Spoken language—none, only signs and gestures

Symbol and flag—a tree on a green background

Cultural characteristics:

The LOGOS never make direct eye contact: it's considered quite rude.

The LOGOS close their eyes and shake their heads from side to side to greet new friends.

Head shaking from side to side means yes.

Head nodding up and down means no.

The LOGOS use small logs or branches to point at anything (a pencil may be used in a pinch), never a hand or a finger which is considered quite rude.

LOGOS are indifferent about sounds and physical contact but any attempt at direct eye contact or pointing of fingers and hands is considered a direct insult or attack.

- After the new cultures have had time to communicate and negotiate, they are brought back together as a class to discuss the experiences and how communication and cultures can clash without ample understanding.

DYNAMIC DIFFERENCES

Laws alone cannot secure freedom of expression; in order that every man present his views without penalty, there must be a spirit of tolerance in the entire population.
—Albert Einstein

We have considered the importance of considering multiple perspectives and all aspects of a problem through numerous activities and academic exercises. Respecting differences takes us one step closer to an appreciation of our human diversity.

CR-CT Skills Developed

Active listening

Appreciation of diversity

Procedure

- Students each interview three classmates and write a short summary about their most interesting traits, talents, pet names, trips taken, etc. on index cards.
- When all interviews are complete, students highlight the interesting facts cards and share some interesting facts about their classmates, with their classmates' permission.
- When the interviews are completed, students are asked to discuss what made the list—were they only the things which the interviewer and interviewee had in common or were differences interesting, as well? How many of the facts that made the list were "difference" facts (for example, a strange pet or hobby, or a trip to an exotic place where most of us haven't been). How many things were the things we all have in common (such as food and clothing)?
- Students share the most interesting facts and the most surprising, and analyze how differences may make life and relationships more interesting.

STRANDED WITH SAME SAM

In order to be irreplaceable one must always be different.
—Coco Chanel

Students consider how a completely homogeneous culture might be limiting to creativity, productivity, and even survival.

CR-CT Skills Developed

Divergent thinking

Inferential thinking

Procedure

- The teacher asks students what would happen if they were stranded on the island of Same Sam—with people who were exactly like you in thoughts, language, and actions, like clones. If we all had the same favorite colors and food, if we all had the same name and were exactly alike, how would it affect our lives and survival?

- Students are asked to answer (in journals or discussion) the following:
  What other people and other skills, interests, or talents would you need to survive?
  How would it feel to be surrounded by hundreds of people who look and sound just like you?
  Who would you send for if you could? What talents would they bring?
  Would they all be exactly like you and the Same Sams, or would you choose different people with different skills, interests, opinions and perspectives?
  What would these people have in common with you? What would be different?
  What are the different things about your friends and community that you would miss? Are they things that the Same Sams wouldn't provide if they were all exactly like you?

THE PARENT PACK

Students in the conflict-positive classroom share their communication studies with parents and family members through this activity. Our research has shown that some of these skills will be used at home and outside of school with a few introductory support activities.

CR-CT Skills Developed

Integrative thinking

Communication

Procedure

- Working in groups, students design a poster and a parent letter to take home that describes their Conflict-Positive Communication and cooperation skills and goals, as well as including conflict-positive conflict resolution steps. A sample is provided below:

Dear Parents,

Our class/school has been studying conflict positive communication and cooperation skills. Students have developed and reached consensus about which skills to include in our parent pack. Please discuss these with your son or daughter when you have time.

Research shows that conflict resolution skills and social communication skills are essential—not only helping students avoid aggression and victimization, but also as life skills in general—often improving academic performance and fostering friendships. We all share the same goals of helping our students to be safe and educated.

As always, we thank you for your interest in our program.

Sincerely yours,

- Students design a Conflict-Positive Chart.
- Students design a take-home version of their Conflict Resolution Chart.
- After reviewing the CPC charts and the conflict resolution steps, students work together to reach a decision about what wording and design to use in the Parent Packs.

TOOLBOX TOUR

Students develop a summary of the essential skills for conflict-positive communication and reflect on those skills.

CR-CT Skills Developed

Metacognition

Procedure

- Students create a list of the skills and strategies that transform communication to integrative or conflict-positive communication.
- After listing the essential "tools" of conflict-positive communication, students give an example of each major strategy.
- If time permits, students reflect on any project, problem, or conflict that was transformed or improved by use of these "tools."

Portfolio Pick

Toolbox Tour

Conflict-Positive Communication:

    Active listening

    ACE paraphrasing

    Asking clarifying questions

    Giving feedback

    Using "I" messages

    Offering ideas

Conflict-Positive Cooperation:

    Criticizing ideas, not people

    Collaborating

    Creating consensus

    Brainstorming

Conflict-Positive Tools:

    Class meetings

    Cooperative critical incident reports

    Integrative problem-solving

    Project plans

    Skill storms

    Check-ins

    Check-outs

    Circling the elephant

Portfolio Pick

Bibliography

American Psychological Association. (1993). *Violence and youth: Psychology's response.* Washington, DC: APA Publishing.

Baron, R., Kerr, N., & Miller, N. (1992). *Group process, group decision, group action.* Pacific Grove, CA: Brooks/Cole.

Barrel, J. (1991). Reflective teaching for thoughtfulness. In A. Costa (Ed.), *Developing minds: A resource book for teaching thinking.* (pp. 207–211). Alexandria, VA: Association of Supervision on Curriculum Development (ASCD).

Baruch, R., & Stutman, S. (1993). Strategies for fostering resilience. Institute for Mental Health Initiatives Paper, Washington, DC.

Beane, J. (1995). *Toward a coherent curriculum.* Alexandria, VA: Association for Supervision and Curriculum Development (ASCD).

Berman, S. (1991). Thinking in context: Teaching for open-mindedness and critical understanding. In A. Costa (Ed.), *Developing minds: A resource book for teaching thinking* (pp. 10–16). Alexandria, VA: ASCD.

Beyer, B.K. (1991). Practical strategies for the direct teaching of thinking skills. In A. Costa (Ed.), *Developing minds: A resource book for teaching thinking* (pp. 274–294). Alexandria, VA: ASCD.

Beyth-Maron, R., Rischhoff, B., Jacobs, M., & Furby, L. (1989). *Teaching decision making to adolescents: A critical review.* New York: Carnegie Papers.

Bloom, S. (1997). *Creating sanctuary: Toward an evolution of sane societies.* New York: Routledge.

Blumberg, H.H., & French, C.C. (1992). *Peace: Abstracts of the psychological and behavioral literature.* Washington, DC: APA Publishing.

Bodine, R. (1996). From peer mediation to peaceable schools. *Update on Law-Related Education, 20, 2,* 7–9.

Brewer, D.D., Hawkins, J., Catalano, R., & Neckerman, H. (1995). Preventing serious, violent, and chronic juvenile offending: A review of selected strategies in childhood adolescence and the community. In J.C. Howell, B. Krisberg, J.D. Hawkins, & J.J. Wilson (Eds.), *A sourcebook: Serious, violent and chronic juvenile offenders* (pp. 61–141). Thousand Oaks, CA: Sage.

Brilliant, K. (1995). Curricula to prevent or reduce violence: Center for violence prevention and control. *Education Development Center Newsletter, 1,* 1.

Caine, R.N., & Caine, G. (1997). *Education on the edge of possibility*. Alexandria, VA: ASCD.

Calaprice, A. (1996). *The quotable Einstein*. Princeton, NJ: Princeton University Press.

Carnegie Council on Adolescent Development. (1995). *Great transitions: Preparing adolescents for a new century*. New York: Carnegie Corporation.

Catalano, R., Hawkins, D.J., Herman, E., Ransdell, M., Roberts, C., Roden, T., & Starkman, N. (1993). *Preventing violence: A framework for schools and communities*. Seattle, WA: Developmental Research Program.

Cawelti, G. (1995). *Handbook of research on improving student achievement*. Arlington, VA: Educational Research Service (ERS).

Committee for Children. *All about Second Step violence prevention curriculum.* (1997). Seattle, WA: Committee for Children.

Costa, A. (1991). *Developing minds: A resource book for teaching thinking* (Rev. ed.). Alexandria, VA: ASCD.

Costa, A.L., & Liebmann, R.M. (1997). *Envisioning process as content: Toward a renaissance curriculum*. Thousand Oaks, CA: Sage.

Crawford, D., & Bodine, R. (1996). *Conflict resolution education: A guide to implementing programs in schools, youth-serving organizations, and community and juvenile justice settings*. Washington, DC: U.S. Department of Justice.

Cropley, A.J., & Dehn, D. (Eds.). (1996). *Fostering the growth of high ability. European perspectives*. Norwood, NJ: Ablex.

Csikszentmihalyi, M. (1990). *Flow: The psychology of optimal experience*. New York: Harper Perennial.

Csikszentmihalyi, M. (1996). *Creativity: Flow and the psychology of discovery and invention*. New York: HarperCollins.

CSPV (Center for the Study and Prevention of Violence), University of Colorado, Boulder, CO. (1996).

Davidson, N., & Worsham, T. (1992). *Enhancing thinking through cooperative learning*. New York: Teachers College Press.

Davis, G.M. (1994). Don't fight, mediate. *Journal of Invitational Theory and Practice, 3* (2), 85–94.

Elias, M.J., Zins, J.E., Weissberg, R.P., Frey, K.S., Greenberg, M.T., Haynes, N.M., Kessler, R., Schwab-Stone, M.E., & Shriver, T.P. (1997). *Promoting social and emotional learning: Guidelines for educators*. Alexandria, VA: ASCD.

Empey, L.T., & Stafford, M.C. (1991). *American delinquency: Its meaning and construction*. Belmont, CA: Wadsworth.

Erickson, L.H. (1995). *Stirring the head, heart, and soul*. Thousand Oaks, CA: Corwin.

Eron, L., Gentry, J., & Schlegel, P. (1994). *Reason to hope: A psychological perspective on violence and youth*. Washington, DC: APA.

Farrington, D.P., Loeber, R., Elliott, D.S., & Tremblay, R.E. (1990). Advancing knowledge about the onset of delinquency and crime. In B.B. Lahey & A.E. Kazdin (Eds.), *Advances in clinical child psychology*, Vol. 13. New York: Plenum.

Fenley, M.A., Gaiter, J.L., Hammett, M., Liburd, L.C., Mercy, J.A., O'Carroll, P., Onwuachi-Saunders, C. Powell, K.E., & Thorton, T.N. (1993). *The prevention of youth violence: A framework for community action*. Atlanta, GA: Centers for Disease Control.

Fishbein, H.D. (1996). *Peer prejudice and discrimination.* Westview, CO: Westview Press/HarperCollins.

Forman, S. (1993). *Coping skills: Interventions for children and adolescents.* San Francisco: Jossey-Bass.

Gabbert, B., Johnson, D.W., & Johnson, R. (1986). Cooperative learning, group-to-individual transfer, process gain, and the acquisition of cognitive reasoning strategies. *Journal of Psychology, 120,* 265–278.

Gardner, H. (1983). *Frames of mind: The theory of multiple intelligences.* New York: Basic Books.

Gibbs, J. (1978). Kohlberg's stages of moral judgement: A constructive critique. *Harvard Educational Review, 13,* 33–51.

Gilhooly, K.J., Keane, M.T.G., Logie, R.H., & Erdos, G. (1990). *Lines of thinking: Reflections on the psychology of thought.* New York: John Wiley & Sons.

Giuliano, J.D. (1994). A peer education program to promote the use of conflict resolution skills among at-risk school age males. *Public Health Reports, 109* (2), 158–161.

Goleman, D. (1994). *Emotional literacy: A field report.* Kalamazoo, MI: The Fetzer Institute.

Goleman, D. (1995). *Emotional intelligence: Why it can mean more than I.Q.* New York: Bantam Books.

Goleman, D., Kaufman, P., & Ray, M. (1992). *The creative spirit.* New York: Dutton, Penguin Books.

Guinness, A.E. (1990). *ABC's of the human mind: A family answer book.* Pleasantville, NY: Readers Digest.

Greenberg, M. (1996). The paths curriculum shows positive effects on social competency of elementary school children. New Haven, CT: *Yale Child Study Center Newsletter of Social and Emotional Learning.*

Greenspan, S. (1997). *The growth of the mind and the endangered origins of intelligence.* Reading, MA: Addison-Wesley.

Hamilton, Gayle. (1994). *Conflict resolution in schools as a drug/alcohol use prevention strategy* (evaluation report). Fairfax, VA: George Mason University.

Harris, R.A. (1998). International Business Consultant.

Hartjen, R.H. (1994). *Empowering the child: Nurturing the hungry mind.* Port Tobacco, MD: Alternative Education Press.

Hawkins, J.D. (1995). Controlling crime before it happens: Risk focused prevention. *National Institute of Justice Journal 95,* 10–18.

Hawkins, J.D., & Catalano, R.F. (1992). *Communities that care.* San Francisco: Jossey-Bass.

Hawkins, J.D., & Catalano, R. (1993). *Communities that care: Risk focused prevention using the social development strategy.* Seattle, WA: Developmental Research Programs.

Hawkins, J.D., Doveck, H.J., & Lishner, D.M. (1998). Changing teaching practices in mainstream classrooms to improve bonding and behavior of low achievers. *American Education Research Journal, 25* (1), 31–50.

Hawkins, J.D., & Lishner, D. (1987). Etiology and prevention of antisocial behavior in children and adolescents. In D.H. Crowell (Ed.), *Childhood aggression and violence: Sources of influence, prevention and control* (pp. 261–282). New York: Plenum.

Hayes, D.A. (1992). *A sourcebook of interactive methods for teaching with texts.* Boston: Allyn and Bacon.

Heydenberk, W., & Heydenberk, R. (1997a). *Creating hope in the conflict positive classroom.* Paper presented at the Right to Hope Conference, Bucks County Community College, Newtown, PA.

Heydenberk, W., & Heydenberk, R. (1997b). *Creating metacognitive listeners.* Paper presented at the 33rd Annual Bloomsburg University Reading Conference, Bloomsburg University, Bloomsburg, PA.

Heydenberk, R., & Heydenberk, W. (1997c). *Conflict positive classrooms in at-risk schools.* Paper presented at the World Peace Organization's 50th Anniversary of the United Nations, UN Plaza, NY.

Heydenberk, R., & Heydenberk, W. (1998). *Creating conflict positive schools.* Paper presented to the Pennsylvania State House of Representatives Subcommittee on Violence in Schools, Philadelphia, PA.

Hirschi, T. (1969). *Causes of delinquency.* Berkeley: University of California Press.

Howell, J.C., Krisberg, B., Hawkins, J.D., & Wilson, J.J. (Eds.). (1995). *A sourcebook: Serious, violent and chronic juvenile offenders* (pp. 61–141). Thousand Oaks, CA: Sage.

Huff-Benkoski, K.A., & Greenwood, S.C. (1995). Use of word analysis instruction with developing readers. *The Reading Teacher, 48* (5), 446–447.

Hyerle, D. (1996). *Visual tools for constructing knowledge.* Alexandria, VA: ASCD.

Izard, C. (1991). *The psychology of emotions.* New York: Plenum Press.

Izard, C., Nagler, S., Randall, D., & Fox, J. (1965). The effects of affective picture stimuli on learning, perception, and the affective values of previously neutral symbols. In S.S. Tomkins & C.E. Izard (Eds.), *Affect, cognition, and personality* (pp. 42–70). New York: Springer.

Johnson, D. (1967). Use of role reversal in intergroup competition. *Journal of Personality and Social Psychology, 7* (2), 135–141.

Johnson, D.W. (1971). Effectiveness of role reversal: Actor or listener. *Psychological Reports 28,* 275–282.

Johnson, D.W. (1971). Role reversal: A summary and review of the research. *International Journal of Group Tensions, 1* (4), 318–334.

Johnson, D.W. (1979). Type of task and student achievement, and attitudes in interpersonal cooperation, competition and individualization. *Journal of Social Psychology, 108,* 37–48.

Johnson, D.W., & Johnson, R. (1981). Effects of cooperative and individualistic learning experiences in interethnic interaction. *Journal of Educational Psychology, 73,* 444–449.

Johnson, D.W., & Johnson, R.T. (1985). Internal dynamics of cooperative learning groups. In R. Slavin, S. Sharan, S. Kagan, R.H. Lazarowitz, C. Webb, & R. Schmuck (Eds.). *Learning to cooperate, cooperating to learn* (pp. 103–121), New York: Plenum.

Johnson, D., & Johnson, R. (1991). Collaboration and cognition. In A. Costa (Ed.), *Developing minds: A resource book for teaching thinking* (pp. 298–301). Alexandria, VA: ASCD.

Johnson, D., & Johnson, R. (1992). Encouraging thinking through constructive controversy. In N. Davidson & T. Worsham (Eds.), *Enhancing thinking through cooperative learning.* New York: Teachers College Press.

Johnson, D., & Johnson, R. (1994). Constructive conflict in the schools. *Journal of Social Issues, 50,* 117–137.

Johnson, D.W., & Johnson, R.T. (1995a). *Reducing school violence through conflict resolution.* Alexandria, VA: ASCD.

Johnson, D.W., & Johnson, R. (1996). Conflict resolution and peer mediation programs in elementary and secondary schools: A review of the research. *Review of Educational Research, 66* (4), 459–506.

Johnson, D.W., Johnson, R., & Holubec, E.J. (1994). *The new circles of learning: Cooperation in the classroom and school.* Alexandria, VA: ASCD.

Johnson, D.W., & Johnson, R. (1995b). Why violence prevention programs don't work—And what does. *Educational Leadership, 52* (5), 63–68.

Johnson, D.W., & Johnson, R. (1995c). Teaching students to be peacemakers: Results of five years of research. *Journal of Peace Psychology, 1,* 417–438.

Johnson, D.W., Johnson, R.T., Stevahn, L., & Hodne, P. (1997). The three C's of safe schools. *Educational Leadership, 55* (2), 8–13.

Johnson, D., Johnson, R., Dudley, B., Mitchell, J., & Fredrickson, J. (1997). The impact of conflict resolution training on middle school students. *The Journal of Social Psychology, 137* (1), 11–21.

Johnson, D., Maruyama, G., Johnson, R., Nelson, D., & Skon, L. (1981). The effects of cooperative learning, competitive and individualistic goal structures on achievement: A meta-analysis. *Psychological Bulletin, 89,* 47–62.

Johnson, D.W., Skon, L., & Johnson, R. (1980). Effects of cooperative, competitive and individualistic conditions on children's problem solving performance. *American Educational Research Journal, 17* (1), 83–93.

Jones, C.F. (1991). *Mistakes that worked.* NY: Doubleday-Delacorte.

Jones, C.F. (1996). *Accidents may happen.* NY: Doubleday-Delacorte.

Jones, M.L. (1990). *The overnight student.* Oklahoma City, OK: Louis.

Karabenick, S.A. (1996). Social influences on metacognition: Effects of colearner questions on comprehension monitoring. *Journal of Educational Psychology, 88* (4), 689–703.

Karpov, Y.V., & Haywood, H.C. (1998). Two ways to elaborate Vygotsky's concept of mediation. *American Psychologist, 53* (1), 27–36.

Katz, M. (1997). *On playing a poor hand well: Insights from the lives of those who have overcome childhood risks and adversities.* New York: W.W. Norton.

Kazdin, A.E., Esveldt-Dawson, K., French, N.H., & Unis, A.S. (1987). Problem-solving skills training and relationship therapy in the treatment of antisocial child behavior. *Journal of Consulting and Clinical Psychology, 55,* 76–85.

Kessler, S. (1994). The mysteries program: School based programs in social and emotional education. *Connections: The Newsletter of Social and Emotional Learning, 1* (1), 4.

Kemper, T.D. (1990). *Social structure and testosterone: Exploration of the social-biosocial chain.* New Brunswick, NJ: Rutgers University Press.

Kennedy, M., Fisher, M., & Ennis, R. (1991). Critical thinking: Literature review and need research. In L. Idol, & B. Jones (1991), *Educational values and cognitive instruction: Implications for reform,* (pp. 11–40). Hillsdale, NJ: Erlbaum Associates.

Koch, M., & Miller, S. (March, 1987). Resolving student conflicts with student mediators. *Principal,* 59–62.

Koch, M. (January, 1988). Resolving disputes: Students can do it better. *NASSP Bulletin*, 16–18.

Kohlberg, L., Levine, C., & Hewer, A. (1983). *Moral stages: A current formulation and a response to critics.* Basel, Switzerland and New York: Karger.

Kohn, A. (1986). *No contest: The case against competition.* Boston: Houghton Mifflin.

Kohn, A. (1990). *The brighter side of human nature: Altruism and empathy in everyday life.* New York: Basic Books.

Lam, J. (1989). *The impact of conflict resolution programs on schools: A review and synthesis of the evidence.* Amherst, MA: National Association of Mediation in Education.

Lantierti, L., & Patti, J. (1996). The road to peace in our schools. *Educational Leadership, 54* (1), 28–31.

Larson, J. (1994). Violence prevention in the schools: A review of selected programs and procedures. *School Psychology Review, 23* (2), 151–164.

LeDoux, J.E. (June, 1994). Emotion, memory, and the brain: The neural routes underlying the formation of memories about primitive emotional experiences, such as fear, have been traced. *Scientific American*, 50–57.

LeDoux, J.E. (1996). *The emotional brain: The mysterious underpinnings of emotional life.* New York: Touchstone.

Lewis, C., Schaps, E., & Watson, M. (1996). The caring classroom's academic edge. *Educational Leadership, 54* (1), 16–21.

Lipman, M. (1993). *Thinking children and education.* Dubuque, IA: Kendall/Hunt.

Lipman, M. (1991). *Thinking in education.* Cambridge, England: Cambridge University Press.

Marano, H.E. (October, 1995). Big. Bad. Bully. *Psychology Today*, 51–82.

Marret, C., & Leggon, C. (1979). *Research in race and ethnic relations.* Greenwich, CT: Jai.

Marzano, R. (1992). The many faces of cooperation across the dimensions of learning. In N. Davidson & T. Worsham (Eds.), *Enhancing thinking through cooperative learning* (pp. 7–28). New York: Teachers College Press.

Mash, E., & Barkley, R.A. (1989). *Treatment of childhood disorders.* New York: Guilford.

Masten, A., & Coatsworth, J. (1998). The development of competence in favorable and unfavorable environments. *American Psychologist, 53* (2), 205–217.

McCord, J. (1994). Aggression in two generations. In L.R. Huesmann (Ed.), *Aggressive behavior: Current perspectives* (pp. 241–254). New York: Plenum.

McKay, M., Rodgers, P., & McKay, J. (1989). *When anger hurts.* New York: New Harbinger.

Meek, M. (Fall, 1992). The peacekeepers: Students use mediation skills to resolve conflicts. *Teaching Tolerance, 92*, 46–53.

Meredith, N. (August, 1987). Kids, communication, and compromise. *Parenting*, 63–66.

Mercy, J. (Summer, 1993). Youth violence as a public health problem. *Spectrum*, 26–30.

Metis Associates, Inc. (May, 1990). *The resolving conflict creativity program, 1988–1989: A summary of significant findings.* New York: Metis Associates.

Miller, J.E. (1987). Peer mediation in Orange County middle schools: Transferring conflict management skills learned in school to home. M.A. Thesis. Queens University, Ontario, Canada.

National Institute of Dispute Resolution. (1998). *Save Our Streets outcome evaluation report.* Washington, DC: NIDR.

National Institute of Dispute Resolution. (1997). *What conflict resolution education offers America's school children.* July/August, IV (3). Washington, DC: NIDR.

National Institute of Dispute Resolution. (1998). *The promise of integrating conflict resolution into the classroom.* (No. 35). Washington, DC: Randy Compton.

Necka, E. (1996). Levels of mind: A multilevel model of intellect and its implications for identification of the gifted. In A. Cropley and D. Dehn (Eds.), *Fostering the growth of high ability: European perspectives* (pp. 95–102). Norwood, NJ: Ablex.

Nummela, R.M., & Rosengren, T.M. (1986). What's happening in students' brains may redefine teaching: Harmonizing new experiences with old in a rich, non-threatening environment helps students learn more naturally and fully. *Educational Leadership, 43* (8), 40–53.

Olweus, D. (1979). Stability of aggressive reaction patterns in males: A review. *Psychological Bulletin, 86,* 852–872.

Olweus, D. (1991). Bully/victim problems among school children: Basic facts and effects of a school-based intervention program. In D.J. Pepler & K.H. Rubin (Eds.). *The development and treatment of childhood aggression.* Hillsdale, NJ: Erbaum Associates.

Ostrander, S., Schroeder, L., & Ostrander, N. (1979). *Super-learning.* New York: Delta.

O'Tuel, F.S., & Bullard, R.K. (1993). *Developing higher order thinking in the content areas.* Pacific Grove, CA: Critical Thinking Press.

Padus, E. (1992). *Emotions and your health.* Emmaus, PA: Rodale.

Paul, R. (1991). Teaching critical thinking in the strong sense. In A. Costa (Ed.), *Developing minds: A resource book for teaching thinking* (pp. 77–84), Alexandria, VA: ASCD.

Pennebacker, J. (1997). *Opening up: The healing power of expressing emotions.* New York: Guilford.

Perkins, D. (1995). *Outsmarting IQ: The emerging science of learnable intelligence.* New York: The Free Press.

Perkins, D., & Salomon, G. (1988). Teaching transfer. *Educational Leadership 46* (1), 22–32.

Phinney, J., & Rotheram, M.J. (1987). *Children's ethnic socialization: Pluralism and development.* Newbury Park, CA: Sage.

Piaget, J. (1997). *The moral judgment of the child.* New York: Free Press.

Pool, C.R. (1997). Maximizing learning: A conversation with Renate Nummela Caine. *Educational Leadership, 54,* 11–15.

Prothrow-Stith, D. (1991). *Deadly consequences: How violence is destroying our teenage population and a plan to begin solving the problem.* New York: HarperCollins.

Prothrow-Stith, D. (1994). Assimilating prevention techniques into the curriculum. *The Fourth R Newsletter of the National Association for Mediation in Education 52,* 1–9.

Prothrow-Stith, D. (April, 1994). Building violence prevention into the curriculum. *The School Administrator,* 8–12.

Regier, D.A., & Cowdry, R.W. (1995). Research on violence and traumatic stress. *National Institute of Mental Health Program Announcement.* Rockville, MD.

Resnick, M.D., Bearman, P.S., Blum, R.W., Bauman, K.E., Harris, K.M., Jones, J., Tabor, J., Beuhring, T., Sieving, R.E., Shew, M., Ireland, M., Bearinger, L.H., & Udry, J.R. (1997). Protecting adolescents from harm: Findings from the national longitudinal study on adolescent health. *Journal of the American Medical Association, 278* (10), 823–832.

Restak, R.M. (1984). *The brain.* Toronto, Canada: Bantam Books.

Restak, R.M. (1994). *The modular brain.* New York: Charles Scribner and Sons.

Roeser, R.W., Midgley, C., & Urdan, T.C. (1996). Perceptions of the school psychological environment and early adolescents' psychological and behavioral functioning in school: The mediating role of goals and belonging. *Journal of Educational Psychology, 88* (3), 408–422.

Rosenthal, R. (1973). The pygmalion effect lives. *Psychology Today,* 56–63.

Rutter, M. (1987). Psychosocial resilience and protective mechanisms. *American Journal of Orthopsychiatry, 57,* 316–331.

Schunk, D.H. (1991). Self-efficacy and academic motivation. *Educational Psychologist, 2* (3 & 4), 207–231.

Seligman, M. (1990). *Learned optimism.* New York: Simon & Schuster.

Sherman, L. (1997). Communities and crime prevention. In L. Sherman, D. Gottfredson, D. Mackenzie, J. Eck, P. Reuter, & S. Bushway (Eds.), *Preventing crime: What works, what doesn't, what's promising.* College Park, MD: University of Maryland.

Snyder, C.R. (1994). *The psychology of hope.* New York: Free Press.

Steele, C.M., & Aronson, J. (1995). Stereotype threat and the intellectual test performance of African Americans. *Journal of Personality and Social Psychology, 69* (5), 797–811.

Sternberg, R.J., (1977). *Intelligence, information processing and analogical reasoning: The componential analysis of human abilities.* Hillsdale, NJ: Erlbaum Associates.

Steinberg, A. (1991). The killing grounds: Can schools help stem the violence? *The Harvard Education Letter, 7* (4), 3–5.

Stephens, R.D., Arnette, J.L., & James, B. (1995). School bullying and victimization. *National School Safety Center, 1,* 1–2.

Sternberg, R.J. (1994). Answering questions and questioning answers: Guiding children to intellectual excellence. *Phi Delta Kappan 76* (2), 136–138.

Sternberg, R.J., & Lubart, T.I. (1991). An investment theory of creativity and its development. *Human Development 34* (1), 1–31.

Stevahn, L., Johnson, D., Johnson, R., & Real, D. (1996). The impact of a cooperative context on the effectiveness of conflict resolution training. *American Educational Research Journal, 33* (3), 801–823.

Stichter, C. (1986). When tempers flare, let trained student mediators put out the flames. *The American School Board Journal, 3,* 41–42.

Stomfay-Stitz, A.M. (1994). Conflict resolution and peer mediation: Pathways to safer schools. *Childhood Education, 9,* 279–281.

Stosny, S. (1995). *Treating attachment abuse: A compassionate approach.* Springer.

Sylvester, L., & Frey, K. (August, 1994). Summary of second step pilot studies. *Committee for Children Reports*, 1–7.

Sylwester, R. (1995). *A celebration of neurons: An educator's guide to the human brain.* Alexandria, VA: ASCD.

U.S. Department of Education. (October, 1998). *Executive summary: Indicators of school crime and safety.* Washington, DC.

U.S. Department of Justice. (March, 1997). *Conflict resolution, 55.* Washington, DC: Donni LeBoeuf & Robin Delany-Shahazz.

Van Slyck, R., & Stern, M. (1991). Conflict resolution in educational settings: Assessing the impact of peer mediation programs. In K. Duffy, P. Olorczak, & J. Grosch (Eds.), *The art and science of community mediation: A handbook for practitioners and researchers* (pp. 257–274). New York: Guilford.

Van Steenberger, N. (Winter, 1994). If only we could . . . *School Safety*, 20–22.

Wallach, L.B. (May, 1993). Helping children cope with violence. *Young Children*, 160–167.

Webb, N. (1985). Student interaction and small group instruction. In R. Slavin, S. Sharah, S. Kagan, R.H. Lazarowitz, C. Webb, & R. Schmuck (Eds.), *Learning to cooperate, cooperating to learn* (pp. 147–172). New York: Plenum.

Wentzel, K.R. (1991). Relations between social competence and academic achievement in early adolescence. *Child Development, 62,* 1066–1078.

Wentzel, K., Weinberger, D.A., Ford, M.E., & Feldman, S.S. (1990). Academic achievement in preadolescence: The role of motivational, affective, and self-regulatory processes. *Journal of Applied Developmental Psychology, 11,* 179–193.

Werner, E.E. (1989). High-risk children in young adulthood: A longitudinal study from birth to 32 years. *American Journal of Orthopsychiatry, 59* (1), 72–81.

Whitman, N.A. (1988). *Peer teaching.* Washington, DC: Eric-Ashe.

Williams, R., & Williams, V. (1984). *Anger kills: Seventeen strategies for controlling the hostility that can harm your health.* New York: HarperCollins.

Wittmer, D.S., & Honig, A.S. (July, 1994). Encouraging positive social development in young children. *Young Children*, 148–156.

Wright, N.D. (1994). *From risk to resiliency: The role of law-related education.* Casabasas, CA: Center for Civic Education.

Zemelman, S., Daniels, H., & Hyde, A. (1993). *Best practice: New standards for teaching and learning in America's schools.* Portsmouth, NH: Heinemann.

Zins, J.E., & Forman, S.G. (1991). Preparing students for the 21st century: Contributions of the prevention and social competence fields. *Teachers College Record, 93* (2), 298–304.

Name Index

Adams, J., 72
American Psychological
    Association, 167
Aristotle, 17, 55
Arnette, J., 8
Aronson, J., 165

Babbage, C., 96
Barkley, R., 4, 20–21
Baron, R., 5
Baruch, R. 8, 14, 19, 20
Beane, J., 17
Beethoven, L., 98
Benedictus, E., 85
Berman, S., 22, 24
Beyer, B., 45
Beyth-Maron, R., 169
Bloom, S., 21, 163, 168
Blumberg, H., 18
Bodine, R., 164–165
Brewer, D., 14
Bullard, R., 9
Bushway, S., 164

Caine, G., 7, 167–168
Caine, R., 7, 167–168
Cappella, M., 97
Carnegie Council on Adoles-
    cent Development, 8
Catalano, R., 5, 14, 167
Cawelti, G., 9, 16, 22, 24, 27
Center for the Study and Pre-
    vention of Violence, 21
Coatsworth, J., 12
Committee for Children, 164

Costa, A., 8, 9, 13, 24, 45, 52,
    167, 5, 24
Cowdry, R. W., 5
Crawford, D., 165
Cropley, A., 6, 108
Csikszentmihalyi, M., 6, 14–15,
    24

Daniels, H., 15–16
Darwin, C., 173
Davidson, N., 5, 9, 16, 21, 23,
    43–49, 166
daVinci, L., 89
Dehn, D., 6, 108
deMestral, G., 85
Deutsch, M., 23, 173
Dewey, J., 9, 16
Doveck, H., 14
Dudley, B., 19, 25

Eck, J., 164
Einstein, A., 87, 30–31, 107
Elias, M., 169
Elliot, D., 6
Elliott, J., 1–2, 229
Empey, L., 8, 14, 15, 20
Ennis, R., 13, 14
Erdos, G., 25
Erickson, L., 9, 115
Eron, L., 5, 8
Esveldt-Dawson, K., 13

Farrington, D., 6
Feldman, S., 14, 19
Fenley, M., 13

Fishbein, H., 171–172
Fisher, M., 13, 14
Fleming, A., 85
Ford, M., 17, 19
Forman, S., 13, 25
Fredrickson, J., 19, 25
French, C., 18
French, N., 13
Frey, K., 169
Furby, L., 169

Gabbert, B., 171
Gaiter, J., 13
Gandhi, M., 30, 31
Gardner, H., 14, 36
Gentry, J., 5, 8
Gibb, J., 4, 6
Gilhooly, K., 25
Goleman, D., 4, 5, 6, 7, 10, 11,
    17, 20, 21, 165, 168
Gottfredson, D., 164
Greenberg, M., 19, 169
Greenspan, S., 16
Greenwood, S., 108
Guinness, A., 5

Hamwi, M., 86
Hartjen, R., 15
Hawkins, D., 3, 8, 20, 14, 52,
    165, 167
Hayes, D., 45–46
Haynes, N., 169
Haywood, H., 24, 25
Hemmett, M., 13
Heydenberk, E., 89

Heydenberk, R., 4, 5, 7, 11, 12, 13, 18, 22, 170–171
Heydenberk, W., 4, 5, 7, 11, 12, 13, 18, 22, 170–171
Hirsch, T., 20
Hodne, P., 165
Honig, A., 25
Huff-Benkiowski, 108
Hyde, A., 15
Hyerle, D., 16, 52, 116

Izard, C., 16, 165–166, 170
Jacobs, M., 169
James, B., 8
Johnson, D., 4, 6, 7, 19, 20, 22, 23, 24, 25, 165–166, 170–174
Johnson, R., 4, 6, 7, 19, 20, 22, 23, 24, 25, 165–166, 170–174
Jones, C., 85
Jones, M., 23, 52

Kagan, J., 49
Karabenick, S., 45
Karpov, Y., 24, 25
Katz, M., 17
Kaufman, P. 4, 5
Kazdin, A., 13
Keane, M., 25
Keller, H., 107
Kemper, T., 21
Kennedy, M., 13–14
Kerr, N., 5
Kessler, R., 169
Kessler, S., 21
King, M.L., 1, 86–87
Koch, M., 165
Kohn, A., 6, 22–23, 172–174
Krisberg, B., 20

Lam, J., 165
Lantieri, L., 165
Larson, J., 19
LeDoux, J., 169
Leggon, C., 3, 6
Levi, S., 85
Lewis, C., 19, 167
Liburd, L., 13
Liebman, R., 24
Lincoln, A., 87, 88, 108
Lipman, M., 4, 8, 15
Locke, J., 72
Loeber, R., 6

Logie, R., 25
Lovelace, A., 96
Lishner, D., 14, 20
Lyman, F., 48

Mackenzie, D., 164
Marano, H., 8, 21
Marret, C., 3, 6
Maruyama, G., 170
Marzano, R., 14, 164
Mash, E., 4, 20–21
Maslow, A., 2, 69–70, 147, 163
Masten, A., 12
McKay, J., 17–18
McKay, M., 17–18
McTighe, J., 48
Meek, M., 20
Mercy, J., 13, 163, 164
Meredith, N., 170
Midgley, C., 166
Miller, J., 5, 170
Mitchell, J., 19, 25
Montagu, A., 173
Mozart, A., 98

Necka, E., 6
Neckerman, H., 14
Nelson, D., 170–171
Nilson, L., 167
Nobel, A., 38
Nummela, R., 168–170

O'Carroll, P., 13
Olweus, D., 20
Onwuachi-Saunders, C., 13
Ostrander, N., 21
Ostrander, S., 21
OTuel, F., 9

Padus, E., 167
Pasteur, L, 85
Patti, J., 165
Paul, R., 23
Penn, W., 53
Pennebacker, J., 169–170
Pergoff, S., 15
Perkins, D., 22–24, 127
Phinney, J., 165
Piaget, J.C., 4, 14, 174
Plato, 55
Polhemus, G., 223–224
Pool, C., 11

Powell, K. 13
Pray, R., 99
Prowthrow-Stith, D., 4, 164

Ray, M., 4, 5
Real, D., 171
Reigier, D., 5
Reiter, P., 164
Restak, R., 21, 163, 169
Rischoff, B., 169
Rodgers, P., 17, 18
Roeser, R., 166
Roosevelt, E., 93, 107
Roosevelt, F.D., 93
Rosengren, T., 168, 170
Rosenthal, R., 3
Rotherman, M., 165
Rutledge, A., 89

Salk, J., 62
Salomon, G., 24
Schaeffer, A., 94
Schaps, E., 19, 167
Schlegel, P., 5, 8
Schroeder, L., 21
Schunk, D., 12
Schwab-Stone, M., 169
Seligman, M., 18–19
Sherman, L., 164
Shriver, T., 169
Silver, S., 85
Simonton, D., 4
Skon, L., 170
Snyder, C., 4, 11, 12, 18, 20
Socrates, 55, 59
Speed, J., 89
Spencer, P.L., 86
Stafford, M., 8, 14–15, 20
Steele, C., 165
Steinberg, A., 165
Stephens, R., 8
Sterling, S., 25
Stern, M., 170
Sternberg, R., 23
Stevahn, L., 165, 171
Stomfay-Stitz, A., 5
Stosny, S., 169
Stutman, S., 8, 14, 19–20
Sylwester, R., 5, 15, 21, 163, 169

Thorton, T., 13
Todd, M., 89

Tremblay, R., 6
Truman, H., 93

Unis, A. 13
Urdan, T., 166
U.S. Department of Justice, 164

VanSlyck, R., 170
VanSteenbergen, N., 13, 164
Vygotsky, L., 9, 24–25

Wahlstrom, R., 18
Wakefield, R., 85
Wallach, L., 12
Watson, 19, 167
Webb, N., 24
Weinberger, D., 17, 19
Weissberg, R. 169
Wentzel, K., 17, 18, 19
Whitman, N., 24
Wilson, J., 20

Wittmer, D., 25
Worsham, T., 5, 9, 16, 21, 23, 48, 49
Wright, N., 7, 8, 14

Zemelman, S., 15, 16
Zins, J., 13, 25, 169

Subject Index

Academic Achievement
  affected by anger, 21
  affected by fear, 21
  and aggression and violence,
    10
  and alienation, 4
  and attachment, 13, 22
  and communication, 2
  and conflict resolution, 4, 20
  and cooperative groups, 15
  and hope/optimism, 19
  and integrated conflict reso-
    lution, 165
  and paraphrasing, 22
  and safety, 2
  and school bonds, 15
Academic controversy,
  159–160
Active listening. *See* Listening
Activism
  related activities, 222–224
Affective vocabulary, 225–226
Aggression
  and conflict resolution, 4
  and learning, 164
  and social skills, 161, 164
Alienation
  and academic failure, 4, 7,
    167
  and creativity, 22
  and emotions, 16
  and flawed thinking, 6
  and gang memberships, 168
  and higher level thinking, 16

  reduced by conflict resolu-
    tion programs, 170
  and school community, 167
Altruism, 167
Analogies
  and increasing comprehen-
    sion, 108
  and increasing creativity, 108
  and transfer of knowledge,
    108
  related activity, 108–114
Anger. *See also* Conflict and
  Emotions
  and attachments and bond-
    ing, 17
  and cognitive rigidity, 169
  and communication, 17, 164
  and learning, 167–170
  and predicting delinquency,
    20
  and social cues, 21
  and success, 7, 20
  and venting, 17
Attachment. *See also* Bonds
  and achievement, 13
  and communication, 7
  and cooperation, 174
  and gangs, 5, 168
  and integrative thinking, 174
  and social skills, 4

Bonds
  and academic achievement,
    14

  and academic failure, 8
  and cooperative communi-
    cation, 5
  and school success, 15
Brain structure
  and climate, 168
  and fear, 168
  and function, 168
Brainstorm
  related activity, 116–121
Bullies, 2, 16, 164
  and deficient cognition, 8
  and social status, 21

Communication
  conflict-positive, 203
  cooperative, 203
  related activity, 209
  style analysis, 203
Class meetings
  related activity, 218–222
Community
  and attachment, 20
  bonds, 4
  and gangs, 20
Communication
  and listening awareness, 27
Comprehension
  and listening awareness, 27
Conflict
  as an academic tool, 174
  attitudes about, 175–177
  and conflict resolution
    skills, 3

Conflict (*cont.*)
  as content, 9
  as a creativity opportunity,
    13
  and diversity, 5
  at home, 5
  as learning tool, 25
  as a natural occurrence, 174
  nature of, 4
  reduction, 20
  resolved by students, 170
  response to, 17
Conflict resolution
  and academic achievement,
    3, 13, 19, 170–171
  determinants of outcomes,
    172
  integrated into curriculum,
    9, 20
  and increased teacher
    morale, 170
  and increased communica-
    tion, 17, 170
  and increased cooperation,
    21, 166
  and increased resilience, 166
  and positive changes in cli-
    mate, 163
  and reducing gang violence,
    164
  and self-esteem, 13
  and sense of safety, 163
  and stand-alone programs, 4
  related activities, 175–201
Critical thinking, 3. *See also*
    problem solving and aca-
    demic achievement
Consensus
  related activity, 216–218
Constitution
  related activities, 72–78
Cooperation
  characteristics of, 16
  and cognitive flow, 15
  increasing metacognition, 25
  and creativity, 6
  and internal laws of control,
    173
  natural tendency, 5
  and the nature of children,
    173

and the nature of society,
    173
  and survival, 173
Cooperative learning
  characteristics of, 16
  and diversity, 171
  and increased achievement,
    170
  and mainstreaming, 171
  and metacognition, 15
  and personality, 174
  positive interdependence,
    171, 172
  and prejudice, 171, 172
  and respect, 174
Core values, 5
Creativity
  and cooperation, 173
Communication
  improved by conflict resolu-
    tion programs, 170
  in a cooperative context, 172
  and academic success, 10,
    23–24
  and conflict resolution skills,
    172
  and hope, 12
  oral communication, 24
Critical concepts
  related activity, 114–115
Critical thinking
  affected by positive emo-
    tions, 16, 170
  and alienation, 16
  and anxiety, 169
  and brain function, 168
  and climate, 169
  and cooperative environ-
    ment, 173
  and cooperative learning, 17,
    171
  curriculum integration, 9
  environment, 6
  increased by social interac-
    tion, 25
  and the integrative class-
    room, 15
  and sense of safety, 3, 163
Creativity
  and cooperation, 6, 15
  and flexibility, 6, 15

increased by positive social
    functioning, 25
Cultural diversity, 229–231

Dispositions
  and intelligence, 13
  and learning, 14
Democracy, 72
Diversity
  and conflict, 4
Decision making
  related activities, 145–157

Emotions. *See also* Anger,
    Affective vocabulary
  and ability to learn, 169
  and academic achievement,
    19
  and aggression, 164
  and alienation, 16
  and brain changes, 7
  and cognition, 169
  and control, 12
  and critical thinking, 16
  and emotional literacy, 21
  inability to express, 169
  and integrative thinking,
    169
  and resilience, 20
Ethics, 9

Gangs
  and alienation, 20
  and attachment, 20
  and community, 20
Graphic organizers
  to identify main idea, 52
  and increased comprehen-
    sion, 52
  related activities, 52–58,
    60–62, 69–71
  to simplify content, 52

Hope
  and achievement, 11
  characteristics of, 12
  and self-efficacy and internal
    locus of control, 12
Homicide, 5,
  incidence, 164
Handguns, 164

Integrative thinking. *See also* Critical thinking, Problem solving
  and attachment, 7
  and cognitive flexibility, 173
  and communication, 7
  and complex reasoning, 174
  and hope, 18
  and sense of community, 174
  and school success, 13
"I" statements
  related activities, 67–68, 193–197

Learned helplessness
  and pessimism, 18
  and social skills, 18
Learning
  and brain function, 168
  and school climate, 168
  and sense of safety, 168
Listening-active, 10, 189–191
  importance of, 21
  percent of time spent, 21
  related activities, 27–35, 40–44
Logical reasoning
  related activities, 127–145

Main idea
  identifying, 54–58
Metacognition
  and conflict resolution, 25
  and cooperation, 15
  developed through cooperative interaction, 25
Minority effect, 21
Multiple intelligences, 14
  interpersonal intelligence, 37
  intrapersonal intelligence, 36

Optimism. *See also* Hope
  and academic success, 19
  and emotional control, 11

Paraphrasing
  as academic tool, 21
  and constructive problem-solving, 22
  and disposition, 23
  and memory, 23
  increasing comprehension, 21–22
  related activities, 55, 58
Portfolios, 27
Prediction, 50
Problem solving
  and aggression, 8
  and attachment, 13
  and cooperative learning, 171
  and discipline problems, 15
  and grade point averages, 19
  and hope, 19
Personality, 174

Questioning
  related activities, 45–50, 52–55, 84–107, 124–125

Restitution
  related activities, 78–82
Resilience, 8

Safety, 2. *See also* Violence
  physical, 18
  psychological, 18
School climate
  affecting academic flow, 167

  affecting cognition, 166
  and ability to learn, 167
  and conflict resolution
  and cooperative learning, 172
  and creativity, 173
  sense of safety, 169
  stimulating cortex, 170
Self-control, 10
  and hope, 12
Self-esteem
  and conflict resolution, 13
  and social skills, 13
Social interaction
  and academic preference, 16
  and brain function, 168
  and construction of knowledge, 167
  stimulating cortex, 170
Social skills
  and academic performance, 16, 17
  and aggression, 164
  and depression, 4
  examples of, 20
  and resilience, 20
  and school bonds, 15
  and sense of community, 2
  and violence, 10, 11
  vs. IQ in success, 4
  and well-being, 12
Summarizing
  related activities, 55–61

Violence
  and academic achievement, 10
  and social skills, 10